D0044866

INNOVATION *by* DESIGN

INNOVATION *by* DESIGN

What It Takes to Keep Your Company on the Cutting Edge

Gerard H. (Gus) Gaynor

AMACOM

American Management Association

New York • Atlanta • Brussels • Buenos Aires • Chicago • London • Mexico City
San Francisco • Shanghai • Tokyo • Toronto • Washington, D.C.

Special discounts on bulk quantities of AMACOM books are available to corporations, professional associations, and other organizations. For details, contact Special Sales Department, AMACOM, a division of American Management Association, 1601 Broadway, New York, NY 10019.
Tel.: 212-903-8316.   Fax: 212-903-8083.
Web site: www.amacombooks.org

This publication is designed to provide accurate and authoritative information in regard to the subject matter covered. It is sold with the understanding that the publisher is not engaged in rendering legal, accounting, or other professional service. If legal advice or other expert assistance is required, the services of a competent professional person should be sought.

Library of Congress Cataloging-in-Publication Data

Gaynor, Gerard H.
   Innovation by design: what it takes to keep your company on the cutting edge / Gerard H. Gaynor.
       p.   cm.
   Includes bibliographical references and index.
   ISBN 0-8144-0696-3
   1. Industrial management.   2. Organizational change.   3. Creative ability in business.   I. Title.
HD31 .G383   2002
658.4' 063—dc21

                                                                    2002001988

Printing number

10   9   8   7   6   5   4   3   2   1

To Shirley

Contents

(1) S – curve
(2) problems in innovation
(3)

Preface

Innovation by Design grew out of concern that organizations that at one time had been outperforming the economy by introducing new-to-the-market products were now relying strictly on incremental innovation, which in many situations does not increase the size of the market

Innovation is a management discipline; it does not come about through a random or hit-and-miss approach, but it requires design. Innovation involves focusing on the organization's mission, searching for unique opportunities, determining whether they fit the organization's strategic direction, defining the measures for success, and continually reassessing opportunities. Innovation doesn't require genius; but it does require total dedication in pursuit of a unique opportunity.

Design is central to the practice of management. Design is also central to the practice of innovation. Science, engineering, medicine, and architecture look to the future with knowledge of the past. These professions look at what could be and use resources to try and make *something new* happen. New products, new systems, and new processes involve design. Design creates change in products as well as lifestyles. Innovation comes about by implementing designs.

Innovation by Design takes a systems approach to guide the governance of organizations that create economic or social value through innovation. Developing an innovative organization does not involve any deep-seated mysteries. There are no recipes, no ten-easy-lessons, and no seven-step panacea. Successful innovation comes from understanding a coherent set of principles and guidelines and then applying them within a specific organizational context.

Innovation requires four complementary elements:

1. Competent people

2. Sound management practice

3. Good innovation design

4. An environment that provides freedom to exercise personal initiative

The competent people include creative and constructive mavericks as well as people with the put-it-all-together competencies. Sound management practice provides operational freedom but with accountability for results and tolerates negative results when necessary. An innovation design meets the requirements that *innovation = invention + implementation/commercialization* and fits the purposes, strategies, and objectives of the organization. And a supportive environment enhances the opportunities for innovation and links the organizational functions and disciplines into a system.

Innovation requires only the right people and an infrastructure that supports the innovators. *Innovation by Design* brings the innovator and the organization into a partnership that aims to develop innovation as a core competence. As Peter Drucker reminds us, "Every organization—not just business—needs one core competence: innovation."[1]

From a national perspective, innovation requires involvement from the complete spectrum of organizational entities—product and service industries, all levels of government, all educational activities from elementary through advanced degree programs, and the general classification of nonprofit organizations. Although *Innovation by Design* focuses on industry, the same principles apply to all organizational entities. In the future few organizations will survive without focusing on innovation. As Tom Peters reminded us in a "California Management Review" article: "Get Innovative or Get Dead."[2]

Innovation by Design involves more than innovation in the traditional sense. Innovation is really about managing the business enterprise. It's about the business system, systems thinking, and new ways of thinking. It's about change and the impact of change on business performance. It's about people. It's about process. It's about optimizing the use of business resources within the context of a specific organizational infrastructure. Too often lack of a supportive infrastructure relegates that new-to-the-market product to the new-product graveyard.

Changing an organization to become proactive about innovation may require a minor revolution in the way the organization conducts its affairs. At the same time the business basics cannot be disregarded. Hanging out the sign "closed until we become innovative" isn't an option. Most people have been conditioned to think in linear terms since childhood. But we now live in a nonlinear world, and those nonlinear ideas are the ones that create wealth.

Because tomorrow's opportunities seldom align with today's organizational boundaries, the process of becoming an innovative organization begins with evaluating the existing business model, getting rid of the restrictive organizational dogma, eliminating those activities that no longer add value, and supporting the champions of constructive unconventional thinking. Managers attempting to build an innovative organization cannot tinker around the edges to foster innovation; they either play the game or watch it from the sidelines.

My objective in writing *Innovation by Design* has been to elaborate on the critical issues that organizations should address as a matter of routine. The complex process of innovation depends on people and their interactions. And what can be more complex than bringing a group of people from diverse disciplines—with all their complementary and noncomplementary characteristics—to focus on a specific issue. We know all about the difficulties usually associated with building even a small productive team that demonstrates collegiality amongst its members.

Innovation by Design raises issues to stimulate new thinking rather than prescribe some definitive methodology. Knowing the fundamentals advances the process. Innovation occurs from developing an *innovation attitude* and not from some executive level dictum. Developing an appropriate attitude requires changing the thinking processes, changing the mind-set, eliminating some of the baggage that no longer adds value, and possibly undergoing a complete metamorphosis. Levels of expectation must be raised to a higher level, and those executives and managers who have been acting like storekeepers and tour directors must reappraise their roles in order to become proactive innovators. Innovation cannot be delegated. In teaching innovation at the university graduate level, I found many managers who were interested in learning about innovation but few who wanted to be the innovators.

Innovation by Design discusses the issues involved in being an innovator and the culture for supporting innovation. Chapters 1 to 3 provide some perspectives of innovation, discuss the types of innovation, and consider the implementation process in various types of organizations. Chapters 4 and 5 examine the basics of the innovation process and present an innovation process design model. Chapters 6 and 7 focus on the issues involved in developing a culture that fosters innovation. Chapters 8 and 9 draw attention to the organizational resources and infrastructure that determine the potential for innovation. Chapter 10 considers the competencies required by the innovator, including skills, characteristics, attitudes, and knowledge. Chapter 11 helps you deal with the virtual innovation prevention department that specializes in creating roadblocks to innovation. The innovation audit in Chapter 12 allows the organization to gain insight into its potential for innovation. The final chapter, Chapter 13, includes guidelines for making innovation a reality.

In *Innovation by Design*, I have tried to distill the critical issues that organizations need to develop if they want to support innovation. Forty years of experience in the management of research, product and process development, manufacturing, and business have provided me with a systems and business-oriented perspective. Experience has been a great teacher, and I have been very fortunate to have worked with people who have given me the opportunity to pursue the unconventional. That experience began in my childhood, and continued through years of schooling leading to a degree in engineering, and positions with several diverse organizations. It culminated in a twenty-five-year career at Minnesota Mining and Manufacturing (3M), where risk-taking was not an impediment to professional or managerial success. My time at 3M included assignments in the United States, seven years of resident foreign service, and extensive global involvement. Those years of experience as a technology and business executive plus fifteen years of consulting, teaching graduate courses in innovation and entrepreneurship, and actively participating in professional society volunteer activities have provided me with insight as to how innovation by design can become a reality.

Notes

1. Peter F. Drucker, *Managing in a Time of Great Change* (New York: Truman Talley Books/Dutton, 1995), p. 134.

2. Tom Peters, "Get Innovative or Get Dead," *California Management Review* 33, 1 (Fall 1990), pp. 9–26.

Acknowledgments

It is not possible to list all the individuals who have affected my thinking about what it takes to be an innovator and the kind of environment that fosters innovation. Most of these colleagues, collaborators, executives, friends, and some casual acquaintances are probably not aware of the lessons they might have taught me. Most of the education was positive, but in the process I also learned what not to do. We don't know why some people develop a questioning attitude and others tend to accept the status quo, or why one person asks *why* and another *why not.* Some of us cannot live without change, while others cannot live with change. Some say, "There has to be a better way" and others live by the dictum, "If it ain't broke, why fix it." Taking an unconventional stand probably came from my father and was judiciously tempered by my mother. In addition to my parents, my sources of inspiration were abundant: several high school teachers who supported my adventures into the unknown, a summer work supervisor during my college years who challenged a group of us to focus on engineering excellence, my many business colleagues and friends, and the many authors who stirred my imagination. I also recognize those tradesmen who fashioned my designs into usable products and the many maintenance and support staff whose services allow innovation to happen.

My sincere thanks to AMACOM's executive editor, Ms. Adrienne Hickey, for her interest in promoting the concept of *Innovation by Design;* to Mike Sivilli, the associate editor; and to Lydia Lewis, the production manager. My compliments to all of them and their staff for their high level of professionalism in making *Innovation by Design* a reality. It's always a pleasure to work with colleagues who pursue excellence.

Finally, to my wife Shirley, my partner who made the decision with me to pursue this effort, my sincere thanks for her interest, research, collaboration, cooperation, and counsel which was so essential to this effort.

Gerard H. (Gus) Gaynor

1

Perspectives on Innovation

There is no doubt that the twentieth century will be credited as the century of innovation. It may not have witnessed the building of the pyramids or the Roman aqueducts or the birth of the Italian Renaissance, but there were monumental achievements that made a profound difference in how societies live and communicate. Whether all innovations helped society achieve an improved lifestyle remains to be established. Twentieth-century innovations had the following effects:

- Changed us from an agrarian society to an industrial society

- Built the infrastructure of the nation

- Revolutionized communication, erasing barriers of time and place

- Reduced the drudgery associated with many jobs

- Almost doubled longevity

- Reduced work hours

- Provided opportunities for personal development

- Overpowered us with data

- Overspecialized some professions

- Caused us to lose some of our work ethic

- Made us a sound-bite society

- Embedded a litigious culture

All of these innovations have changed our lifestyle—some were for the greater good, while the benefits to society of others can be questioned. The critical failing may be that society, as a whole, has not increased its intellectual capability to cope with the demands of new technologies and the changes created by those technologies. We process billions of bits of data but we have limited ability to discriminate the useful from the useless. We purchase all types of gadgets that often force us to question the impact on effectiveness and efficiency. At the same time the fight continues to introduce the metric system, and agreement could not be reached to use statistical sampling for the 2000 census. Life has become simpler in many ways, and at the same time more complex. Are all our organizations ready to apply the basics of innovation?

Figure 1-1 is a pictorial description of the factors that affect innovation. Innovation depends on four major elements: resources, infrastructure, culture, and process. All four are equally important. In *Innovation by Design,* we direct attention to integrating these four elements into a cohesive, systematic approach to improving the re-

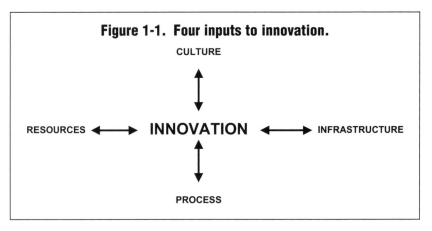

Figure 1-1. Four inputs to innovation.

sults from investing in innovation. Each of these elements interacts with the others to form an effective and efficient means for pursuing innovation. Innovation cannot take place if any of these four elements are missing. Obviously, each of these elements will not meet all the expected requirements. Resources require a supporting infrastructure and a supporting infrastructure requires resources. A supporting culture and an effective and efficient process provide organizations with a means for expanding innovation throughout the organization.

Innovation by Design defines innovation as invention plus implementation/commercialization. Invention involves the process of taking an idea and developing it into a concept, which finally leads to an innovation. So, where do we go from here?

Innovate Now or Pay Later

Most discussions about innovation focus on computer hardware and software, the Internet, e-commerce, and all the electronic gadgetry that is supposed to make life easier and more productive. Arguments cannot be made against this perspective of innovation, but innovation includes more than these limited technological accomplishments. Most innovation does not reach the public eye. The public seldom recognizes innovation in the chemical and pharmaceutical industries, in manufacturing processes, in the building of local and national infrastructure, in space exploration, in agriculture, in medicine, and even in government and academic organizations. Innovation is taken for granted and seldom recognized. Society only sees the results. Yet, major organizations that have neglected innovation have had a profound negative impact on its people, communities, and the national economy.

Too often innovation is considered solely the purview of those involved in the organization's technological activities. Although technological innovation drives most organizations, the proof of technological innovation resides in the marketplace. Technological innovation without comparable levels of innovation from all sectors of an organization significantly reduces the benefits from investing in innovation.

Innovation involves all entities of an organization, with no exceptions. Is there any justifiable reason why human resource departments should be exempt from being innovative—not just promoting innovation but doing innovation? And what about innovation in the accounting department—not through a wave of creative accounting but through new approaches to reporting and eliminating financial reports, accelerating the project approval process, or verifying the return from investing in new manufacturing facilities? Also, is there any reason why administrative functions should be exempt from introducing innovations, such as purchasing departments simplifying their processes and reducing the time from request to delivery? These innovations will most likely be incremental but can have a major impact on organizational performance. Bureaucracies are an important part of any organization, but they need to be effective and efficient. Maintaining the status quo is not acceptable.

Innovation includes the whole organization—no single group or function has a monopoly on innovation. Executives and managers cannot be excluded, since they cannot expect innovation from others if they are not the innovators in some sphere of the organization's purposes and objectives. Every member has the potential to be the innovator. Every external contact has the potential to support the innovation process. The sources are unlimited. The critical issue lies in recognizing the opportunities. The road to successful innovation often presents what might be considered insurmountable challenges but the innovator pursues the challenges relentlessly. The innovator knows that the shortest distance between two points is not a straight line; detours are the name of the game.

Innovation has taken on significantly greater prominence in recent years. People from academia, business and industry, government, and the nonprofit sector have spent a great deal of time attending conferences on innovation, hiring the gurus, and talking about it. However, it is necessary to differentiate between reality and the media hype. Innovation involves more than gaining knowledge, promoting continuous learning, or thinking deep thoughts—it involves translating knowledge and thinking into action. Yes, all are important, but individually they are insufficient. A more appropriate approach to innovation can be expressed by paraphrasing the 3M statement related to introducing innovative products:

Make a little, sell a little, make a little more, sell a little more, and so on to learn a little, do a little, learn a little more, do a little more, and so on.

Learning is absolutely essential but must be followed by doing. That "make a little, sell a little" has gotten much bigger in recent years, and likewise the "learn a little, do a little" has become an interdisciplinary exercise.

Most innovation takes place incrementally. Even though a concept may be recognized as a potential breakthrough, innovation success comes about incrementally over time. Innovations generally are not planned. Management cannot call a meeting and decide it wants to innovate. Planning is anathema to the innovator, not because of lack of interest but because until the concept has been defined—which very often includes experimentation in its broadest sense and verification and validation of a long list of parameters—very little is known about the interaction between the technology and the market.

Tom Peters, who with colleague Robert H. Waterman, Jr., wrote *In Search of Excellence* in 1982, eventually became the innovation guru. He went on to recommend such actions as celebrating failures, hiring and protecting renegades, recognizing small wins, implementing a "performance culture," committing the organization to lifelong learning, reading the right books, getting beyond rational analysis, and looking at failure as a part of life. One cannot argue with Peters' recommended actions. That's the way innovation comes about. It's not accomplished from nine to five. It's not accomplished without risk to personal careers. It's all about having the courage to introduce change. People who cannot live without change become the innovators. Innovators do not live in the organization's comfort zone.

There are no formulas for developing an innovative organization. There are principles that need to be followed in order to introduce innovations on time. The innovation from organizations such as Proctor & Gamble, 3M, Hewlett-Packard, Corning, Apple, Compaq, Dell, BancOne, Wal-Mart, CNN, *USA Today*, Honda, Sony, and others did not come about through some orderly set of plans. Principles were followed but tailored to the specific needs of the organization and to the particular innovation. In each of these organizations innovation came about by focusing on the marketplace. Innovation involves a process but is not dominated by process. Too often industrial organizations have emphasized technology but the test of technological innovation is in the marketplace, not in the laboratory. This industry perspective also applies to academia, government, and nonprofit organizations. Each lives in the province of the marketplace. Although academia and government are slow in responding to market forces, the nonprofit organizations clearly now realize that their future depends on providing services that meet user needs—needs of their supporters and their clients.

Choice or Chance

Leaving innovation to chance may be a dangerous strategy as world markets continue to expand. Although the general wisdom is that the world is getting smaller, I suggest that just the opposite is true. The world may appear to be smaller because of our capacity for instant communication, but the business opportunities, while demanding more control of resources, are expanding significantly. As organizations and nations lose their uninhabited markets, competition will increase for products that add value.

Although innovation cannot be left to chance, no one can dictate just when it may occur. No one can say, we will innovate and make it happen. Innovation involves people and springs from their intellect, imagination, and motivation rather than from executive dictums. However, the organization's executives are accountable for providing the flow of products that comes about only through its innovators. If innovation was clearly understood and easy to accomplish, chances are there might be more of it.

Discussion of any topic needs to be based on a framework that allows looking at the pieces in relation to each other and also in relation to the whole. Without a frame of reference it becomes difficult rationally to reach logical conclusions. However, we need to be cautious about applying too much structure, logic, and rational thinking when considering innovation. The new, the unconventional, and the off-the-wall proposals that alter the status quo of an organization are not amenable to conventional wisdom. The voices of conformity and conventional thinking are not the voices of innovation.

The Innovation Continuum

Innovation does not take place by some well-defined linear process. Innovation lies on a continuum of events that begins with a raw idea, which is developed into a concept, which then yields some type of invention, and which is finally implemented and commercialized. These are progressive and iterative stages that describe the innovation process. Too often the words like idea, concept, invention, and innovation are used interchangeably. We may even hear such comments as, "What an innovative idea!" But ideas, concepts, inventions, and innovations are all different. So just what do we mean when we speak about this continuum from idea to innovation? The innovation process begins with a raw idea, after which the work begins.

Ideas

Raw ideas provide little value unless someone pursues them. So an idea is just an idea and nothing more unless it's acted upon. Relatively few idea generators take the time to adequately describe the idea, and many organizations, though not suffering from a lack of raw ideas, suffer from a lack of interest in pursuing them. Those suggestion boxes may be full, but those "suggesters" will most likely not pursue the ideas to a conclusion.

A raw idea is just what the name implies, a raw idea: a spur of the moment thought, a reflection of some visual or audible stimulus, or the result of daydreaming. A raw idea needs hard thinking to determine its significance. Ideas need to be framed in some acceptable manner in order to be communicated to others. Somehow documenting an idea brings out the implementation difficulties and forces greater introspection and thought. Developing the idea requires many iterations. The final idea may be quite different from the original one.

People who say "I had a great idea last night" probably won't do anything about it. Working an idea involves writing it down, turning it inside out and outside in and upside down and downside up, and thinking about it to determine its complexities and significance. Whereas there may be no shortage of creative people or idea generators, what is lacking are people willing to articulate the idea from a systems perspective and then pursue the idea to a successful conclusion. That original idea may not be recognizable as it goes through the development process.

Implementation of ideas requires some deep thinking. We all know that the more we think about an idea the less we know about it. The original idea may be our answer to a major problem or opportunity before the thinking machine goes into action, but after descending from cloud nine and facing the realities the work begins. According to Theodore Levitt, "The trouble with much creativity today is that many of the people with the ideas have the peculiar notion that their jobs are finished when they suggest them; that it is up to somebody else to work out the dirty details and then implement the proposals. Typically, the more creative the man, the less responsibility he takes for action."[1] Even though Levitt noted this phenomenon in 1969, it prevails today in most organizations, including at the executive and management levels. It takes a lot of interest, energy, and staying power to work out the many details to fashion an idea into something new and useful.

Some statistics help demonstrate how many raw ideas are required to generate a commercially acceptable product. A Universal Industrial Success Curve[2] shows a seven-stage segmentation scale of ideas. From 3,000 unwritten raw ideas, 300 would end up being formalized in some written form, which would lead to a *single* success. That's not a very good success rate. There is something wrong with the idea-generating process if only one out of 300 ideas can be considered successful. There must be a better way.

Evidently, the various brainstorming processes are yielding quantity rather than quality. Although much has been written about various forms of brainstorming and ideation activities, most writers underestimate the effort required to articulate an idea into some workable reality. Generating ideas requires some deep and disciplined thinking. A group may meet for two hours and brainstorm a solution for resolving some specific problem, but there are few examples of brainstorming sessions yielding the idea for a breakthrough product, technology, or something that would provide a significant economic or social benefit. Brainstorming sessions generally don't promote deep thinking. Those two-hour brainstorming sessions may provide an answer to some nagging problem that can be decided based on known facts. But looking into the future will not be accomplished in two hours.

When brainstorming sessions deal with a new product or process, they require extensive preparatory work, followed by a three- to five-day immersion session, and by subsequent evaluation, reexamination, and redesign sessions. There's nothing magical about the three to five days for the session. Such sessions require a select group of mentally alert and disciplined people willing to work around the clock if necessary to build on each other's ideas. Why around the clock? It takes time to work through an idea, consider the issues and alternatives, and determine its viability from many different perspectives. Once a group is on a roll, the discussion must continue until the critical factors have been identified. These are not sessions to promote a particular concept but opportunities for exploring and seeking resolution of a major organizational issue.

Topics could include strategy, effectiveness and efficiency, new products and processes, entrance into new markets, dealing with competitive issues, and expansion into global markets. The list of potential topics is unlimited but they must be topics that require concentrated thinking time. After the initial session has been summarized (within twenty-four hours), another session is scheduled approximately two weeks later with sufficient time to review the results of the previous meeting and to develop a plan. These are not sessions for pursuing personal agendas or promoting a specific idea or solution. Those promoting a particular approach without participating in thoughtful discussion should be asked to leave the session. These are not sessions for selling ideas; they are sessions for exploring ideas, for doing the hard work.

At one point in my career, I organized a group of four people to brainstorm concepts for designing automatic assembly equipment. I had worked with this group for many years, and our freewheeling discussions often lasted into the early morning hours. The objective was to develop a workable concept that met the system requirements. This group, from the first meeting onward, developed a collegial relationship. Nobody arrived with the purpose of convincing the group of any preconceived solution. The sessions focused on exploring various ideas and developing a workable and value-adding concept. At one time we brought two additional people into these sessions—what a disaster. Immediately they began pushing their preconceived concept without any thought of exploring options.

After a few hours they were politely told to either put on their thinking caps or leave.

Launching a successful product, process, service—whether related to industry, government, or academia—involves more than just the idea; success also depends on resolving the interrelated human issues in the operating system. An excellent product idea cannot be a market success without the support of all other organizational functions. A recognized idea in some government agency provides little if any value unless the cross-functional implementation difficulties are resolved. Academia cannot transform itself into an innovative organization without considering the social construct in which it operates. So, an idea is only an idea unless it is acted upon. In an ideal situation the needed passion to go forward in pursuing the idea would come from the idea generator.

From Idea to Concept

Transforming an idea into a workable concept involves taking account of the system in which the idea will be implemented. In the formative stages of the concept, the available information may be limited but it needs to be considered. In addition, new information needs to be gathered and factored into the decision processes. The work effort to develop a concept includes the following tasks:

- *Identifying the available resources*—the required resources from either within or outside the organization

- *Understanding the organizational infrastructure*—the infrastructure that supports innovation

- *Assessing the competencies and capabilities of the organization*—individual, team, and various group competencies that are required to develop into organizational capability

- *Interpreting economic and global demographic information*—information related to the context of the concept under consideration

- *Evaluating the competencies of all the support functions*—the skill levels of the organizational support functions, noting the deficiencies

- *Managing the interfaces*—those involved in bringing any concept to fruition

- *Integrating individual and team and group competencies into organizational capability*—individual competence that develops into organizational capability

Transforming that idea into a concept—whether in academia, government, or business and industry—is not possible without concentrated work effort. The organizational capability must be greater than the sum of the individual competencies, and that involves managing with discipline.

Organizational resources, infrastructure, and capability in marketing, sales, and distribution cannot be disregarded in academic or governmental organizations. As in industry, these organizations also have interfaces with contradictory objectives that are very difficult to reconcile. While academia emphasizes independent thinking, it also lacks interest in interdisciplinary participation—each unit typically operates independently of the other with no integration of thought or action. Governmental entities depend on rules and regulations, policies and procedures, and the environment is generally averse to innovation. Not-for-profit organizations also require a full understanding of their resources, infrastructure, and the ability to market and distribute their products.

Assuming that an idea has been clearly identified, developing it into a concept requires a significant amount of effort. Just what is that effort? There are few ideas that can be developed within a single discipline. A technology idea may not be worth pursuing unless some investigation is performed regarding its need. If the investment is made, how will the technology be used—what line of products will reach the market using the technology? Who are the customers? What are the features, advantages, and benefits? How does the technology help sustain the organization's future? As you can see, making the transition from idea to concept goes beyond just the formulation or the defining of the idea.

A viable concept requires more than a description on paper as to what it will do for the organization if implemented—it requires a proof of concept. A proof of concept is just what the phrase implies—it must show that the concept is workable. This means that the known and the unknown need to be identified. The known issues require some level of validation. The unknown issues require resolution, which may involve some experimental studies to develop prototypes that demonstrate the underlying principles.

Proof of concept can be accomplished through the simplest and most primitive of techniques, depending on the needs. As a physicist from the University of Chicago taught me many years ago, concepts are proven with rubber bands, pins, beeswax, string, and all the mundane things found in society. Of course the mundane things now involve more sophisticated resources, but they can probably be found in somebody's high-tech junk box. Developing a concept (we need to keep in mind that this takes time) is really coming to grips with the undefined, the uncertainties, and the unpredictable issues and circumstances related to moving from an idea to a well-structured and understandable concept.

Assuming that an idea has been clearly articulated, here are some of the questions that must be answered on the road to developing a concept. All of these questions apply to industry, academia, government, and nonprofit organizations.

- How does the defined concept advance the organization's purpose, mission, objectives, and strategies?

- Does pursuing this concept fit the organization's long-term strategy? How will successful implementation of the concept differentiate the organization from the competition?

- Has the concept been analyzed from a systems perspective?

- Are all the technologies available internally? If not, are they available from outside sources?

- In what stage are the technologies on the continuum, from ready-to-be-retired to leading edge to unproved?

- Are the marketing, sales, and distribution organizations in place to pursue this particular concept? If not, what are the alternatives?

- What are the competitive issues?

- Are all the resources available?

- Does the infrastructure support the concept?

- Have the knockouts been identified and resolved? What will prevent this concept from being implemented?

- Is there a realistic financial analysis?

- What are the investment tradeoffs?

- Have the uncertainties been considered?

- Have the unknown issues been resolved?

- Have the risks been evaluated?

A clearly articulated concept requires responses to these questions. The responses will have various levels of uncertainty that must be seriously questioned during the initial stages of transforming an idea into an articulated concept. But that uncertainty can be either diminished or increased as new information and knowledge are gained. The point is that one does not sit down and define the concept on paper. Articulating a concept involves extensive search for new information. Why is it so difficult for society to agree on a viable health care system? Why is it so difficult to resolve the issues facing the educational community? Why is it so difficult to introduce change in any organization? The answers to these questions lie in developing alternative concepts that can be articulated in some logical way. It is the work effort that requires a total commitment of energy and time.

Invention

The word *invention* should not require any explanation, but we may look at the definition from different perspectives. The following descriptions provide perspectives from a management scholar, an eminent educator, and an economist:

A management scholar:
We discover what before existed, though to us unknown; we invent what did not exist before.[3]

An eminent educator:
The invention process covers all efforts aimed at creating new ideas and getting them to work.[4]

An economist:
Every invention is (a) a new combination of (b) preexisting knowledge which (c) satisfies some want.[5]

So, we invent what did not exist, create new ideas and get them to work, and satisfy some want in the process. These descriptions focus on preexisting knowledge in some form. Invention is not science. Components, assemblies, mechanisms, and various types of equipment used in daily living are recognized as inventions. All of these are some combination of preexisting knowledge. Although we normally associate inventions with patents, we need to recognize that many inventions are never patented. As an example, many organizations do not patent their processes but instead treat them as organization-confidential; once a patent is issued, knowledge of the invention becomes available to all who choose to search the patent literature. Counting numbers of patents does not provide much security for beating out the competition. There are patents and then there are patents. The optimal solution is to have patents that add value, significant value.

It is considerably more difficult to associate invention with the academic and government communities. While academic institutions create many inventions as a result of their scientific and engineering research efforts, finding new ways of organizing education has been less successful. Approaches such as programmed learning and distance learning have met with varying degrees of success, usually better when related to training than to education. The success of various levels and approaches to Web-based learning will be determined in the future. One point is certain, however; not all education will go electronic. There are some excellent tools in the marketplace, but those tools need to be evaluated as to their potential benefits to the academic community and the learner.

It is difficult to identify inventions in government-related organizations except in functions dealing with space exploration, defense, and various groups dealing directly with technology. However, there should be ample opportunity if the focus were on effectiveness, efficiency, and economic use of resources. Of course, such a focus would involve introducing change that would most likely eliminate over 50 percent of existing policies and procedures. Just thinking of making organizational bureaucracies productive in any organization provides mega-opportunities for invention.

Innovation

What do we mean by innovation? The word *innovation* first appears around 1297, according to the *Oxford Dictionary*. In 1561, T. Norton of Calvin's Institute said, "It is the duty of private men to obey, and not to make innovation states after their own will." In 1824, L. Murray said, "The spirit of innovation has extended itself to other parts of grammar, and especially to the names of Tenses." In 1939, J. A. Schumpeter said, "Innovation is possible without anything we should identify as invention, and invention does not necessarily induce innovation."

A great deal of controversy exists as to what comprises an innovation. Ideas, concepts, and inventions are the precursors of innovation. Ideas and concepts cannot generally be implemented. Inventions, even though supported by a patent, require significant expenditures to make them operational. The following comments provide some insight as to a description of innovation:

Edward B. Roberts:
The first generalization is: innovation = invention + exploitation. The invention process covers all efforts aimed at creating new ideas and getting them to work. The exploitation process includes all stages of commercial development, application, and transfer, including the focusing of ideas or inventions toward specific objectives, evaluating those objectives, downstream transfer of research and/or development results, and eventual broad-based utilization, dissemination, and diffusion of the technology-based outcomes.[6]

Peter F. Drucker:
Its [innovation's] criterion is not science or technology, but a change in the economic or social environment, a change in the behavior of people as consumers or producers, as citizens, as students or as teachers and so on. Innovation creates new wealth or new potential for action rather than new knowledge.[7]

Gifford Pinchot III:
Invention is the act of genius in creating a new concept for a potentially useful new device or service. In innovation, that is just the beginning. When an invention is done, the second half of innovation begins: turning the idea into a business success.[8]

Theodore Levitt:
Generally speaking, innovation may be viewed from at least two vantage points: (1) newness in the sense that something has never been done before, and (2) newness in the sense that something has not been done before by the industry or by the company now doing it. Strictly defined, innovation occurs only when something is entirely new, having never been done before.[9]

These descriptions of innovation focus on different aspects but at the same time are not contradictory. Although invention in all disciplines and in all industries has the same meaning, innovation because of its all-encompassing scope, from introducing new materials through developing macro systems, requires contextual considerations. So where do all of these descriptions lead? The following descriptions summarize what innovation involves:

- Innovation is creating new ideas and getting them to work.
- Innovation is not science or technology.
- Innovation creates new wealth rather than knowledge.
- Innovation is turning an idea into a business success.
- Innovation is a change in the economic or social environment.
- Innovation must be user-focused.
- Innovation = invention + exploitation.
- Exploitation = everything involved in implementation or commercialization.
- Innovation is newness in the sense of not having been done before—but with a little bit of slack.

All of these descriptions build on the fact that:

INNOVATION = INVENTION + IMPLEMENTATION/
COMMERCIALIZATION

Innovation begins with an idea that is transformed into a concept that includes some new combination of what is already known and can be implemented to serve some purpose. Invention and innovation involve creativity. They require thinking about the possible. They require thinking about what could be, about doing things differently, and about combining known facts into new combinations. They require the ability to put it all together. Invention and innovation also need people with some level of dissatisfaction with the status quo, namely new pathfinders with the ability to move the status quo.

Sources of Innovation

Too often innovation is considered solely the purview of those involved in the organization's technological activities. Although technological innovation drives most organizations, the proof of technological innovation resides in the marketplace. Innovation involves more than the introduction of new computer hardware and software. Technological innovation without comparable levels of innovation from all sectors of an organization significantly reduces the benefits from investing in innovation. The critical issue lies in recognizing the opportunities. The road to successful innovation often presents what might be considered insurmountable challenges but the innovator pursues the challenges relentlessly. The innovator knows that in pursuing innovation the shortest distance between two points is not a straight line—detours are the name of the game.

Perhaps all organizations need to follow Peter F. Drucker's dictum:

> Every organization—not just business—needs one core competence: innovation.

Drucker is not suggesting that everyone can or should be an innovator. If all employees were innovators without adequate support from staff, chaos would reign supreme. It is safe to say that there would be no innovation.

Organizational Governance

Innovative organizations are governed by four major considerations:

1. Understanding the innovator's characteristics and working relationships

2. Developing an environment that fosters innovation

3. Integrating the organizational activities, functions, and disciplines

4. Managing from a systems perspective

Building the innovative organization requires competent innovators, collaborative peers and colleagues, a supporting management, and consideration of the internal management system and the external system in which the organization operates.

Innovators do not meet some idealized description or specification. Generally they tend to be constructive mavericks that have a passion to pursue some particular activity—their eyes and minds are on the future, on what could be. They are probably independent thinkers who challenge ways of doing things and cannot live without change, which does not suggest that they are necessarily the change makers.

Organizations attempting to develop an environment that fosters innovation need to recognize the complexity of the task. Balancing freedom and discipline, short- and long-term results, and resources to maintain a competitive edge requires multidimensional decision processes. Innovation will not thrive in an organization with a command-and-control mentality nor in an organization that believes in total freedom. There must be a balance between levels of freedom and levels of discipline. The extreme ends of this continuum are reserved for special circumstances.

Why integration? Innovation involves many different disciplines. That is a fact. No single discipline can develop an innovation. Technological complexity requires input from many disciplines. Knowledge of electronics without knowledge of mechanical systems will not yield innovation. Knowledge of medicine without knowledge of electronics and materials technology will not produce a new heart pacemaker or an implantable heart valve. Knowledge of computer software without knowledge of computer hardware will not produce an Internet. Knowledge of information systems without mechanical or electrical knowledge will not design a complex automation system. Knowledge about technologies without knowledge of marketing and distribution will not produce a commercially successful innovation. When organizational functions and disciplines are integrated, that integration can multiply the benefits in a working group manifold. Innovation demands integration.

Innovation also depends on accepting the systems approach to management. The concept of a "system" is not new. The practice of the systems approach began in the 1950s as a result of the expansion of the defense industries. The system is no more than a collection of all the components and a resolution of the impact of the combination on a customer, user, or society. Managing the pieces without considering the interaction of the pieces not only lengthens the time-to-market but also generates a significant amount of rework. Innovation is not solely a technological issue. Solely relating innovation to technology without considering the marketing and distribution requirements will not yield innovation. It takes the whole organization to bring about a successful innovation.

The process for implementation, often considered complex, requires understanding the principles and applying them within a specific organization or organizational unit. Organizations tend to pursue some single issue that has been recently anointed by an academic or industrial guru or the business press as though it were the answer to competitiveness and business sustainability. These single-issue approaches to management began decades ago and have spanned the years from scientific management to reengineering the corporation. As single issues, no approaches have been able to optimize the use of organizational resources and their related infrastructure. Pursuing any single issue ignores the basics for creating economic value and developing competitive advantage.

From a practitioner's perspective, creating economic value and competitive advantage are grounded in individual competence that can be integrated into organizational capability. This perspective requires a mental attitude that focuses attention on optimizing the system rather than maximizing the output of selected business entities or activities. Managing the enterprise means exploiting the resources and the infrastructure of the enterprise and transforming them into unique capabilities. This can only be accomplished through a call for enterprise-wide innovation.

Innovation Must Be Nourished

The chances of developing a theory or a theoretical base for innovation in the classical scientific sense will probably not occur. There are different industries, different competencies and capabilities, different motivations, and different priorities. But a systematic categorization of activities certainly will not deter innovation. Academic researchers need to continue their efforts in providing longitudinal studies that at some future date may offer more quantitative analysis of the innovation process.

The extent to which innovation can differentiate the successful from the unsuccessful organizations depends on how we define innovation and how we define success. Too often success is solely defined in quantifiable financial terms. Financial success is essential, but the learning that takes place during the process of innovation cannot be disregarded. The innovation efforts that fail often provide the starting point for new innovation, as illustrated by the example of 3M's Post-it Notes. The knowledge gained in these so-called failed innovations is a corporate asset when documented and available for future use. These failures are the organization's intellectual property—they represent organizational learning. At the same time the future cannot be dedicated to learning from failures.

Innovation does not occur in an organization that supports the status quo and denigrates the forward thinkers. Chances are that if the stimulus for innovation does not come from within the organization, pursuing it outside the organization may not provide the desired effect. Industrial campuses don't necessarily motivate. 3M still maintains one of its original buildings, the Benz Building, which has been the physical location of many of 3M's major innovations. However, whether the modern research buildings with all their architecturally refined spaces provide more fertile environments for innovation is questionable. In the final analysis, innovation depends on people and their interactions. Innovation begins with a mental model.

Culture is important. When an organization does not provide an environment that fosters innovation and does not provide an organizational infrastructure to support innovation, none will occur. When an organization does not support the constructive mavericks and make concessions for failure, innovation is dead. Culture is not so much about the organizational culture but about the subculture in which the innovator practices the art of innovation—innovation is part science, part theory, and a lot of art. But a culture that supports innovation is not a touchy-feely culture. On the contrary, an innovation culture is a supportive one with discipline that promotes high expectations and challenges its people.

The organization that takes the biggest innovation risks may or may not realize the highest payoffs. This depends on the short- or long-term orientation of the organization. Technologies can lie dormant for many years. Chester Carlson invented the xerographic process in 1938. A copy machine was unveiled in 1948, but it took another decade for Haloid-Xerox to deliver a practical rotary-drum office copier.

Innovation Myths

Beware of the innovation myths! There are few if any yes or no responses to issues facing the innovators. Research shows that although innovation has been studied from many different perspectives, attempts to define, dissect, and characterize innovation models have resulted in perpetuating many myths. Kuczmarski and colleagues list four myths that are associated with innovation:

1. Individuals drive innovation.

2. Innovation begins with brainstorming.

3. Innovation requires creative people.

4. An innovation process will give the results you need.

They counter with the following characterizations:

1. Innovation is a team sport.

2. Innovation begins with understanding the customer.

3. Innovation requires effective problem solvers rather than creative people.

4. The innovation process is only one tool for successful innovation.[10]

All of those myths lie someplace on a true to false continuum. Although no theoretical base exists for innovation, some specific requirements must be present for innovation to occur. Innovation cannot occur without resources and a supportive infrastructure. Innovation cannot occur if management doesn't support it. In the early stages, individuals do drive innovation although teams are required as the project progresses. Although customer input is essential, innovation also begins with those individuals who are inquisitive, intuitive, and have demonstrated powers of observation. While problem solvers are important, it takes some level of creativity to put those disparate pieces of technology and markets into a new product or system. Problem solvers by their very definition display various levels of creativity. However, problem finders who have the initiative and motivation to become problem solvers are in short supply. Problems associated with introducing an innovation are not found in a handbook.

Organizational culture is important. It's difficult to innovate in an organization that essentially closes the door to new ideas. Why are companies like Hewlett-Packard and 3M always listed as the most innovative organizations? Very simply, over time they have developed a culture that fosters innovation. They recognize that innovation requires individual as well as team performance, that customers are important but are not the sole sources of ideas, that culture is important, and that any use of a rigid process without thought just doesn't work.

You may ask what's the importance of discussing these innovation myths if each can lie someplace between the true and false extremes of the myths continuum? Each myth has some degree of truth, but organizations cannot guide their thinking at the extreme ends of that continuum. It's impossible to think of innovation as only a team sport. The "0" and "1" structure of computer programs doesn't work. Innovations come in all sizes and shapes, from all geographical centers, and with very specific requirements. One size does not fit all. Managers need to be cognizant of the fact that definitions can be either related to short-term or to long-term positions, and that balancing the relationship is the art of management. An organization that is considered innovative today may not be so tomorrow if the passion for innovation dies.

Summary

- Innovation depends on four major elements: resources, infrastructure, culture, and process. All four are equally important and need to be integrated for successful innovation.

- Organizations will innovate now or pay the price at some time in the future. Innovation is not a matter of chance, but of choice.

- Innovation involves a continuum from ideas, to concepts, to invention, to innovation.

- In simple terms *innovation = invention + implementation/ commercialization.*

- Sources of innovation are unlimited.

- Innovation must be nourished by a supportive culture.

- The innovation myths lie on the true-to-false continuum.

Notes

1. Theodore Levitt, *The Marketing Mode* (New York: McGraw-Hill, 1969), pp. 155–170.

2. Greg A. Stevens and James Burley, "3000 Raw Ideas = 1 Commercial Success!" *Research Technology Management,* May–June 1997, pp. 16–28.

3. Robert A. Burgelman, Modesto A. Maidique, and Steven C. Wheelwright, *Strategic Management of Technology and Innovation* (Chicago: Irwin, 1996), p. 1.

4. Edward B. Roberts, *Generating Technological Innovation* (New York: Oxford University Press, 1987), p. 3.

5. Jacob Schmookler, *Invention and Economic Growth* (Cambridge: Harvard University Press, 1966).

6. Roberts, *Generating Technological Innovation,* p. 3.

7. Peter F. Drucker, *Management, Tasks, Responsibilities, Practices* (New York: Harper & Row, 1973), p. 788.

8. Gifford Pinchot III, *Intrapreneuring* (New York: Harper & Row, 1985), p. 11.

9. Levitt, *The Marketing Mode,* p. 54.

10. Thomas Kuczmarski, Arthur Middlebrooks, and Jeffrey Swaddling, *Innovating the Corporation* (Lincolnwood, Ill: NTC Business Books, 2001), pp. 32–37.

2

Innovation Types and Product Classes

Innovations vary in scope, time for completion, and organizational and societal impact. Categorization of any kind usually involves areas of duplication, where the lines between one category and another overlap. This lack of distinct categories complicates the classification process. These levels need to be rationalized, especially when we deal with the higher levels of innovation. There are significant difference in the complexities between what are normally considered incremental innovations and those that include major investment of resources, significant capital investment, and long lead times.

Standard Categories of Innovation

The generally accepted innovation categories include incremental, discontinuous, architectural, system, radical, and the more recent disruptive. Later in this chapter, I propose a simplified, three-category perspective, but first let's look at the standard classification scheme.

Incremental Innovation

Incremental innovations include the nuts and bolts kinds of innovation—the modification, refinement, simplification, consolidation, and enhancement of existing products, processes, services, and production and distribution activities. The majority of innovations fall in this category, and their importance should not be minimized in any way.

Some examples of incremental innovation include:

- The many versions of Sony's Walkman—not the original but all the models that followed and were built on a common platform

- Versions of nylon thread and cloth—from coarse products to refined products—with the nylon products of 2001 showing dramatic improvement over those of 1940

- Most automobiles, with annual minor improvements that over years provided significant benefits in safety, efficiency, and user comforts

Discontinuous Innovation

Discontinuous innovation has many corollary implications. It tends to make the skills of engineers, scientists, accountants, patent attorneys, and other professionals obsolete unless they recognize the impact of the diminished value of their knowledge and experience. Discontinuous innovation also tends to make technologies and processes obsolete. At the same time discontinuous innovation provides significant opportunities for those who have prepared for the next paradigm shift or recognize the need to make the transition.

Some examples of discontinuous innovation are:

- From the horse and buggy to the automobile, making many workers and professionals obsolete

- From candles and gas lights to oil lamps to electric light bulbs in many types to suit specific purposes, which provided society with luxuries previously unknown and which required new skills and competencies in all disciplines. Consumers now want light bulbs that meet their specific needs and wants.

- From manual typewriters to electric to word processors to personal computers. It is difficult to find people who can type ninety words per minute today, carpal tunnel syndrome was not in the vocabulary, and what would we do without cut and paste?

Architectural Innovation

Architectural innovation reconfigures a system of components that constitute a product, process, or service. Design components are linked together in a new way using many core design concepts in a new architecture. Architectural innovation requires knowledge about the components and how they are linked.

The following are some examples of architectural innovation:

- The transistor as a replacement for the vacuum tube. Remember those days when drug stores provided all the vacuum tube testers? The reliability of electronic products has increased by several orders of magnitude.

- Material substitutions, such as plastics replacing steel and aluminum. What would we do without plastics?

- From airplane radial engines to jet engines, with greater reliability and significantly greater efficiencies.

Systems Innovation

Systems innovation includes activities that require significant resources from many different disciplines; that involve many different businesses, academic, and governmental entities; and that take many years to accomplish. These are innovations that are plagued with government and societal regulations and often with significant interface problems.

Some examples of systems innovation are:

- *Communication Networks.* With the number of phone messages occurring daily, the old switchboard systems would probably require that every citizen function as switchboard operator.

- *Satellite Operations.* These are significant investments that have at times proved to be failures and have raised social issues related to confidentiality, intellectual property, and access.

- *World Wide Web.* There is no end of regulations and concerns about freedom of speech and intellectual property rights, about our dependence on it as a source of information, and about the impact created when maintenance problems arise.

Radical Innovation

Radical innovation involves introducing new products or services that develop into major new businesses or spawn new industries, or that cause significant change in a whole industry and tend to create new values.

Some examples of radical innovation are:

- Computer industry, going from kilobytes to gigabits and more. What would happen if all the computers would shut down for some unknown reason—remember those little stickers that airlines used for seat assignments—or how about the grocer who added everything mentally, no adding machines just pencil and paper

- Banking—not everyone subscribes to electronic banking—some don't trust the banks and want to personally deposit their checks—those are choices but the banking business has gone through at least a mild metamorphosis—ATM machines, funds available just about anyplace in the world with the appropriate plastic card

- The Internet—radical innovation or not, depends on your perspective—in one sense radical in another not—the Internet was touted that it would transform industry, government, and all social institutions—the Internet is really just another complementary technology—we need to learn to use it with increased levels of effectiveness and efficiency

Disruptive Innovation

Disruptive innovation brings a new value proposition, as suggested by Christensen.[1] Although Christensen refers to these as disruptive technologies, they are really disruptive innovations. If technologies are defined as artifacts, then the term disruptive technologies may be applicable. Disruptive innovation has some specific characteristics. These innovations generally underperform current products at the time they are introduced, they have features that attract a select group of first-to-adopt customers, they are usually more expensive, they offer new features and benefits, and the marketplace initially awards them little recognition. It takes time before these innovations gain market acceptance.

Some examples of disruptive innovation are:

- Silver halide film to digital photography—digital photography continues to have difficulty in meeting the standards of silver halide, but the marketplace has accepted the product because of additional benefits such as easy distribution

- Full-service stock brokerage to on-line brokerage—on-line brokerage has gained acceptance, but many people continue to prefer working face-to-face—like electronic banking the personal touch continues to predominate

- Standard retailing to on-line retailing—on-line retailing is having its ups and downs and at some time the formula for successful on-line retailing will be implemented

The Innovation Matrix

The innovation matrix (Figure 2-1) considers the type of innovation and the related activities. The matrix provides a means for determining the issues involved in each category. Attempting to develop a major systems innovation could prove to be destructive if the governing issues are not considered. Likewise, applying the conditions and requirements for a systems innovation to an incremental innovation may be equally destructive. We also need to recognize that categorizing an innovation is not a science and any one innovation can be positioned into different categories. What can be incremental to one organization may be disruptive to another. So categorization must be viewed in the context of the organization. What may be a best practice in one organization may be totally inappropriate in another.

Defining the position in the matrix helps the innovator understand the required resources and infrastructure for an activity fitting in that particular position. Each position in the matrix has different requirements. It's easy to understand the differences as we go from incremental to disruptive. Systems, radical, and disruptive innova-

Figure 2-1. Innovation matrix.

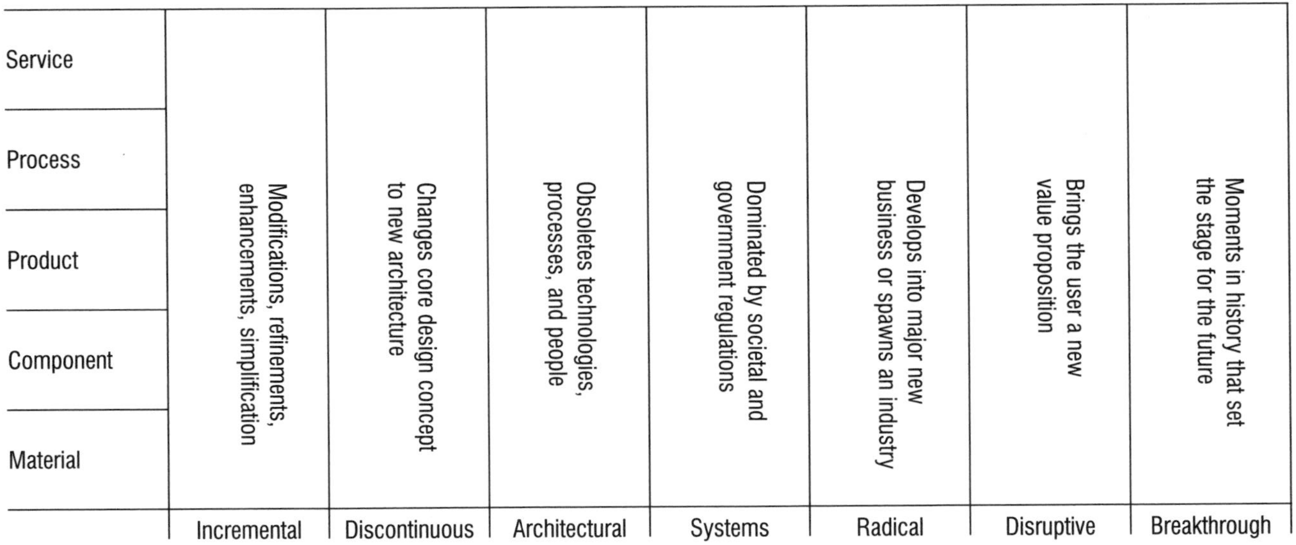

	Incremental	Discontinuous	Architectural	Systems	Radical	Disruptive	Breakthrough
Service							
Process							
Product	Modifications, refinements, enhancements, simplification	Changes core design concept to new architecture	Obsoletes technologies, processes, and people	Dominated by societal and government regulations	Develops into major new business or spawns an industry	Brings the user a new value proposition	Moments in history that set the stage for the future
Component							
Material							

see p. 73

tions will most likely be driven from the top down. However, most incremental and many architectural innovations can be and should be driven from the bottom up. That's the challenge to the professional community regardless of discipline.

Classification Inconsistencies

The classification of innovation on the incremental to breakthrough continuum requires simplification for operational purposes. A debate about where an innovation may lie on the continuum provides little benefit. These classifications allow consideration of innovation scope and they serve that purpose. Although it may be disheartening to some, an analysis of the whole innovation continuum from discontinuous to disruptive shows that most innovations can be classed as incremental. The first Sony Walkman was a major innovation, but all subsequent versions were incremental modifications, designed for new applications, and general product improvements. The first yellow pad of Post-it Notes may have been a breakthrough product for 3M, but subsequent renditions were incremental and obvious. The same applies to HP and its computer printer business. The technology was developed, the marketplace accepted the product, and then it became a question of how its use could be expanded and how many new configurations could be developed. In each of these examples the product lines expanded into a class of products that developed into major businesses. This does not in any way minimize the contributions of these products to their respective organizations.

The horse and buggy gave way to the automobile. Yes, major improvements have been made, but the automobile remains much the same after a century of major improvements—four wheels, an internal combustion engine, a steering wheel, and of course all the comforts of home from climate control to high fidelity audio systems to heated leather seats. I'm not minimizing the improvements, but the concept of the automobile remains essentially the same after almost one hundred years.

It also took about one hundred years to advance the music record business. Most people probably do not remember the Edison cylinder recording devices or the phonograph records that were more than a quarter of an inch thick. Those initial technologies took us from 78 rpm to 33 1/3 rpm, to 45 rpm, to wire recording, to tape recording, to CDs. Wire recording was not very popular and 45 rpm records were introduced to satisfy the market for inexpensive records. So over the course of about one hundred years, only four major improvements were introduced in how we listen to recorded music. That's one major innovation every twenty-five years. Once again there were major advances in materials technology and significant modifications and improvements in performance, but it was incremental innovation as far as the recording technique was concerned. Use of magnetic tape was a significant departure from plastic records: there were new technologies, new competencies, and new user benefits. The introduction of CDs presented a major departure from the traditional use of magnetic media, and once again there were new technologies, new competencies, and new user benefits.

An examination of systems, radical, and disruptive innovations also shows that they do not occur that often. The Internet may be considered a disruptive innovation, but in essence it's a new way of doing business—a new tool to accomplish the same result. Xerography may be a radical innovation, but after the first rotary drum copy machine became the office copier all improvements, advancements, and additions were incremental. Digital photography is a disruptive innovation by definition, but its impact on silver halide photography remains to be seen.

A Simplified Classification

These generally accepted categories of innovation contain many inconsistencies but at the same time provide some general guidance as to complexity and impact on the organization's business and society. With the exception of incremental innovation, all others do cross boundaries. Although the transition from the horse and buggy to the automobile is considered to be discontinuous, it is certainly radical and disruptive. Although the transistor as the replacement for vacuum tubes is considered to be architectural, it is certainly discontinuous, radical, and disruptive. Development of computer technology and its ancillary implications, although considered radical, can also be classed as disruptive, discontinuous, and perhaps architectural.

No classification system is perfect. I suggest the simplified classification system shown in Figure 2-2 because it fits the majority of organizations and the majority of their innovations. The simplified classification includes only three categories: incremental, new-to-the-market/society, and breakthrough. Incremental remains incremental. Discontinuous, system, radical, and disruptive now become one category: new-to-the-market.

Incremental innovation is described as improvements to current products, processes, services, and systems. Incremental innovations:

- Span a continuum from minor to major

- Can be short- or long-term

- Can be single or multidisciplinary

- Involve technology and/or markets

- Have high or low impact

New-to-the-market/society innovations deliver new products, processes, services, and systems, and they usually:

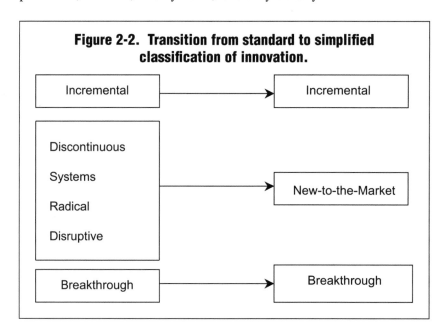

Figure 2-2. Transition from standard to simplified classification of innovation.

| Incremental | → | Incremental |

| Discontinuous
Systems
Radical
Disruptive | → | New-to-the-Market |

| Breakthrough | → | Breakthrough |

- Involve a major organizational effort

- Continue for long time periods

- Require multidisciplinary input

- Involve major marketing decisions

- Involve leading-edge technologies

- Have high impact on results

- Deal with uncertainty and create anxiety

- Require innovation management expertise

The new-to-the-market/society concept here can be expanded or limited. It's a convenient expression because all innovation depends on the marketplace, whether in industry, academia, or government. New-to-the-market includes discontinuous, architectural, system, radical, and disruptive innovations.

Breakthrough innovations fall into two categories:

1. Innovations specific to a particular business

2. Innovations that develop new industries

Both categories are really quite rare. Innovations specific to a business depend on the size of the business. An innovation that yields a billion dollars in sales in an organization whose annual revenue is $15 billion would be considered a breakthrough. But in that same organization an innovation generating $200,000 would not meet the requirements. However, an innovation that yields $100,000 in an organization whose annual revenue is $250,000 would certainly be a breakthrough.

Organizational breakthroughs are really in the eyes of management but must be appraised realistically. Breakthrough innovations require significant amounts of capital and can span many years before reaching expectations. Innovations that spawn new industries require long-term decisions and significant amounts of capital investment. Programs like the Boeing 747, xerography, communications, satellite operations, microprocessors, and most material innovations, such as the general category of polymers, have required major investments of resources over many years.

Industry breakthroughs are less common than we think. Figure 2-3 illustrates some of the innovations that built new industries in the past one hundred years.

Product Classifications

All classifications including product classification systems leave something to be desired. There is no one generalized classification that fits all industries. Furthermore classification is full of gray areas, which means that 2 + 2 seldom equals 4. So why talk about them? We talk about them to gain a better perspective of how to consider investments, to describe the potential benefits taking into consider-

---

Figure 2-3. Examples of industry breakthrough innovation.

Electric light bulbs	Power-generating equipment
Fluorescent lights	Power transmission
Steam engine	Diesel locomotives
Photography—X-ray and graphic arts	Color photography
Rubber	Synthetic rubber
Radio	Television
Telex transmission	Facsimile
Radar	Internet
Aircraft	Jumbo jets
Helicopters	Rockets
Gasoline engine	Jet engine
Steel-belted tires	Disk brakes
Automatic transmissions	Power brakes and steering
Plastics	Nylon
Polyester	Wrinkle-free fabrics
Plexiglas	Polymer-based plastics
High-impact plastics	Derivatives of petroleum products
Robotics	Automation
Xerography	Computers—hardware and software
Microprocessors	Lasers
Magnetic tape	Videocassettes
Optical disks	Ballpoint pens
Medical technologies	Computer-aided tomography
Gene technology	Space exploration

ation the uncertainties, to determine the availability of resources, and to discover the limitations of the organizational infrastructure.

New products can be classified as a(n):

- Improvement to a current product or class of products

- Novel replacement product

- New-to-the-market product

- Breakthrough product

- Me-too product

Improvement to a Current Product or Class of Products

Continuous product improvement cannot be avoided. These improvements sustain the organization even though all have a limited life cycle. The improvements, however, must be more than cosmetic. They must provide a defined benefit to the user but not necessarily be classified as innovative. Examples of continuous product improvement are:

- *Copiers.* Consider the enhancements to copiers, from the slow single-page copier to collators, staplers, size reduction and expansion, and color copiers.

- *Appliances.* These are now computer controlled and they provide for variable requirements, as illustrated by today's typical domestic dishwashers, stoves, and refrigerators.

- *Automotive.* Four wheels, a combustion engine, and a steering wheel continue to be the standard, but major improvements have been made in the form of disk brakes, steel-belted tires, new safety features such as air bags, and comfort features such as seat warmers.

Negative results often occur from improving products or adding new features. For example, the improvement to copiers created many customer complaints and service problems. An appliance manufacturer was required to replace the compressor on certain home refrigerator models because of problems associated with the original design—a major improvement but not fully tested to meet the reliability requirements of the marketplace. The automobile industry has been faced with recalls for major operational and safety problems.

Novel Replacement Product

A novel replacement product serves the same purpose as a current product and may include some enhanced features. Innovative replacement products do not occur very often. Significant improvements and addition of new features happen frequently, yes, but not replacement. The Kodak disk camera system represents a major attempt at introducing a replacement product/system even though it was a marketing disappointment. It was presented as a replacement for the type 110 film and camera system that had been on the market for over ten years and was a dominant format in amateur photography. The disk camera concept was not only innovative but provided many benefits in the cycle from purchase of film to delivery of prints. The camera could fit in a small purse or a shirt pocket. There were significant savings in processing of film and prints. But it never met marketing expectations. This is a good example of an excellent concept that failed to meet customer expectations because of technical problems—initial field complaints required 100 percent inspection of all film packages. In addition Kodak, Fuji, and others misread the oncoming changes in the 35-mm format market that began to offer significant competition because Japan introduced inexpensive higher quality 35-mm cameras. The sales projections for the disk camera system never materialized. In late 1989, the disk system that was projected to represent more than 30 percent of Kodak's amateur photography business represented less than 10 percent of sales, with many problems. The concept was certainly innovative but the implementation never met expectations.

New-to-the-Market Product

It's difficult to find new-to-the-market products in most established organizations. This is usually the domain of the upstart entrepreneurial organization or an established firm that emphasizes internal innovation and entrepreneurship. In most organizations that have been built on established technologies, processes, and products, it becomes difficult to stray from the path that led to the firm's success. At one time they may have mortgaged all their resources to pursue a technology or market, but the pioneering spirit decreases very quickly after organizations reach a certain level of maturity. During those intervening years, from the neophyte stage to being a major factor in the marketplace, the organizational mentality changes. Management tends to become risk aversive.

The following examples illustrate new-to-the-market products:

- Optical disks

- 3M's Post-it Notes

- Computer-aided tomography (CAT scanners)

- Nuclear magnetic resonance imaging (MRI scanners)

- Apple Computer

- Industrial robots

- Medical implant devices, like pacemakers

Breakthrough Product

Product or process breakthroughs seldom occur. Although organizations search for those market, technology, and product breakthroughs, and often invest significant resources in pursuit of the breakthrough, achieving the breakthrough is often somewhat problematical. So what are breakthrough products?

"Breakthrough" means coming up with something new—something that has not been achieved up until now. A breakthrough usually involves both technology and markets. In recent years it's been difficult to identify breakthrough products, technologies, or markets. E-commerce may be an example of a breakthrough market, though it is still too early for a definite conclusion. Authors Nayak and Ketteringham describe product breakthroughs as follows:

> The act of doing something so different that it cannot be compared to any existing practices or perception. Breakthroughs, whether in commercial enterprise, science, or politics, are moments in history. Innovations are events behind the scenes that set the stage for history.[2]

Breakthrough products also spawn new industries or totally change philosophies of operation. The origins of 3M and Hewlett Packard were born with a philosophy that recognized innovation and internal entrepreneurship as essential for building successful organizations. Even though a company like General Electric is considered a prime example of managerial expertise and receives kudos for its financial and managerial performance, the question remains, Is GE innovative? Has GE produced any breakthroughs?

Each industry needs to describe "breakthroughs" in its own terms and within its business and industry context. Nayak and Ketteringham consider Post-it Notes a breakthrough product for 3M. Breakthrough products are also new-to-the-market products that go on to build an industry (see Figure 2-3).

Me-Too Product

A me-too-product is just what the name implies: a product introduced into the market in direct competition with one already in the marketplace. It may or may not provide new features or advantages but it is introduced in direct competition with an existing product. A decision was made to compete in a particular market even though nothing new could be offered. Such a decision can be based on some particular function the organization feels it can perform more effectively than its competitors. It may have a better distribution system, it may have superior manufacturing facilities, or it may consider that some aspect of the organization will provide significant advantages over the competition. As a rule, this is not a very good strategy unless significant benefits can be clearly identified. Pursuing the me-too approach does not provide for long-term organizational growth.

Just how product classifications arise is not known. Somehow the management literature, in an attempt to provide clarification, encumbers the system with unnecessary detail. The same situation applies to innovation. Figure 2-4 shows a simplified classification of products. Improved products can be classed as incremental improvement. Novel replacement and new-to-the markets products are combined in one class, new-to-the-market. Breakthrough products continue to be classified as breakthrough. The me-too category is not included since it seldom provides any long-term benefit.

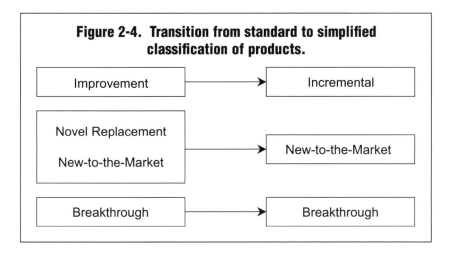

Figure 2-4. Transition from standard to simplified classification of products.

Relation of Innovation to Product Classification

Innovation is pursued in relation to products, processes, and services. Figure 2-2 lists the classification of the types of innovations and Figure 2-4 lists the classification of products, processes, and services. The three classes of innovation are essentially equivalent to the three classes of products, processes, and services. Incremental innovation relates to improvements to a current product or class of products. New-to-the-market/society innovation, which includes discontinuous, architectural, systems, radical, and disruptive innovation, relates directly to novel replacement. Breakthrough innovation leads to breakthrough products.

Classification never approaches an ideal. There are always inconsistencies. The introduction of the ballpoint pen can certainly be considered a disruptive innovation. At the same time it was also certainly a new-to-the-market/society product, a novel replacement product, it was original and unavailable, and would be considered a breakthrough product. Any particular product can fit many different categories.

New-to-the-market/society innovations produce breakthrough products. Discontinuous innovation (from the horse and buggy to the automobile), architectural innovation (from the vacuum tube to the transistor), systems innovation (communication networks), radical innovation (copying machines and computers), and disruptive innovation (silver halide film to digital photography) can all fall into the new-to-the-market/society products category. However, not all novel replacement products or original and unavailable products can be classified as breakthrough. The disk camera was a novel and original and unavailable product but not a breakthrough. The APS (advanced photo system) camera system is novel, it is not really original and unavailable (just a different configuration), and it is also not a breakthrough. Steel-belted tires, disk brakes, and other major automobile improvements were more than product improvements. These were real advancements in technology, safety, and performance.

Product Platforms

The long-term success of a product-driven organization depends on developing a stream of new products. Old products become obsolete and are replaced with new products with added features and benefits. New markets open up in geographical areas that provide additional business opportunities. New technologies in all organizational functions surface and provide additional benefits. These linear-type activities prevent organizations from reaching their full potential. Yet, developing and introducing one product at a time is the norm for most organizations. This single-product approach often involves developing totally new processes for bringing the product to market.

Meyer and Lehnerd describe a product platform as follows: *A product family is a set of individual products that share common technology and address a related set of market applications.*[3] They suggest that creating streams of products one at a time usually fails to meet the organization's goals in the long-term. Every product must justify its own existence, not taking into account commonality, compatibility, standardization, and modularization. They suggest that building an entire family of products on a common platform leverages the organization's resources and improves effectiveness and efficiency. Companies like Black and Decker, Hewlett-Packard, Compaq, and 3M have become masters of using the product platforms.

Most product portfolios evolve over many years and become a collection of technologies, materials, processes, and market segments. Black and Decker, a manufacturer of consumer power tools, provides an excellent example of using product platforms. When

Black and Decker organized its activities around product platforms, it basically captured a major share of the market. In a period of five years, companies such as Stanley, Skil, Pet, McGraw Edison, and General Electric all left the consumer power tool business.

Like many organizations, Black and Decker's product portfolio grew from developing one product at a time over many years. By 1970, Black and Decker was faced with thirty different motors with specialized tooling for each design, sixty different motor housings, 104 different armatures with specialized tooling for each, and a multiplicity of switches, connectors, hardware, and bills of material. The development of the common platform involved developing a universal motor with a broad range of power requirements using plug-in connectors, fixed-diameter laminations but allowing variation in length, and standardized housings. These design changes allowed for automatic assembly of the power tools. A change in power requirements from 60 watts to 650 watts was accomplished by adding additional length to the motor but with the same laminations.

Savings accrued by using common tooling, reduction of the number of parts in inventory, reduced warehouse space, simplified purchasing, reduced number of production processes, common packaging, and general overhead costs that occur when processes are simplified and the number of individual piece parts are significantly reduced.

Hewlett-Packard accomplished similar benefits from its platform approach to inkjet printers. The original product was a black-and-white printer. It migrated to a color printer and then to a dual pen system. This was followed by portable printers and then by cost reductions. New product platforms were eventually introduced for the HP 600 and 800 series of printers.

Compaq Computer Corporation provides another example of using the product platform strategy. Compaq entered the personal computer market in 1982 and established itself as a major player. It began with a line of PCs, the Compaq Deskpro series, and leveraged the PC into a product platform. Deskpro was targeted at the corporate and technical microcomputer market. From the Deskpro subsystems it leveraged a new architecture that provided flexibility for memory, faster processing, drives, and personalized requirements. Compaq continued its vertical scaling to the upper levels of the corporate market.

3M, the company with $16 billion in sales and 50,000 or more products, is built on product and process platforms. 3M has about thirty product platforms based on specific processes. They are experts in coating and cutting up the material into all kinds of shapes and sizes. Whether it's sandpaper, reflective sheeting for highway signs and safety wear, surgical drapes, adhesive-based products, professional cleaning materials, or films of different kinds, the coating expertise and all the related technologies come from a series of technology platforms.

Lehnerd provides additional evidence of the benefits accruing from approaching products from the product platform perspective.[4] For example, a midwest manufacturer was the beneficiary of a program that required approximately one year using the product platform approach. This manufacturer over a period of many years ended up with products that were developed to provide special needs. The number of products proliferated to the point where identifying actual production costs is problematic. The analysis, classification, and subsequent design by a dedicated team reduced the product line to three classes: a "Basic" good-quality product, a "Standard" product that is better than the Basic, and a "Premium" or best product. Figure 2-5 shows the benefits that can be achieved from using product platforms. The new product line provided an expanded list of customer options and improved profit margins based on incentives associated with the new product lines.

Meyer and Lehnerd have developed "thought architecture" for effectively pursuing product line renewal based on platform technology.[5] There are five principles:

1. *Product Family Planning and Platforms.* This requires looking to the future for market opportunities and derivative products and planning for the successive generations.

Figure 2-5. Benefits from implementing product platforms.

	Piece parts/unit	Material ($)	Direct labor ($)
Basic (good)	85 to 28	13.10 to 11.83	2.84 to 0.82
Standard (better)	43 to 27	21.70 to 19.08	1.61 to 0.81
Premium (best)	48 to 29	33.99 to 24.22	1.77 to 0.81

2. *Simultaneous Design for Production.* Integrate manufacturing needs in the design process at the beginning of the project, not at the end. There is no room for designs that cannot be manufactured economically.

3. *Global Product Design and Market Development.* Globalization often requires product modifications because of local codes or restrictions. Design those requirements into the product.

4. *Discover Latent, Unperceived Customer Needs.* Identify the needs that customers have not as yet articulated. This is a combination of science, art, and experience.

5. *Elegance in Design.* How many new and improved versions will the customers accept? Design for simplicity. The challenge is to make the complex simple, which includes integrating the subsystems and interfaces into the systems design.

This thought architecture approach produced the simplification of the Black and Decker consumer line of products. Approaching a product line from the product platform perspective provides significant opportunities for innovation. Like any tool or technique, the approach to product platforms is not accomplished in ten easy lessons. The process requires a dedicated team supported by management.

Making a Better Mousetrap

Lehnerd also provides an excellent example of composite design that builds on the principles of product platforms.[6] Competitive product design cannot be disregarded. We are all familiar with the Victor mousetrap, which is not exactly a high-tech product. It was invented in 1896, and the most recent configuration was patented in 1913. Lehnerd relates the opportunities from using composite design to optimize form and function. The Victor mousetrap includes the following elements:

- Wooden base
- Steel spring
- Copper-plated steel tripping plate
- Copper-plated spring steel latch bar
- Copper-plated spring steel jaw

- Two sizes of copper plate wire staples

- Red and black ink

Just consider the number of parts, the number of subprocesses, and the many operations involved in manufacturing this mousetrap. The Victor mousetrap is not without it flaws, but millions are produced and sold annually.

In 1991, The Better Mousetrap came on the market. It includes a plastic upper jaw, lower jaw, a trigger/bait plate, and a steel garter spring. Lehnerd considered this transformation of the simple mousetrap as *product elegance.* Plastic parts are made in a single-step family mold. Attaching a label and the garter spring completes the assembly. The simplicity of The Better Mousetrap not only does not impair its functionality, its performance exceeds that of the Victor mousetrap. It's a winner on safety, simplicity of design and manufacturing, reliability, ease of arming, disposal, and reuse. Not many products are as simple as the mousetrap. The payoff of design elegance increases with the complexity of the product. Consider the possibilities of reducing complex products by the same ratio as the mousetrap comparisons.

Platform Teams

Robert Lutz, former President of Chrysler, reorganized Chrysler's engineering department to operate as platform teams.[7] According to Lutz, platform teams are task oriented. All engineering disciplines are integrated to work on a vehicle. In a typical balkanized automobile environment, you have a brake department, and the brake department has to focus on brakes on every single vehicle. Then you've got the electrical department, and they do the electrical work on every single vehicle that goes through. Then you've got locks, handles, and mechanisms, and every single project has to pass through locks, handles, and mechanisms. It's all highly sequential. And if you have several projects coming through at once, each may hit a manpower limit in each of those departments. Managers either ask for more heads or say, "Put it in the in-basket and we'll get to it."

According to Lutz, such an environment creates a comfort zone because workers could spend their whole career in locks, handles, and mechanisms and rise to the top of the locks, handles, and mechanisms department working for some old bull of the woods. A new kid on the block might say, "By God, if I just stick around here long enough and keep the old guy satisfied, when he retires I'll become head of locks, handles, and mechanisms and I can be the guy to tell the program managers to get lost."

Summary

- The generally accepted innovation classification system that includes incremental, discontinuous, architectural, system, radical, disruptive and breakthrough as shown in Figure 2-1 has been reduced to incremental, new-to-the-market, and breakthrough. The categories from discontinuous to disruptive have been combined into one class, new-to-the-market.

- This same simplified classification (incremental, new-to-the-market, and breakthrough) has been applied to product classification to avoid the microsegmentation often used that only provides more data with diminishing value.

- The development of product platforms directly improves the financial returns from manufacturing and also reduces significant costs associated with product distribution and related administrative activities.

Notes

1. Clayton M. Christensen, *The Innovator's Dilemma* (New York: HarperBusiness, 1997) p. xv.

2. P. Ranganath Nayak and John M. Ketteringham, *Breakthroughs* (Amsterdam: Pfeiffer, 1994), pp. 1–3.

3. Mark H. Meyer and Alvin P. Lehnerd, *The Power of Product Platforms* (New York: The Free Press, 1997), pp. xi–xii.

4. Alvin P. Lehnerd, "Product Platform Renewal." in *Handbook of Technology Management,* Gerard H. Gaynor (New York: McGraw-Hill, 1996), pp. 25.1–25.15.

5. Meyer and Lehnerd, *The Power of Product Platforms*, pp. 15–22.

6. Alvin P. Lehnerd, "Building a Better Mousetrap," *Today's Engineer* 1, 2 (1999): 40–43.

7. Peter M. Tobia, "Robert Lutz Gives Engineers the Nod." *Today's Engineer* 2,1 (1999): 6–11.

3

Genesis of Innovation

No individual or organization has a monopoly on innovation. Innovation is open to anyone who has the courage and stamina to face the challenges of introducing something new that upsets the status quo. However, the type of organization does affect how the innovator functions and how the organization views the innovator. Established organizations with an established comfort zone and organizational structure view innovation from a more formalized perspective. The independent innovator will view innovation as a matter of life and death, approaching it with total dedication while mortaging assets to their limit and maintaining great hopes for the future.

In this chapter, we will consider the following topics central to the genesis of innovation:

- Innovation in established organizations

- Top-down and bottom-up innovation

- Innovation in the start-up

- Characteristics of independent innovators

- The role of teams in innovation

- How individuals become teams

- How innovators break the rules and change the game

- Managing the dynamic tensions in innovation

Innovation in Established Organizations

Established organizations as a class are probably not the most innovative. The 1980s downsizing demonstrated the difficulties in pursuing innovation. How was it possible that major organizations suddenly needed to decrease their total employment by 30 percent or more? How could such established organizations be so unskilled in developing a continuous stream of products? How could these organizations, once dominant players in their industry, reach such a state of disarray? How could organizations with established technical, marketing, and business competencies go into a black hole?

Blame was usually placed on the economy, management, the bureaucracy, short-term orientation, Wall Street, and lack of a guiding vision. The reasons could be numerous. The real difficulties lie in the fact that organizations reach a relaxed and unacceptable comfort zone. Success often leads to basking in past accomplishments without recognizing that success can often be short-lived.

Under these circumstances implementing change becomes almost impossible and discipline is replaced by pursuing touchy-feely approaches to management. Remember when CEOs were talking about delighting the customer? What did that statement really mean? I once remarked to a CEO of a *Fortune 100* company that as a customer I really didn't want to be delighted; or I just wanted my order to meet specifications and be delivered on time and at the agreed cost, with no excuses. Organizations say they listen to the customer, but do they fully understand if the customer is adequately delineating future needs? The customer must be defined; is the customer the end user, the purchasing agent, or a golf or social colleague? Organizations also have a tendency to believe their public relations releases. Those releases often lack credibility and the reality is far different. However, there are organizations that provide innovation leadership, and even though fluctuations in the economy may reduce total revenues, these organizations manage to weather the situations without major catastrophes.

Top-Down Innovation

In established organizations, innovation usually comes from the top down or from the bottom up. Each requires a different approach and each has its own set of parameters and peculiarities. *Top-down innovation (TDI)* has the advantage that the people in power set the pace—they set the targets and the objectives and provide the funding. The implementation is left to the many functions and professional disciplines that will interact in order to meet the objectives. Those working on the project do not have to beg for funding. This approach takes the form of a directive, such as: We will explore that new market. We will eliminate some segment of our current product line. We will compete in some new market segment with a new-to-the-market product. We will invest in this new technology for the future. We will make an investment in automated manufacturing. Such directives leave no doubt as to where the organization will find its future.

The only limits of top-down innovation are the people resources. In most situations the funding and direction will be provided. Nonaka and Kenney compared the approaches of Canon, Inc. and Apple Computer regarding innovation.[1] Both are examples of top-down innovation, but with some differences: One is organized, and the other is individualistic, self-governed, and freewheeling.

Canon

In 1982, Canon began reconceptualizing the plain-paper copier (PPC) business and investigated the opportunities for lightweight compact copiers. Management knew that the new copier would not come into being by minor improvements in component and assembly designs; it would need a thorough analysis of the market to establish the required features, advantages, and benefits. Canon approached the opportunity with a high-level project team. The team included:

- Project manager—the director of the Reprographic Products Development Center (RPDC)

- Advisor to the project—managing director of the RPDC

- Director of the corporate technical planning and operations center

- Representatives from quality control, finance, and marketing

- Task force to examine the color copying issues

Kei Saito, the deputy general of RPDC summed up the philosophy that would guide the project: *Good products are created when production engineering and design become fused for their development.* By integrating design with production engineering it is possible to propose uniform parts design and resolve issues related to assembly during the design process—the assembly steps and the sequence. If design is isolated from production, difficulties are bound to arise when it comes time to plan manufacturing facilities. Emphasis was placed on eliminating rework of designs and subsequent problems in manufacturing. This fusion of related disciplines presents many challenges, but when directed from the top creates far fewer problems during implementation.

Apple Computer

Apple Computer's approach to innovation was quite different. Operations were more fluid, with not as much organization. Here was a start-up that began in a garage in 1976 with an idea that generated $750 million in sales by 1982. The market did not accept some of the attempts to extend the product line, such as the Apple III and the Lisa, but the company was still cash-rich even following those failures. Management continued in the hands of the founders, and financial and operational discipline was lacking. Nonaka and Kenney describe Apple as being in a state of confusion with no direction and too many projects.

In 1979, Steve Jobs left the Lisa project and was attracted to the Macintosh development group. By 1981, Jobs replaced the original Macintosh project leader and began to build a project team. Jobs became the project champion. The original Macintosh goal was to be smaller, faster, more powerful, and less expensive than the Apple, and many new features were added to expand those specifications. Jobs recruited people from Xerox Parc and even used some of their technology. The Macintosh team of about twenty-five people was separated from the rest of the organization; the final configuration was not defined, and a development schedule did not exist. Jobs was the product visionary, the champion, and the final decision maker.

The success of the Macintosh is now part of product development and innovation history.

Canon and Apple Comparison

The above examples from Canon and Apple are presented as two distinct methods to fulfill the requirements of the innovation equation:

$$INNOVATION = INVENTION + IMPLEMENTATION/$$
$$COMMERCIALIZATION$$

Canon managed innovation with an integrated executive level team with agreed-upon objectives, target dates, and expectations, and was also able to circumvent 600 Xerox patents in the process. Canon's effort began with the proverbial blank sheet of paper and the reconceptualization of the plain-paper copying business by introducing lightweight compact copiers. They became the market leaders. At Apple, the activities were isolated from the rest of the organization and management was ambivalent about the project. Jobs had the vision, but objectives were not clearly articulated, and resources were limited. Nonetheless, the Macintosh reached sales of $4 billion.

The transformations at Canon and Apple were quite different. Canon focused on the up-front work with a disciplined approach. It then developed a corporate program, provided the necessary resources and infrastructure, and established the objectives and the performance targets—basically a systematic way of managing innovation. Canon introduced innovation by design. In today's parlance, this is called the Canon model or template.

The Macintosh emerged from a somewhat chaotic environment, eventually received management's support, and was very successful. As Moritz stated: "False starts, diversions, mistakes, experiments, rebellion, and competition formed the stuff of the machine."[2] Apple's history seems to run in cycles with changing management and direction, but always with an element of the unexpected.

Not all top-down innovation will be staffed with such high-level executives. However, when projects originate or receive the blessing from the top of the organizational pyramid, the operational problems are significantly reduced. How many organizations use the top-down approach to innovation is not known. We could also ask, Are the Canon and Apple case studies examples of innovation or just good management? Both cases meet the requirements of innovation = invention + implementation/commercialization, but in very different ways.

Executive-level involvement in innovation usually focuses on new-to-the-market type activities. Incremental innovation is generally the responsibility of the immediate organizational unit. As shown previously, incremental innovation can have some long-term impact on providing additional features and benefits of an existing product line. Incremental innovation in manufacturing processes also becomes the responsibility of the organizational unit's management. However, if new plant and equipment are required, support from the executive levels of management will be essential.

Bottom-Up Innovation

Bottom-up innovation (BUI) is just what the name implies—innovation originating someplace in the bowels of the organization. Everyone is welcome to participate in bottom-up innovation. BUI provides the greatest challenges to innovators—those people (the productive mavericks) who think differently, who ask many questions, who have many interests, who are dissatisfied without change, who are considered arrogant, who bring a different perspective, who ask "why not" more often than "why," who create problems for first-level managers, but who are the lifeblood and future of the organization. These are the people who come up with ideas and are willing to go through the laborious process of first convincing themselves and then convincing several levels of management of the value of those ideas.

3M

3M is probably the best example of bottom-up innovation—innovation is part of the company's culture that has been fostered for more than seventy-five years. That culture, while providing freedom of action and opportunities for exploring new ideas, was guided by operational and financial discipline. The history of some of the products that now represent its major divisions includes mild threats of termination from management if the person championing the product did not cease spending time on it. That history also reveals that those threatened individuals continued to pursue their efforts in some form in spite of management's objections.

3M is a unique and dynamic company that continues to reinvent itself. The reinvention process began shortly after it attempted to mine corundum in 1902. The owners realized the company was founded on a mistake. The mining effort that should have yielded corundum, a natural material from which to produce sandpaper grit, turned out to be another mineral not fit for abrasive applications. A share of 3M stock couldn't buy a shot of whiskey. But that first mistake yielded other mistakes, and the company today has in excess of $16 billion in sales with net income of over 10 percent.

Innovation continues to be the driving force at 3M. It now operates in 63 countries and promotes that same entrepreneurial spirit worldwide. 3M is a leader in coated and nonwoven abrasives; tapes of unimaginable compositions; transportation and personal safety; medical, pharmaceutical, and health care information systems; a leading supplier of connecting, insulating, and protective products for the electronic related industries; Post-it Notes; and many other related products. When 3M says people are the greatest asset, they practice it.

Lew Lehr, a former 3M CEO, was one of the principal developers of surgical drapes, one of the first products in the health care business. When sales faltered, Lehr was told by his superiors to drop the product line, and of course he agreed. Lehr then had a convenient memory lapse and forgot to tell the factory to stop production until after they had built up substantial inventory. The rest is history since sales increased, and Lehr's decision paved the way for the creation of a health care products group whose sales now exceed $3 billion annually.[3] This is not an atypical 3M experience. But such actions take courage. Top management does not always have the answers.

Many 3M innovators bootleg resources to the greatest possible extent. Bootlegging resources is part of the 3M culture. Pursuing any idea requires resources and those resources are not always available when something new comes to light. Although 3M expects its managers to be open to new ideas whether they relate to technology, markets, products, or business issues, the reality is quite different. As previously emphasized, it takes time to develop an idea to the point where it can be communicated. Talking about the idea or writing about it may not be the most effective way to convince managers to provide the resources. The idea may require a physical demonstration—a "show and tell" kind of communication.

An argument can be made that such bootlegging techniques should not be necessary—they are a waste of time and inhibit many potential innovators from taking up the cause. However, most innovations in their early stages would be considered a waste of time and resources. Accepting something new will always meet resistance from some organization sector. With all of our sophisticated management tools for reaching decisions, shouldn't we be able to evaluate ideas more appropriately and then decide whether or not to provide the resources? The answer to this question is both a maybe yes and a definitely no.

The "maybe yes" is from the standpoint of determining the market viability and technology needs. But this assumes that the idea and the flow of products from the implementation of the idea can be defined in relation to all the interconnecting parameters. It assumes that projections can be made regarding product acceptance. It assumes that the original idea can be described in detail. Unfortunately, the process from idea to commercialization does not allow for such assumptions. After an idea goes through many iterations, it often has little relation to the original.

The "definitely no" is from the standpoint that innovation doesn't come about from assignments. Innovators display a certain passion in pursuit of some goal, whether directed from the top or pursued by the lone innovator. That passion is difficult to transfer to the vast majority of employees. The innovators with a passion to pursue some goal may not exhibit the same level of passion if given a specific assignment. The passion is generated from their absolute ownership of the ideas that they brought to light. Innovators live the idea 24 hours a day, 365 days a year. Ideas become obsessions.

Challenges and Limitations

Taking an idea and developing it into a definable concept provides the greatest challenges to the bottom-up innovators. Any successful effort of consequence demonstrates the naiveté experienced in the early stages of transforming an idea into a workable concept. In the beginning, all the questions seem to have answers. As ideas go through many iterations, the level of confidence in the answers diminishes significantly, which creates a dilemma for the innovators. The once-great idea born for its simplicity has become very complex. Every day presents new avenues for investigation. Innovation is without any doubt a learning process. More thought raises new questions and complexities.

Bottom-up innovation has its limitations. It depends on a specific type of individual—one who will not take no for an answer, one who has the drive to pursue a goal in spite of a possible negative career impact, one who is willing to put in personal time and effort toward reaching a goal. Not too many people will pursue an effort when they are told to stop by someone in authority. Also, not every person has the same capacity to disregard the criticism often associated with pursuing a new idea. In the final analysis, innovation is about change and change creates high levels of discomfort. Someone's ox is bound to be gored. A manager who comes from the technical side of the business may be very skeptical about market innovation. Likewise a manager with a background in marketing may be very skeptical about promoting a new product idea that is based on non-traditional technologies. A CEO who comes from the financial side of the business may only be concerned about the numbers. Under any of these scenarios, the innovator has an uphill battle.

Innovators are not always the idea generators. Innovation is all about integration—integrating data, information, knowledge, and experience from many different sources. It is not about being a technical or marketing specialist. Innovators need one overriding competence—the competence to put it all together. It's the competence that brings to the table sufficient knowledge of the marketing and technical issues, looks at innovation from a business perspective, wears the business hat when necessary, and considers innovation from a strategic business perspective.

Innovation in the Start-Up

Innovation in a start-up organization presents a situation similar to that of bottom-up innovation. There are some exceptions:

1. Chances are that the head of the start-up is the innovator.

2. Innovation becomes the precursor of the entrepreneurial organization.

3. The objectives are (or should be) defined and focused.

4. Every employee wears many hats, and that provides them with a broad perspective of the operation.

5. The organization operates more like a team.

6. The communication lines are much shorter and usually direct.

7. Working groups are more easily aligned.

8. The CEO is really not the CEO but another worker.

9. Levels of management are ambiguous—there aren't enough people to worry about titles. (Note that titles can actually decimate a start-up because titles begin to segregate staff by level of importance. That "lowly" technician may be the most important person in a start-up.)

10. Funding is generally insufficient.

It takes a particular type of person to work in a start-up. If you're concerned about working with uncertainties and risks, you'll most likely not become involved with a start-up; if you do become involved, it will be painful. Money is generally in short supply. One of the conditions we face in the new millennium is that too many start-ups want to begin big. They often begin with unreasonably high expectations, lack of knowledge and experience, and misunderstanding of what it takes to build something from the foundation up. Building a sound business foundation is absolutely essential.

Independent Innovators

Innovation also begins in the family garage, the kitchen, or the basement, and perhaps in all three locations. Hewlett Packard and Apple Computer both began as private enterprises that grew into major corporations. Chester Carlson, inventor of the xerographic process (from Haloid Xerox to Xerox) was turned down by the best and brightest of *Fortune 100* companies when searching for funding. After all, what was wrong with carbon paper? Who would ever need a copying machine? Today, there are probably other Hewletts, Packards, Carlsons, and Jobs searching for funding for a product that might become the next major industry.

The spirit that guides these innovator/entrepreneurs presents us with a challenge. Why are there so few of them? Granted, for every successful one many others never survive. That is the shakeout process of competition. In the early 1900s, there were over one hundred automobile manufacturers in the United States. Today, the United States is really down to two, and only a handful remain worldwide. The computer industry has had a similar shakeout, but primarily because of rapidly changing technologies.

The independent innovators resemble the corporate bottom-up innovators in many respects. They have a dream. They're driven to accomplish that dream. They'll pursue it relentlessly. Innovators are no different than those who pursue excellence in any profession, be it the arts, sports, or education. They're willing to dedicate their time and effort in pursuit of something that they think will in some way have an impact on society. Very simply, they have a vision and will dedicate themselves to fulfilling it.

Role of Teams in Innovation

For many years, significant emphasis has been placed on teams and team performance. The academic and trade press continue to focus on teamwork. Research papers abound on the topic of how a particular organization used teams to accomplish great things. In spite of the emphasis on teams, less than 10 percent of projects are completed to specification, on time, and at cost, which is not a very good track record. There are reasons above and beyond the use of teams that have created this situation.

Corporations send their management teams to all types of conferences in order to teach team building—they climb mountains, they run the rapids, and they bear their souls in behavioral modification sessions, all for the purpose of getting to know each other and function as a team. Peter Senge describes the management team as a collection of savvy and experienced managers from different functions and areas of expertise. He's concerned about the appearance of a cohesive team when in reality it is anything but cohesive. In essence the major issues are never raised, disagreement is squelched, going against the flow is a heretical act of disobedience. According to Senge, "Most management teams break down under pressure."[4] Chris Argyris, a veteran about learning in management teams, says, "The team may function quite well on routine issues. But when they confront complex issues that may be embarrassing or threatening, the 'teameness' goes to pot."[5] Argyris further notes that "the consequence of such actions results in skilled incompetence—teams full of people who are incredibly proficient in keeping themselves from learning."[6] Senge also asks a valid question about teams: "How can a team of committed managers with individual IQs above 120 have a collective IQ of 63?"[7]

These comments are not to be construed as eliminating the team concept. But they represent what occurs when teams need to resolve complex issues. One of those complex issues is innovation. Does the organization invest in innovation or not? Does it provide the environment that fosters innovation? Does it tolerate those people who think outside the traditional box and tend to ignore the interpreted wisdom of those in charge? More and more literature focuses on innovation being a team effort—innovation begins with one person and eventually requires a team. It is difficult to identify a single innovation that originated with a team. Yes, at some point a team with the required skills and disciplines fulfills the requirements of the innovation equation: innovation = invention + implementation/commercialization. But innovation begins with the individual—the source of the idea.

Those who have been involved in innovation or have attempted to introduce change in any form know firsthand of the difficulties. There are always reasons for another study, for touching base with some other person or group, for considering the impact on the organization, for not being politically possible, and for not being technologically feasible. The final blow comes with comments such as "You're really creating a problem." These are but a few reasons for delaying a decision. The bottom-up innovator ignores such remarks and continues to move forward.

From Individual to Team

Research has not as yet discovered how ideas come into being. Innovation begins with some perhaps momentary thought called an idea that eventually is transformed into a real-life concept. 3M's Post-it Notes provide an excellent example. Art Fry, the inventor, sang in the church choir for many years. Like all his predecessors, he fumbled with those little pieces of paper that marked the hymns of the day. But on this particular Sunday, he concluded there had to be a better way. Why hadn't this thought come to him long before this particular Sunday? Probably because Art Fry finally became sufficiently frustrated to be motivated to find a better way. Without becoming involved in the psychology of idea origination, we do know that frustration is often the mother of invention. Perhaps we should leave it at that.

Another example to consider: A *Fortune 100* company we'll call Company A acquires Company Z, a major manufacturing company outside the United States, with an acceptable product line but with antiquated manufacturing facilities. The objective is to expand Company A's market penetration globally. The management team made the decision that no major problems would occur in integrating the two cultures. Unfortunately, integration required more effort than anticipated; as attempts were made to integrate the two organizations, incompatibilities in research direction, manufacturing capability, and marketing operations were quickly identified. Company A's operational philosophy—that subsidiaries must be managed by the national employees—ruled out any major involvement in Company Z except for three or four people. For many years, little progress was made and year after year losses increased.

During this period, Company A sent its so-called best and brightest to turn the organization into a profitable venture. Unfortunately, the best and the brightest never resolved the issues necessary to move to a profitable position, and for many years Company Z continued to generate significant losses. Company A was seriously thinking of divesting its interest in Company Z. As in any organization, politics played its role for both positive and negative reasons. A high-level manager who had just been removed from his position in Company A was sent to Company Z as the managing director. He was sent there as a kind of penance.

What the new managing director found in a few months was that the best and brightest never dug into the details. The best and brightest were sent from highly profitable operations of Company A and never really had to struggle to meet their quota of new products or their sales and profit targets. As a matter of fact, they usually surpassed them. They never really had to dig into unpleasant situations and get their hands dirty. They managed from the front office, and since their markets were basically uninhabited, they set the rules of the game. In this situation they were not the lead players

Company Z certainly had its problems—an excess of people, totally antiquated manufacturing facilities, a supposedly unmotivated sales organization, and a set of policies and procedures that would break the bank. A short study revealed that many customers received very specialized and costly services for which they were never billed—special product modifications that had been priced without acknowledging the added costs. The lack of even adequate manufacturing facilities increased the rework. Defective products and waste and scrap continued to increase.

The new managing director of Company Z recruited a chief engineer and a process engineering manager from Company A. The vice presidents of engineering openly fought the appointment of the chief engineer. The team now included the managing director, a new Company A marketing and sales director, the chief engineer, the process engineering manager, and the Company Z management for research and development, manufacturing, finance, and human resources. Within one year, a plan was developed by the team and funding approved by Company A (The Mother House) for additional research staff, new production facilities, a major reduction of staff through consolidation of activities, a realignment of the product line, incentive programs, and all the minutiae that are included in major investment programs. Two years later, the tide began to turn and Company Z went into the profitable column. This first investment was only the beginning. Over the next ten years, major investments were made in new production facilities. New competitive products were introduced, the sales organizations reoriented, and Company Z became a profit contributor to Company A.

What made the difference? The new Company Z team took a hands-on approach. This was about doing. The U.S. contingent from Company A, and the Company Z contingent developed into a real operational team and formed a real partnership. Their backs were up against the wall and it was a matter of survival. This was no eight-hour-a-day job. The initial planning took place at many around-the-clock sessions. There wasn't any point in just upgrading the manufacturing equipment. Basically, the group began with a clean sheet of paper and started the thinking process at the very beginning. This was not a single-issue program; stretch targets were established for everyone and every participating group. The group adopted the systems approach from day one. Every function was involved and recognized their role in this process. The purpose was not to provide new manufacturing facilities; the purpose of the effort was to build a successful business. The vision was established, the resources were provided, and the work began.

This turnaround was accomplished by breaking the rules. Company A had no idea what was involved in bridging the gap between the two companies and their two cultures. Most of the management team never learned the language and never recognized their limits. Two cultures must develop into a common culture that has parts of each. It takes a level of flexibility to develop that common culture. Moreover it takes a special group of people to develop into a functioning team that focuses on the final objective—not functional objectives, but business objectives. In this case, Company A and Company Z finally found common ground.

Innovators Break the Rules and Change the Game

Innovators not only break the rules of the game but also change the game itself. They're the new game in town—new ballpark, new coaches, new players, new market, new philosophy of operation, and a new spirit and interest that attacks the traditional bureaucratic approaches to management. Here are some examples of the *new game in town*:

Lever Brothers

In 1936, Lever Bros. introduced Spry to compete with P&G's Crisco, a product that had been introduced in 1912. In one year, Spry reached half the market share of Crisco.

Canon

In the early 1960s, Canon entered the photocopier field then dominated by Xerox. By the early 1980s, it was a close second to Xerox—even though IBM and Kodak attacked the same market.

Texas Instruments

TI entered the calculator business in 1972, although the market already included HP, Casio, Commodore, Sanyo, and others. Within 5 years, TI is the market leader.

Apple

In 1976, Apple introduced the Apple II in direct competition to Wang, IBM, HP, Atari, Commodore, Tandy, and others. Within five years, Apple became a market leader.

Yamaha

In the late 1980s, Yamaha tried to revitalize its declining piano business by developing digital technology so customers could either record live performances by the pianist they'd chosen or buy recordings on diskettes and play the same composition on their pianos.

Gannett

In 1982, Gannett introduced *USA Today* in a field of 1,700 daily newspapers. By 1993, it had five million daily readers.

Howard Schultz

In 1987, Howard Schultz bought Starbucks Coffee from the original owners. In five years, he transformed the company from a chain of 11 stores and sales of $1.3 million to 280 stores and $163.5 million in sales.

We can add to this list Dell Computer, Hanes Corporation, Nucor Steel, Toyota, Perdue, Timex, Southwest Airlines, and BancOne. All of these examples have one thing in common: The competition was attacked without the help of radical technological innovation.

Managing the Dynamic Tensions in Innovation

Innovation creates mental and emotional tension. Change creates tension. Appointment of a new chief executive officer or a new manager creates tension. Attempting to develop a culture that supports innovation creates tension. Most humans prefer the status quo. How often do you hear the comment: "If it ain't broke, why fix it"? If it "ain't broke," someone better take a look at how long it will continue to work. Managing the following dynamic tensions determines the level of innovation:

- Change and stability

- Creativity and routine

- Leading and following

- Freedom and constraint

- Short-term and long-term focus

- The status quo and the change makers

Change and Stability

No organization can undergo continual change. Normally periods of change need to be followed by periods of stability. Organizations cannot be kept in continual turmoil, always focusing on the next round of anticipated changes. This becomes evident as organizations find it necessary to recruit people with new and different skills. New technologies will require new technical competencies. Entering new markets will require new knowledge of how those new markets function. Introducing new products that continue to become more complex will require new approaches to customer education and training. Those new products will also require education of internal levels of management.

The reluctance to accept change at various levels and types spans the complete organization, from the top-level executives to those who carry out the nitty-gritty details that allow the organization to keep its doors open. But accepting change will not come about without some change in education. Just how does an organization educate its members about accepting change and promoting it? There is no need for Managing Change 101. The most simple and direct way involves keeping members apprised of the organization's performance. When members of any organization understand the implications of a slowing economy, growing competition, their underperformance, or other major factors, chances are they will accommodate to those changes. But the knowledge must be available before the crisis arises. In many situations, accepting change is not a matter of choice, but people need to be prepared to accept change or suffer the consequences.

Accepting change begins at the top of the organization. Those behaviors determine how the rest of the organization accepts change. If top-level executives shy away from change and fail to support the change makers, change will not occur. The organization will continue to function normally until some crisis arises. Attitude begins at the top of the organization. That positive attitude will be emulated throughout the organization.

How do change and stability affect innovation? Incremental innovation does not or at least should not create any significant tension—it just requires the ability to manage projects effectively and efficiently. But where innovation begins to obsolete competence and skills, it threatens the lifestyle of its members. Addressing competence and skill may be one of the manager's major responsibilities.

Maintaining long-term stability may not be a viable strategy. We are all victims of our past, and it's difficult to part with those methodologies, processes, routines, and attitudes that have provided a high level of comfort. In a competitive global economy and in the face of new demands and expectations from the market, if Company X will *not* change and Company Y *will* change, then the demise of Company X may be imminent. That's the reality of a free-market economy.

Creativity and Routine

No individual, at least in the traditional sense, is creative 24 hours a day or 365 days in the year. If this were true we really wouldn't need too many creative human beings. Experience teaches that periods of creativity are followed by periods of routine, which are needed to transform the idea into some form of physical manifestation. Creative people work at their craft be it art, writing, or innovation. The artist must paint, the writer must write, the innovator must innovate. Each of these requires doing. Thinking about the next piece of artwork, the next book, or the next innovation is not sufficient. There comes a time when the real work must begin if the thinking process will result in something other than a thought, and the "doing" phase involves much routine.

Henry Mintzberg used the metaphor of the potter in relation to crafting strategy.[8] The potter provides an excellent metaphor for describing the creative process. The potter begins with a lump of clay, some tools, past experience and knowledge, and an idea. At some time, after many attempts to fashion a design, a product emerges. That original lump of clay may have taken many different shapes—creativity followed by doing and creativity followed by more doing until the result meets the expectations of the potter. The mind and the hand must work together. Creativity without doing the doing remains only an idea. Creativity involves integrating thought and action.

Can everyone demonstrate some level of creativity? An emphatic yes! Can everyone be creative? Probably not. Creativity is hard work that requires dedication and a level of passion that not many people are willing to try to reach. It requires the discipline to excel at the routine. Why did Michelangelo paint the Sistine Chapel? Why is Leonardo da Vinci—renowned artist, engineer, and author—considered the preeminent example of creativity? Thomas Edison, Alexander Graham Bell, and the many high-tech entrepreneurs of recent times not only demonstrated high levels of creativity but also took those ideas and molded them into products. Creativity that results in innovation requires doing the routine—doing what is often considered the dirty work.

Leading and Following

Like being creative, anyone can be a leader but few take the initiative. Leadership usually means going against the traditional, bringing people along to a new way of thinking, or recognizing what needs to be done that nobody else recognizes. It does not mean taking a poll and then making a decision—that's not leadership; that's just going along with the flow. Leaders are actually difficult to find. Some CEOs are leaders, but not all. Position doesn't automatically bestow capability.

Innovators possess leadership qualities. They go against the traditional. They think beyond the immediate needs of the organization. They have an end target in view but take the detours when necessary. They exploit the available resources. But leadership for them is neither the command and control type nor the type of leadership described by the human relations school of management.

Abraham Zaleznik brings us into the real world, where managers often subordinate the challenges of real work to the demands of "psychopolitics."[9] Psychopolitics is a condition shaped by the human relations school of management, in which social relations take precedence over customers and clients and where process becomes king at the expense of productivity. Zaleznik warns that as more emphasis is placed on psychopolitics, less emotional energy is directed toward the real work—of thinking. Thinking is described as work related to acting on ideas about products, markets, and customers.

Innovators abhor psychopolitical leadership. They recognize that leadership in innovation is about thinking. They understand that leadership has its pitfalls—it can alienate, it creates controversy, it destroys friendships, and it changes the ground rules, but it's absolutely necessary to sustain performance. Leadership is built on the foundation that different disciplines are required to bring an idea to a successful conclusion, and that final step requires someone who has the put-it-all-together skills, which translates into leadership.

Leaders in innovation require followers—disciplined and competent in their discipline, with an understanding of the needs of other disciplines. But followers in this sense are not non-questioning disciples or do-what-you're-told robots. These followers are thinkers in their own specific disciplines and they exercise their will on the leader. At times these followers take on specific leadership roles. They are leaders in and masters of their discipline.

Freedom and Constraint

We all expect or want freedom to exercise our creativity and be masters of our own destiny. Freedom places significant responsibilities on the individual. The questions we need to answer as individuals are: How much freedom can I handle? and What type of freedom do I want—freedom to choose the work I do or freedom to do the assigned work in my own way?

My years of experience with competent engineers and scientists demonstrated that most people cannot accept total freedom. I hired a very competent electronics engineer who not only had the credentials but also had an exemplary track record in new product innovation. We'll call him Mike. For about six months Mike more than met expectations and was a good role model for his associates. He walked into my office one day asked if I had a few minutes to discuss an issue. I suggested that if he had the time that we could do it immediately. We sat down and after a few introductory comments by both of us, Mike said, "Gus, I don't feel that I'm doing the best that I can for you. I've got these projects that I'm working on and they're good projects, but I need more freedom to choose what I should work on if I'm going to be creative." I suggested that if he was interested, I'd reassign his projects to others in the group, and give him ninety days to work on whatever he wished to work on. If he wanted to continue after the ninety-day period, we'd reevaluate the situation. I gave Mike total freedom and asked him to just keep me informed. Mike thought this was a great idea and left the office enthused and exhilarated. From past experience I wondered just how long this excitement would last.

Within ten days, Mike was back in my office asking for an assignment. What happened? The fact is that very few people can accept total freedom. Total freedom may be a wish, but it's difficult to function in an environment where expectations are not defined. Mike didn't know what I expected from him at the end of ninety days. Had I told him of my expectations, it would have been the same as assigning some type of project. Total freedom places demands on the individual—but few people can accept it. Innovators, who are mavericks and independent thinkers, must be able to accept total freedom. Innovators accept this as a challenge. This is why we have so few of them.

Freedom to accept an assignment and execute it *in my own way* presents other problems. In today's global economy, the pressure will continue to complete most work activities in the shortest period of time. Everyone cannot begin a project at the bottom of the learn-

Circulation Summary
SDCC/SCS Library
Mon, Mar 10, 2008 11:20 AM

---------------------Patron--------------------
    Name: Fordjour, Charles
       ID: 087766200
----------------Checkouts----------------
Evolve! :   Apr 21, 2008
Innovation and entrepreneur   Apr 21, 2008
The innovator's solution :   Apr 21, 2008
Innovation by design :   Apr 21, 2008
Heads up :   Apr 21, 2008
-------------Available Holds------------
None
---------------------Fines---------------------
Balance Owing: $0.00
   Estimated: $0.00

For info or renewals 619-441-2200 x1227

ing curve. It is absolutely necessary to develop some flexible approach of balancing freedom with some constraints.

Here is a "lessons learned" example: A young engineer assigned to a project was supposed to solicit vendors for a particular component. He went to the catalogs and selected the names of sixty-five potential suppliers and followed up with letters and specifications. (This was before the Internet.) Within this group of potential suppliers, there were probably no more than five or six suppliers who would be capable of meeting specifications, a fact of which his manager was well aware. Do lessons like this have to be learned and relearned by everybody? This is an example of a manager not coaching the young engineer appropriately. Extend this same attitude to a design engineering effort, and young engineers will end up designing a component or an assembly that cannot be manufactured. Obviously extinguishing the young engineer's enthusiasm and excitement needs to be taken into consideration, but managers must remember that one of their functions is that of teacher. Extend this same thinking to the marketing department. A new employee begins a market study without any guidance or understanding of the area under consideration. Not only will the study take an excessive amount of time but will most likely miss some of the essential information.

Short-Term and Long-Term Focus

The arguments regarding short- or long-term orientation have not generated any new insight toward resolving the issue. The issue is not one of either/or, but both—it *must* be both. Every employee wants to receive their pay on time, they want their medical insurance premiums paid on time, and want to receive all other perks that their organization offers. The organization meets these obligations by paying attention to the quarterly results. So short-term results become a necessity. Management needs the competence to balance these short-term requirements with the future needs of the organization. Statistics demonstrate that sales lost in one quarter are seldom recouped in subsequent quarters. It's like project scheduling: If the schedule begins to lag it is usually recouped only by eliminating certain agreed-upon requirements. So short-term success, in spite of Wall Street's demands, is essential. That's the real world. Future obligations must be accommodated.

Providing adequate resources for long-term activities requires planning. Long-term sustainability will not occur if a conscious effort is not made to invest in innovation. Funding must be provided on a consistent basis. The organization cannot open the money tap and then arbitrarily and periodically shut it off and expect innovation to flourish. The investment may not be large but it must be continuous. The allocation of funds for guaranteeing the future of the organization through innovation cannot be left to chance. It is impossible to set some standard for investing in the future. Successful organizations include those with major investments in research and development and those with relatively modest funds. Money by itself is insufficient.

The Status Quo and the Change Makers

Can you imagine an organization where everyone was an innovator? Can you imagine an organization where 25 percent of the staff was innovators? Keep in mind we're talking about innovators and not idea generators. Such an organization would be described with one word: chaos. Innovators create change and it makes little difference whether those changes are related to the technology functions, the marketing and sales functions, or the many administrative functions. Even the executives could not manage the chaos. Innovation by its very nature creates change. Someone working to introduce change will upset those who oppose it. There is a limit as to how far the boat can be rocked.

Change can be considered as a good or as a disruption of the accepted way of life. However, introducing change forces people to think—to think about the future and recognize its impact on the person and the organization. With today's availability of information, the world does not stand still. Why did the best and brightest in industry fail to perceive the impact of global competition? Why was the entire downsizing necessary? How did all of those people manage to get on the payroll? Why did it become necessary to start all of those quality programs? Companies began counting quality circles and the number of suggestions in the suggestion box as though these were measures of improved quality. The answer is quite simple: It was easier to maintain the status quo than seek new opportunities. Change didn't seem to be an option. The academic community and the consultants and the industrial training organizations took up the cause and began touting change as the single issue that would transform organizations. Change cannot be created by dictum or by some seven-step process. An organization that is adverse to change requires a totally new orientation.

Rosabeth Moss Kanter provides insight into Eastman Kodak and its attempts to change from a paternalistic bureaucracy into an innovative giant.[10] Kodak, in its attempts to establish a more entrepreneurial culture, set aside one percent of revenues for new ventures, which included a new venture process, acquisitions, and certain equity investments. Kanter suggests that Kodak established a pioneering model that other organizations flocked to examine and model. This pioneering model was really the seventy-five-year-old 3M model that involves bottom-up innovation. It's impossible to force innovation, especially if innovation is not demonstrated at the top of the organization. With the recruiting of more CEOs without knowledge and understanding of the industry or the business, these executives turn to the so-called experts to fill in the gaps.

What happened to this attempt to nurture new ventures? Hirsch reported on the results as Kodak attempted to institute its entrepreneurial spirit.[11] Kodak started fourteen ventures: Six were shut down, three were sold, four were merged into the company, and one operated independently.

Why did the entrepreneurial approach fail? Over the decades Kodak developed a comfort zone for its employees—king in the photographic industry without major competitors, control of the marketplace for introducing new products, and excellent employee benefits. This is not typically the type of environment that fosters innovation and entrepreneurship. Words like "stretch" and "push" and "performance" probably seldom surfaced. There was no need, because Kodak was king of the hill.

One of Kodak's entrepreneurial leaders mentioned that he supposedly was in control but was forced to use Kodak engineers and researchers and other employees as assigned to him. He had no choice in the selection. He also noted, "Kodak people would take their eight-hour workday and go home." Innovative and entrepreneurial organizations are neither built nor sustained when participants watch the clock.

Kodak was a well-respected organization. It could do no wrong.

It was not only a profitable company, but it was also oriented toward the social needs of the community and society in general. Using Kodak as an example illustrates the difficulty in changing a culture. The problems arose because management at the top did not understand what is required to change a culture. The transition from a paternal and bureaucratic organization to one that lives innovation does not occur by dictum. The change process not only requires reorientation; it also creates a need to bring new people who will drive the organization in the desired direction. It takes time to reorient an organization to accept change when required.

Change makers at any level in the organization need a vision. Innovators need a vision. But that vision must be grounded in the real world. I don't know where the idea of developing an organizational vision came from, because the synonyms appear to be so fragile that the word could not be associated with the idea of what an organization wants to be or where it wants to go. Consider these synonyms for "vision" that appear in Roget's Thesaurus: dream, mirage, pipe dream, illusion, figment of the imagination, make believe, apparition, hallucination, and utopian.[12] There may be more. Not very appropriate descriptions for tough-minded executives. However, these synonyms fit many organizational visions. They are visions without a defined means for achieving them. These vision statements usually include a beginning phrase such as: We will be the something or other in this industry—lowest cost producer, preferred supplier of this or that, or some similar statement. There is no linkage between the vision statement and reality.

Even though other words or phrases like new horizons and mental models seem appropriate, they lack the force that states just what an organization wants to be. Perhaps we should just use the phrase, *what does the organization want to be*, and back it up with a plan that recognized the resources required to get there. These comments may seem extreme but innovation requires a change in attitude and innovation requires a change from the typical step-by-step approach to the process. Tomorrow will not be the same as today. The creative and contributing mavericks must be accommodated. Those who cannot live without change must also be accommodated. At the same time, innovators are just one part of the innovation process, and there comes a time when the creative and contributing mavericks must recognize that concepts that turn into innovations at the proper time need input from many disciplines.

Summary

- No organization has a monopoly on innovation. It only thrives when people have the courage to challenge the status quo.

- Innovation can occur from the bottom-up or be sponsored from the top-down. Each approach has its set of do's and don'ts.

- Innovation in a start-up organization is similar to bottom-up innovation in the established organization, but with the need to often mortgage family security.

- Innovation requires the individual with the passion to pursue an idea, but a team to move forward to implementation/commercialization.

- Innovators break the rules of the game and manage the dynamic tensions.

Notes

1. I. Nonaka and M. Kenney, 'Towards a New Theory of Innovation Management: A Case Study Comparing Canon, Inc. and Apple Computer, Inc." *Journal of Engineering and Technology Management* 8,1 (1991): 67–83.

2. M. Moritz, *The Little Kingdom* (New York: Morrow, 1984).

3. Ernest Gundling, *The 3M Way to Innovation* (Tokyo: Kodansha International, 2000), p. 180.

4. Peter M. Senge, *The Fifth Discipline* (New York: Doubleday Currency, 1990), pp. 3–25.

5. Ibid.

6. Ibid.

7. Ibid.

8. Henry Mintzberg, "Crafting Strategy," *Harvard Business Review*, July–August 1987, pp. 67–75.

9. Abraham Zaleznik, "Real Work," *Harvard Business Review*, December 1997, pp. 53–62.

10. Rosabeth Moss Kanter, *When Giants Learn to Dance* (New York: Simon and Schuster, 1989), pp. 40–43.

11. J. S. Hirsch, "At Giant Kodak, 'Intrapreneurs' Lose Foothold," *The Wall Street Journal*, August 17, 1990, pp. B1, B8.

12. *Roget's International Thesaurus* (New York: Harper & Row, 1977).

4

The Innovation Process

Management research has provided very little insight into how innovation occurs. Most research studies have focused on the history of innovation, not how or where or why innovation occurs. Anecdotal information tells us how some innovations emerge, how they develop, how they are implemented, and how they are terminated. In essence, there is no research that leads to a theory of innovation. There are no road maps, no seven steps, and no algorithms to define just how ideas are born and how they mature into an innovation. At the same time, there really is no mystery about what is required to become an innovative organization.

Experience tells us that:

- Innovations do not proceed through a series of orderly well-defined stages.

- The many variables in the innovation process prevent predicting outcomes.

- Although the desired outcome can be specified, the route to achieving the outcome not only includes changing direction frequently but also often involves scrapping approaches and starting over.

- The process consists of an idea that comes from some recognized need that's developed into a concept, followed by invention, and then taken through development, production, and diffusion and adoption by end users.

- Innovation involves more than implementing the prescribed linear processes suggested by researchers into the management of innovation.

Process Considerations

Process plays an important role in any achievement. Is there any one specific process for innovation? Probably not, but that doesn't mean that no process exists. In this chapter we'll explore some of the issues discussed in the academic research on the innovation process. The innovation process will be guided by the type of innovation, the importance of the innovation, the elapsed time and expected time of introduction, sources of the innovation (top-down or bottom-up), the availability and the adequacy of the organization's resources, the character of the organizational infrastructure, and the number of technology and market unknowns.

Type of Innovation

The application of the innovation process will vary depending on where the innovation lies on the innovation continuum, which ranges from incremental to the more intensive new-to-the-market and breakthrough innovations, as described in Chapter 2. There's see p. 29 quite a difference between making an incremental product improvement and introducing a new-to-the-market product. The scope involves different levels of both technological and marketing complexity. The specific process steps required to develop the concepts and sell those concepts up the management ladder will entail varying levels of frustration. Although elements of the process may be the same, the application will vary depending on the specific innovation—single discipline, multidiscipline, system, or macro system projects.

Importance of the Innovation

How is the potential innovation perceived not only by management but also by peers from all disciplines? Keep in mind that innovation involves invention plus implementation/commercialization. Management must somehow perceive the innovation as adding value to the bottom line even though the measure of that value may be qualitative and indirect. Innovation is seldom done because it's a good thing to do. There must be some justification and that justification must be apparent. The estimated contribution by the innovation must be measured in relation to the organization's size.

Timing and the Expected Time for Completion

Timing of any innovation requires consideration of the amount of change that the innovation creates. Too early and too late have similar consequences. Too early means the market may not be ready to accept the innovation. Too late may give the competition an opportunity to gain a greater market share. This holds true for introducing a new product or process as well as introducing organizational change. The latest product innovation, if introduced before the users have the competency to take full advantage of its benefits, can often ruin future prospects. The market must be expecting some innovation and be ready to buy the product.

Sources of Innovation

Theoretically all members of an organization are sources of innovation. But innovation will seldom involve more than 5 or 10 percent of the staff even in the most innovative organizations. External influences can also stimulate innovation. As discussed in Chapter 3, the innovation process can begin from the top down or from the bottom up. The process in each case will be quite different. If management has made a decision to pursue a particular activity (top down), the usual challenges of acquiring funds, convincing top management, and finding support become less significant issues. After all, the executive tower has spoken. In contrast, the bottom-up innovator faces an uphill battle.

The Innovation Moment

Innovation research has not shown why ideas become apparent at a specific moment in time or how ideas are transformed into an innovation. Why did someone think of an idea at some specific moment in time and go on to pursue it? Behavioral scientists may have some insight, but that insight does not provide much guidance for increasing these magic moments. For the time being, organizations struggle with finding ways to motivate people to become innovators.

Organizational Infrastructure

If the organizational infrastructure does not support innovation, then innovation may not be a strategy to sustain performance. The organizational infrastructure includes such areas as purpose of the organization, its objectives, its strategies, management attributes, and its support for innovation. The road to changing the culture and mentality of an organization may be difficult, but it can be done. The infrastructure needs to support the innovators, especially if a stream of new products is essential to the organization's future performance. The history of decreased levels of performance when organizations fail to renew themselves is well documented.

Organizational Resources

Organizational resources include more than people and money; they include intellectual property, access to information, capability, time, customers, suppliers, plant and equipment, and financial reserves. All of these resources involve people and their interactions. Unfortunately, too few organizations really know the competencies of their people resources. Selection of participants usually involves too much emphasis on credentials rather than on past performance. Learning that focuses on developing breadth of knowledge, which takes place under many different circumstances and is so important to the innovation process, should be the principal criteria for determining innovation competence.

The Number of Unknowns

Product innovation involves technology and market unknowns. Those unknowns must be dealt with. Too often the effort to resolve these unknowns ends up on the to-do-later list. The process involves dealing with these unknowns in a timely manner and the proper time is now, not after major investments of time and money have been made. What is unknown today may be a known tomorrow, but then new unknown issues will arise and need to be resolved. The process may be perfect, but the people who have responsibility for implementing processes are human. No one has the crystal ball that holds all the answers.

Process Models

Some background from academic research provides a base for considering the innovation process. Research on innovation usually focuses on questioning top-level executives. But most executives are not innovators. The preferred approach might include studying the innovators in their daily efforts to fully understand the process and gain firsthand knowledge of the problems encountered on that innovation journey, but the process itself would influence the results. While academic researchers have presented many models from their studies, four have been selected as representative:

- Roberts and Frohman

- Quinn

- Van de Ven

- Cooper

The models developed by these researchers will be considered from the perspective of innovation sponsored from the top down and sometimes blessed or at least tolerated from the bottom up.

Roberts and Frohman

Much of the management literature on innovation attempts to place the innovation process into a stage-by-stage process. The Roberts and Frohman model has six stages, and is representative of many models found in academic research.[1] It includes:

- Recognition of the opportunity

- Idea formulation

- Problem solving

- Prototype solution

- Commercial development

- Technology utilization and/or diffusion

The authors acknowledge that innovation is not a linear process and that it's conceivable to be in the commercial development stage and find it necessary to return to the problem-solving stage or any period that preceded it. This model disregards the fact that the innovation process involves doing several actions simultaneously. Recognition of an opportunity and idea generation are often simultaneous actions. Thinking of technologies and markets are also simultaneous activities. Resolving a design problem and at the same time thinking how that design fits into the system is not a choice; it's a must. It's true that one can search for an opportunity and then find a solution, but innovators tend to think in chunks. The Roberts and Frohman process model may fit an organization that is directed top down—someone recognizes an opportunity and after much discussion and deliberation manages to formalize a project as an organizational venture.

The Roberts and Frohman model stops after technology utilization. They consider this model as a process for technological innovation and in so doing do not meet the definition of innovation = invention + implementation/commercialization. Innovation is not just about technology and markets. Organizational behavior plays a major role. Innovation involves change, and change creates not only high levels of discomfort but also significant amounts of dissonance.

The Roberts and Frohman model supposes that innovation is a totally rational process with some prescribed methodology. Such a rational process assumes a stable economic and competitive system, but these systems are dynamic. Uncertainty and innovation are synonymous at least in the early periods where general rules of experimentation, work, and conduct do not apply. This is not to suggest the process as described by Roberts and Frohman is not workable, but like other researchers, they assume that the innovation is driven from the top of the organization and lives in a well-organized and static environment.

Quinn

James Bryan Quinn refers to the innovation process as controlled chaos.[2] He doesn't really focus on the details of the process but rather on the mental attitude of the independent innovator and the restrictions placed on the corporate innovator. Quinn considers innovation from two perspectives: 1) the independent innovators who begin in the kitchen or garage or the attic (Quinn refers to these as the garage innovators) and 2) the innovators working in a corporate bureaucracy (organizational innovators).

Quinn suggests that garage innovators, or independent innovators:

- Perceive probabilities much higher than others do

- Can live with frustration, ambiguities, and setbacks

- Avoid early planning

- Use sweat capital—time is not important

- Beg, borrow, and steal—such as by taking a temporary unauthorized loan

- Disregard formal planning tools

The organizational innovators operate in two different realms: those who work on ideas from the bottom up and those who work on innovations directed from the top down. Quinn identified seven barriers to innovation that include:

1. Top management isolation

2. Intolerance of fanatics

3. Short time horizon

4. Assessment of all overhead charges

5. Too much rationalism

6. Excessive bureaucracy

7. Inappropriate incentives

Successful bottom-up corporate innovators behave very much like Quinn's independent innovators and possess the same characteristics, except they don't have to work at the kitchen sink or in an already overcrowded garage. The corporate bottom-up innovator generally faces an uphill battle, fighting the negative responses at all levels even among peers and those just fundamentally against change—the "don't-rock-the-boat" people. There is no doubt that the restrictions often placed on the corporate innovator working from the bottom up lead to a reduced innovation effort. Why would anyone want to fight the corporate bureaucracy to help the organization, especially the bureaucratic managers who are inclined to play it safe and may not even understand the need for pursuing innovation? The real life bottom-up innovator just accepts this as another challenge and a fact of life in the innovation game.

Top-down innovation places relatively few roadblocks for the innovator or the innovation team. The greatest pressure will be on timing. After the entire project has been given the organizational blessing, detractors may find it necessary to reconsider their attitudes. The resources will probably be made available and executive pressure can be applied for gaining support. These types of projects usually stem from ideas that somehow reach the executive level or are generated at the executive level. Executive management recognizes that the idea somehow meets the strategic directions of the organization. What the innovation might be is not known, how to achieve it is not known, but the end result is specified. The resources will be provided.

Van de Ven

Van de Ven and his associates have studied and done considerable research in innovation over many years. They published the results of seventeen years of research that synthesized the findings from the Minnesota Innovation Research Program, which focused on the question, "How and why do innovations develop over time from concept to implementation?" This longitudinal study included hearing health, therapeutic blood filtration, naval systems, school site-based management, computer company start-ups, commercialization of space, nuclear safety standards, government strategic planning, advanced integrated circuits, hybrid wheat development, corporate mergers and acquisitions, state education reform, multi-hospital systems, and human resources management.[3]

Van de Ven found that innovation is a repetition of convergent and divergent thinking, that innovation projects were not consistent from project start to finish, and that outcomes were only partially stable and often were precursors to other ideas. The organizational structure of these projects generally included a group of loosely bound practitioners with a drive toward some specific goal. Innovation involves dealing with unknowns, unpredictable events, and ill-defined and ambiguous goals—*mental chaos in a technical sense.* Only a few of the organizations in the Van de Ven study include industries involved in manufacturing. Most are organizations providing services. Van de Ven verified through research the assumptions accepted as fact by those involved in innovation.

Van de Ven proposes a model that includes three periods in the innovation process:

1. Initiation

2. Development

3. Implementation/termination

Van de Ven acknowledges that innovation does not occur through some linear or mechanistic process but shows that common elements exist in the various innovations. The research provides additional information about innovation but doesn't provide a theory of innovation. It provides another perspective that needs to be taken into consideration by organizations whose future viability depends on innovation.

Initiation. The initiation period is the time of churning ideas and attempting to develop them into a workable concept. An innovator doesn't come up with an idea to fulfill some unmet need and then develop a solution. The effort to define the concept is an iterative process. Most of what you may learn today, you discard tomorrow until the concept makes sense. If innovation occurs from the bottom up, there are no plans. There isn't sufficient information to develop a plan. The plan involves discovery.

Van de Ven's research shows that certain commonalties occur in the initiation period. Not every process characteristic was observed in every innovation, but there was general support for the following process patterns:

1. The process has a gestation period that may last several years and is not initiated on the spur of the moment.

2. Some internal or external trigger usually shocks the individual or the organization into recognizing some significant opportunity or dissatisfaction.

3. Plans are developed and submitted to those who control the resources.

Points 1 and 2 have been generally accepted by practitioners without proof but from personal observations of their own involvement. Point 3, from this practitioner's perspective, is valid when the innovation is directed from the top down. Bottom-up innovators seldom begin with formalized plans; their plans are mental models.

This initiation period is considerably more complex than Van de Ven suggests. Imagine after going through this gestation period and finally recognizing some unfulfilled need that stimulates your curiosity. You think that all the questions have been answered but some new piece of information creates new conflicts that need to be resolved. You acknowledge that this initiation period requires a daily battle of what works and what doesn't work. Van de Ven doesn't describe the deliverables at the conclusion of this period.

Development Period. Van de Ven's development period also provides some commonalities among the investigated projects:

1. The initial idea proliferates into many ideas and activities that proceed in divergent, parallel, and convergent paths.

2. Setbacks and mistakes are part of the process because unanticipated events alter the original assumptions and can snowball into vicious cycles.

3. Changing criteria for success arise that create additional problems between the doers and the resource controllers—controllers are seldom aware of just what innovation implies.

4. The lack of full-time personnel assignments results in experiences that range from euphoria to pain.

5. Major problems usually require resolution by managers or by external sources funding the program.

6. Innovation units develop relationships with other organizational units and negotiate for resources, the required competencies, and other proprietary assets that involve a complex web of interests.

7. Innovators are often involved in activities with competitors, suppliers, and government agencies to create a supportive infrastructure for implementation.

There is no doubt that these seven points need to be considered. But this development period more appropriately refers to following the best practices related to project management. These are common activities and consequences that all projects, not just the ones focused on innovations, encounter.

Implementation/Termination Period. The implementation/termination period also displays certain patterns that need to be reconciled. These patterns often occur throughout the developmental period by linking the new with the old or by reinventing the innovation. Innovations stop when they are implemented or when the flow of resources has been curtailed in such a way that prevents continuing the activities. The success or failure is acknowledged and generally affects the careers of the innovation participants.

In the real world of innovation, implementation absorbs significant resources. It is a complex process of integrating the resources and infrastructure to meet some predetermined requirements. While Van de Ven has found that an innovation activity stops when the resources are curtailed, this doesn't fit with my personal experiences. Passionate and committed innovators don't stop; they find a way to pursue their challenge either within or outside the organization.

The Innovation Journey. Van de Ven concludes the description of what he refers to as "the innovation journey" with: "How might we explain these process observations?" Van de Ven's study documents empirically an innovation journey that is considerably different from the prevailing view. Van de Ven calls into question some of what he considers to be commonly held beliefs about the innovation process. These beliefs according to Van de Ven include:

- Innovation development proceeds in an orderly periodic progression of periods or phases or in a random sequence of chance or "blind" events.

- Innovative behavior that is unpredictable implies an underlying mechanism of randomness or "many variables."

- Innovation development processes converge to a common outcome regardless of their initial condition.

- The innovation journey occurs in a predictable, cybernetic manner.

The pragmatic view of the innovation journey that Van de Ven describes probably never existed, at least not in the minds of the innovators. The history of innovation documents that innovation does not take place in an orderly progression of periods or in a stable and predictable cybernetic manner—it's all about success and failure, euphoria and pain, change and status quo, and passion and commitment. However, innovation covers a spectrum of complexities and the different types of innovation will of necessity be treated differently. It's conceivable that incremental innovation may—and probably should—occur through an orderly process, but those innovations on the portion of the continuum ranging through breakthrough innovation play in a different ballpark. Very often what may be called an incremental innovation is just another upgrade of an existing product and follows nothing more than the best practices associated with managing projects. Such innovation usually involves solving defined problems where technologies and markets remain essentially the same.

Cooper

Robert Cooper introduced the stage-gate system for moving product innovation to the marketplace more rapidly.[4] The process describes a series of stages with defined decision points. As a development reaches certain stages, a decision is made to either continue or discontinue the effort. The six stages include problem identification, ideation, conceptualization, development, testing, and launch.

1. *Problem identification* begins with identifying a particular problem or opportunity.

2. *Ideation* focuses on ideas that might be employed to resolve the problem or pursue the opportunity.

3. *Conceptualization* considers developing all the aspects of a proposal for consideration—technologies, market growth issues, potential revenue stream, available resources, organizational fit, and the competition.

4. *Development* includes all the design and development activities—parts, assemblies, product, manufacturing, marketing, administrative issues, product prototyping, and resolving the marketing development issues.

5. *Testing* involves all the necessary tests in order to verify the needed requirements, reliability, quality, and identification of the actual users.

6. *Product launch* focuses on the commercialization or implementation of the innovation—full-scale manufacturing and selling.

Each of these six activity categories will be subdivided into many subcategories depending on the scope of the innovation. Any single stage could have many decision points. Product launch will include many decision points depending on the organization's philosophy of introducing new products. If market testing drives the marketing decisions, then geographical market testing, income level testing, and general demographic dimensions may need to be analyzed.

As the product goes through these six stages, certain criteria are established to make the go/no-go decision. The objective is to quantify these criteria. These criteria will include issues related to product uniqueness, customer need and perception, market size attractiveness, strategic fit, value for long-term sustainability, availability of internal technologies, usability of the current distribution system, and financial return. These criteria need to be tailored to the scope of the innovation. The list of criteria may be very long for some cases and very short for others. And with experience, they may become second nature—they are givens that the organization follows.

A stage-gate approach to innovation disregards the need for flexibility in making decisions. Using a strict go/no-go procedure provides little opportunity for improving the performance level and scope of innovation. If the evaluation process follows strict guidelines, a majority vote during a review kills the project. Many potentially significant innovations may never be allowed to proceed using the stage-gate system. It's too easy to kill a project at the problem identification or ideation stage. In addition, no innovation follows such an innovation pattern. This does not suggest that there's no need for project reviews, but project reviews at least in the early stages of an innovation require open but disciplined minds that tolerate ambiguity in projecting the state of the innovation and its possibilities. A project could be killed on Friday afternoon, but a few more days of effort may present a different picture. Innovation cannot be fostered by such numerical machinations. Time lines and fulfillment of those time lines are essential but need more than numbers to fulfill the objectives.

Limitations of Process Models

My experience shows that all four views of the innovation process emanating from academic research must be reconciled. The approach of Roberts and Frohman may work well in a top-down organization. Management decides on a course of action and basically assigns the work. Whether the result involves innovation is really not known. Innovation may or may not result. Management may dictate that Project X has a high priority, provides the resources, establishes the work schedule, and makes the assignments. At least the message has been passed to the organization—we want this done. Whether the equation, innovation = invention + implementation/commercialization will occur cannot be determined at the outset of the project.

Quinn, on the other hand, considers innovation both from the individual innovator/entrepreneur working with personal resources and the corporate innovator/entrepreneur facing bureaucratic interference. These two scenarios are quite different. While Quinn considers innovation as "controlled chaos," from a practicing innovator's perspective the chaos arises not in the physical process of innovation but within the mental processes required to transform a raw idea into a defined concept that is pursued to a successful invention and then on to an innovation.

Van de Ven verifies through longitudinal research what most practitioners believe intuitively. This does not in any way discount the findings. The difficulty with this longitudinal study over seventeen years concerns the variety of organizations included: start-ups to established organizations, health care to education, naval systems to government strategic planning, and from human resource management to advanced integrated circuits. Inclusion of these different types of innovation could conceivably lead to a theory of innovation, but diversity of types of innovation, innovator characteristics, and type of industry militate against such a result. A theory to be useful must apply to all situations.

Van de Ven and his associates, like Roberts and Frohman, do not carry innovation through to a conclusion. Roberts concludes with technology utilization and/or diffusion, which means transfer to manufacturing. Van de Ven stops the innovation process prior to implementation. But introduction into the marketplace, adoption, and continued improvement are part of the innovation process—at least for those who take a system approach. Innovation = invention + implementation/commercialization.

The stage-gate approach to innovation presents a tidy way for making decisions. But that's not the way innovation occurs. The problem identification stage may go back and forth with the ideation stage and reach into the conceptualization and development stages. There is no evidence to show that if problem X is identified, then the launch ends with product Y. It's conceivable that an identified problem could reach the testing stage and possibly go back to the conceptualization stage. If the innovation under consideration is of significant value, chances are that many uncertainties will have to be rationalized. All of the required information will not be available at the problem identification stage—it will be developed as the innovation moves through the various stages. While a major innovation may take several years to complete the cycle, the economy and the marketplace will not stand still. Major changes in technology and the marketplace needs could scuttle an innovation. Innovation requires constant vigilance of the marketplace and upcoming technologies.

Summary

- Top-down innovation eliminates most of the frustrations that face the bottom-up innovator. Management has given its blessing, so the innovation process will be funded.

- Bottom-up innovation probably requires bootlegging resources for defining a concept. It's generally an uphill fight and requires a high level of ingenuity for co-opting the required resources.

- The innovation process needs to take into account the type of innovation, the timing and time to completion, the sources of innovation, the organizational infrastructure, the organizational resources, and resolving the unknowns.

- Knowledge of why and when and how innovation occurs is limited. Those supposed "eureka!" moments are preceded by much thought, with ideas that somehow emerge at unexpected times.

- The Roberts and Frohman model focuses on technological innovation and appears to be mechanistic and limited to top-down innovation. They define innovation as the transfer of technology to research, development, manufacturing, or other, leaving out the crucial step of implementation/commercialization.

- James Bryan Quinn's approach to innovation as controlled chaos more closely defines the innovation process as long as it is limited to mental chaos, which should be reaching its end as the innovation enters the project stage.

- Van de Ven presents the results of a longitudinal research study and a scholarly analysis of those results. He subdivides innovation into the initiation period, the development period, and the implementation/termination period, but considers innovation as ending before launching the product into the marketplace.

- Cooper's stage-gate system provides a restrictive process that does not seem compatible with the needs of fostering innovation. The process also seems more appropriate for top-down sponsorship of innovation than bottom-up.

- Metrics for measuring performance have not been discussed in any of these four models. But metrics need to be developed before significant resources are provided. Measurements of success are just part of the successful innovation equation.

Notes

1. E. B. Roberts and A. L. Frohman, "Strategies for Improving Research Utilization," *Technology Review*, March–April 1997, pp. 33–36.

2. James Bryan Quinn, "Managing Innovation: Controlled Chaos," *Harvard Business Review*, May–June 1995, pp. 73–84.

3. Andrew H. Van de Ven, Douglas E. Polley, Raghu Garud, and Sankaran Venkataraman, *The Innovation Journey* (New York: Oxford University Press, 1999), pp. 21–66.

4. Robert G. Cooper, *Winning at New Products: Accelerating the Process from Idea to Launch* (Reading, Mass.: Addison Wesley, 1993), pp. 109–120.

5

Innovation Process Design

Chapter 4 provided background information about several approaches for managing innovation that originated from academic research. As noted, these models lack a certain sense of reality and look at the management of innovation from a limited perspective. All innovation begins with the individual. "Eurekas" usually occur only after a great deal of thought. Different sources of information (people, events, new learning, and observation) may have triggered an idea, but articulating the idea is not a group effort. My years of working in innovative organizations coupled with years of experience as a consultant have verified my conclusions. Ideas build on ideas and some person eventually articulates them. The systems approach to the innovation process makes this assumption and involves four stages:

1. Idea-concept-invention (ICI)

2. Pre-project

3. Project

4. Project-product launch/follow-up

Figure 5-1 illustrates the four stages of the systems approach to the innovation process. The ICI stage involves what Quinn described

Figure 5-1. The four stages of the systems approach to the innovation process.

Idea-Concept-Invention ICI Stage	Pre-project Stage	Project Stage	Project-Product Launch
The innovation stage—managing the unknown, the uncontrollable, and the unpredictable	Validating design parameters and preparing project plans—requesting funds many times	Innovation ends—follow project management principles—business plans	A systems approach—depends on industry and firm's business practices
Opportunities Concept Knockouts Strategic fit Resources Infrastructure Metrics Deliverables	Funding Concept framework Design iterations Integration Prototypes Models Simulations Project plan	Framework Scope Funding Competencies Technology Marketing Distribution Implementation	Marketing plans Commercialization/ Implementation Line extensions Exploiting Technologies New markets Product platforms

as controlled chaos but is more appropriately called mental chaos—trying to keep multiple thoughts in balance at any one time, knowing that many possibilities exist, and making the right decisions. Innovators discipline their thinking and doing by recognizing that although input from other disciplines complicates the innovation process, their input is essential because innovation is a multidisciplinary activity.

The pre-project stage includes the activities required to develop the idea into a workable concept that is worth pursuing. This stage considers the many questions that require answers in order to provide some level of confidence. Prototypes or models are built and tested. Critical technology and marketing issues are resolved. The concept must meet a sufficient number of organizational requirements so that it can be recognized as a potentially viable project and receive additional funding through normal organizational channels.

The project stage involves what the name implies: application of the fundamental principles of good project management. But project management in this context means integration of research projects, product development projects, manufacturing projects, and marketing projects. The integrated approach takes into account the needs of all the functions and disciplines. The project cannot be managed as though it were made up of series of smaller and functionally directed projects, or months of work may end up being invalidated. In other words, this is no longer a period of chaos. This is the time to apply sound design engineering principles, follow marketing fundamentals, and design manufacturing processes that will provide a product that meets quality and reliability standards. This stage involves routine management of resources and infrastructure—skills from Management 101.

The project-product launch/follow-up stage includes all the activities related to launching the product. This is probably the most critical element of the innovation process. The product exists, it has been tested and retested, it supposedly meets all the requirements, but this is the first time it's in the customer's hands. The technologies have been proven and the markets are consistent with the organization's prior activities. Few problems should arise if the innovation is incremental. Any product in the innovation continuum beyond the incremental faces greater obstacles and requires greater attention.

Idea-Concept-Invention Stage

The majority of creativity takes place or at least should take place in the Idea-Concept-Invention (ICI) stage. This does not exclude considering new ideas any place along the concept to implementation chain, but changes must be considered in relation to their impact on meeting the project objectives. Introducing changes or allowing the project scope to creep as the innovation moves toward implementation discounts the future benefits of the innovation. The ICI stage ends when an idea has been translated into a well-defined concept and proof of concept has been established—not just for the technologies but also for the market and the system. This stage integrates some combination of new and old technologies into something new and projects the market potential. During the ICI stage, the name of the game changes. Innovation requires a new ball (the concept), new players (qualified innovators), a new ballpark (new culture), new coaches (proactive managers), and new customers (early adopters).

Figure 5-2 presents a typical feedback process for taking an idea and developing it into a concept. The idea is subjected to inputs 1

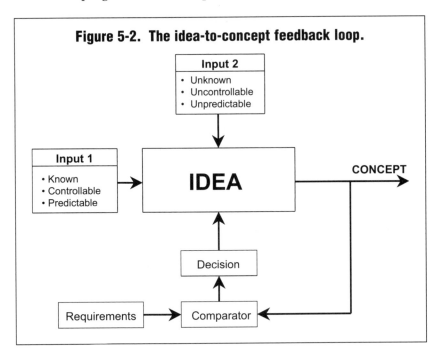

Figure 5-2. The idea-to-concept feedback loop.

and 2, followed by a comparison to the requirements and a decision to determine the corrections that may be required for developing the idea into a viable concept. The ICI stage includes coming up with the idea, developing the idea into a workable concept, demonstrating technical and market feasibility, and obtaining pre-project funding. This is a stage ruled by unknowns, uncontrollable events, and unpredictability. The decisions made during the ICI stage are based on available information, and, as new information (verifiable facts) is uncovered, directions may change and the concept may be redefined, or possibly completely eliminated. This is not a simple continuous or unbroken multi-step process. The ICI stage is often characterized by one step forward followed by two or more steps back.

As an idea begins to take on the form of a concept, the technical and marketing feasibility should not be in doubt, at least to the extent of available and verifiable information. There will be changes in the future, but the issues should be clearly identified. The work must have progressed to the point where peers and immediate management are in accord with the concept. The work should also have gone far enough to understand the known constraints and the significance of the unknown parameters as well as any other potential uncertainties. At some point in time, real money must be approved.

The ICI stage is dedicated to activities that define the:

- Concept

- Knockouts

- Market opportunities, customer base, and needs

- Strategic fit

- Resources, infrastructure, and confidence level

- Deliverables of the ICI stage

An argument can be made that these six activities restrict the innovator from attending solely to the technical or marketing issues. But experience has shown that if some preliminary consideration is not given to these issues, resources can be wasted that could be dedicated more appropriately to other programs. Responding to these issues does not suggest that definitive and complete answers will be confirmed but these issues must be considered in the thought processes. The feedback loop of Figure 5-2 helps control and rationalize those unknown, uncontrollable, and unpredictable inputs.

Innovation is about maintaining or building businesses, not just creating technologies or products. There is little benefit in going through the frustrations of developing a concept only to find that the marketing channels do not exist. If new technologies are required, they need to be identified. Innovation that is not closely linked to the organization's purposes and objectives needs special attention to understand the complexities.

Define the Concept

Every concept begins with an idea. Often there are conflicting ideas because innovators often are able to visualize many different opportunities at any one time—Quinn's controlled chaos. The problem lies in making a choice. Generalizing as to how the choice will be made will most likely never be possible. It is probably not a totally rational process, and to the extent that it is rational, it's probably biased in some way and is based on feeling and a gut reaction. This is not to suggest that the decision is a roll of the dice. The innovator has most likely thought seriously about the issue.

Anyone involved in solving problems realizes that very often the process includes many failures both large and small. An immediate solution to a problem is not usually the final one. It is seldom possible to conceive and understand all the parameters involved and the interactions between those parameters. As new knowledge is acquired, prior decisions must be reconsidered. Problem solving doesn't come about via a prescription. Yes, there is a certain methodology, but that methodology is limited to the facts and the interpretation of those facts at the time the decisions are made. That interpretation of facts changes as new knowledge raises new questions about past decisions and creates new unresolved issues. New options become available as new information is discovered. What was comprehensible yesterday may be incomprehensible today.

Always remember that developing an idea into a concept that can be clearly articulated takes time and requires patience and the ability to deal with continuous setbacks. No one will disagree that xerography was a breakthrough innovation. Chester Carlson in-vented the xerographic process in 1938, but the first copy machine wasn't unveiled until 1948. Another twelve years elapsed before the rotary drum office copier was delivered. Twenty-two years elapsed from the creation of the idea to its effective utilization and commer-cialization.

Developing the concept also requires experimentation in its broadest sense. Experimentation helps to assess concept feasibility. Models of certain components may have to be tested. Various simu-lation techniques may have to be used. Those areas where no avail-able solution appears may require extensive experimentation. Acquiring information from all possible sources helps provide legiti-macy to the concept. The principles underlying the innovation must be understood. So, the innovator must be prepared to deal with the small successes and often the big disappointments. Both are real, and lessons can be learned from those failures.

In many respects, developing the concept is equivalent to devel-oping a project definition and a framework by which to define the work effort. It becomes more complicated because as an innovation it will most likely include resolution of many more unknown factors related to design, technology, and market considerations. This is not a defined step-by-step process. The objective is to end up with a proof of concept that includes not only the technology issues but also the production and marketing issues.

What is proof of concept? As the name implies, its goal is to prove through some means that the concept is workable. The proof can be demonstrated either mathematically or through some physical con-figuration. Proving the feasibility of the concept forces the innovator to focus the effort on achieving some specific result and helps iden-tify the problem issues. Innovators can often spin their wheels and accomplish low levels of performance because they haven't taken the time to write down just what this innovation is all about. Reading that description over and over provides a means for finding the prob-lems and the benefits in the particular description, and it often forces the innovator to reappraise the original assumptions and the means for accomplishing the tasks at hand.

A realistic approach must be taken when developing a proof of concept. Don't expect perfection. This is just the first try; there will be many more before the idea has been transformed into a workable concept.

Identify the Required Technologies

Whether the innovation relates to a product, a process, a service, or the implementation of some administrative routine, technology will be involved. In many cases, the technologies may already exist and be obvious choices, while at other times in order to provide a significant benefit, it may be necessary to determine the benefits and the limitations of moving to leading-edge technologies. Also, the innovators must identify the technologies required to pursue the concept, and determine which of those are known and available in-house, which ones must come from outside sources, and which do not yet exist at an acceptable level for implementation. This effort becomes a major stumbling block in the innovation process because many innovators and managers as well as technical specialists over-value their organization's technical competencies.

Technologies can be looked at from the perspective of those that include the results from science and engineering, and those that include tools, techniques, and methodologies. The main concern involves the technologies that result from science and engineering, which are the core technical competencies that add value. But those core competencies must not only be core but proprietary and not available to other organizations if they are to provide a value-added benefit. Too often core competencies are nothing more than a listing of technical competencies without regard for their value in competing in a global economy. Competencies that are recognized as standard fare across an industry can hardly be considered as adding value. Somehow those core competencies either individually or in some combination must differentiate an organization from its competitors. As a colleague once reminded his organization, "Our process technology is so confidential that all our competitors now have considerable value-added benefits from new process technologies—they get better yields and greater output per work effort." This is an excellent example of management myopia.

So, part of the innovation process requires that innovators identify the required technologies and their status—their usability, their performance, their limitations, and maturity. They should also relate the technologies to their origin, such as heat transfer, electronics, optics, dynamics, fluid mechanics, materials, and so on. Innovators also need to classify the required technologies according to whether they are core, supporting, or emerging, defined as follows:

- *Core technologies* are the key and critical technologies that drive the firm's business, and are typically not available to competitors.

- *Supporting technologies* are essential to maintaining the business. This list can be extensive and adequate expertise must be available to deal with them.

- *Emerging technologies* are those that determine the future technology directions or provide entry into new markets.

Technologies can also be classified as leveraging, leading, pacing, or exploratory. The idea is not to place excessive emphasis on classification but to understand the current and future state of the technologies involved in developing the concept. What an innovator may consider as a core technology may be a technology already being exploited by the competition.

The technologies must also be considered from a system perspective. Focusing only on the immediate product technologies related to the product or process can lead to significant time delays in the future as well as significant financial losses. Here are a few examples of the other issues that should be considered and may help to emphasize this point:

- Safety and environmental issues

- Government regulations at international, national, and local levels

- Maintenance issues

- The user's knowledge and level of understanding

- Potential savings from life-cycle product management

It is too late to consider these issues after the design has been completed and the product is being tested and moving into manufacturing.

Evaluate the Technology Competencies

What are the innovation competencies of the innovator and the organization? Innovators need to understand their own limitations. This is especially true as an idea progresses toward a definable and workable concept. Innovators cannot be experts in every discipline associated with an innovation, especially in the case of new-to-the-market or breakthrough innovations. Innovators need to exploit their own skills, competencies, and experiences and supplement them with input from other professionals. Those complementary competencies reduce the time from idea to implementation. I stress the need for the expertise of others because some innovators often tend to become enamored of learning new disciplines rather than focusing on the problem at hand. Innovators also need to recognize the role that leadership and communication skills play in the process. If they are not capable of providing them, a surrogate can take the responsibility.

Since innovators can't do it alone it's important that they know who has the technical competency to support their effort. Choosing colleagues with the appropriate expertise requires knowledge about the organization's competencies. Searching the typical organizational master file to identify these potential associates probably will not provide direction. Too often such databases are not updated and the original input regarding skill level might have been problematic at best. The objective is to find support from colleagues with the expertise, the track record of accomplishments, and the work habits and attitudes that support the innovation.

Innovators need colleagues competent in their own field of expertise (not that of the innovator) and who have demonstrated:

- Discipline knowledge—a leading-edge type of person who has a track record of accomplishments
- Creativity and innovation in their own discipline
- Conceptual skills—comparable to or better than those of the innovator
- Subject and disciplinary knowledge
- Multidisciplinary understanding and experience
- Process of knowing in depth
- Ability to analyze and synthesize

- Good powers of observation

- Interpersonal skills

The purpose of this exercise is to evaluate the organization's level of expertise. Is it surface, in-depth, or leading edge—and who are the people associated with the know-how? They're the tickets to the future.

Describe the Knockouts

Knockouts include anything known that would cause a "no-go" decision at some time in the future. Evaluating the knockouts is a continuous effort. What appears to be a knockout today may not be one tomorrow, and today's analysis of the knockouts may not be applicable tomorrow. Synergy with other organizational activities may not be evident today, but may be tomorrow. What was thought to be a requirement yesterday might not be one today. What was deemed unnecessary yesterday may be absolutely essential today. These are the tradeoffs that successful innovators make every day. The knockouts include issues related to technology, product distribution, marketing, sales, physical distribution, and customer service.

Technology. What are the technology issues that would prevent this effort from being a success? Identify them now. This does not imply that an innovator gives up on developing the concept. On the contrary, it does mean that the innovator becomes aware of a required technology that may not exist at the level of development required for the specific activities involved. Validating the state of technologies prevents misguided effort from being expended by the innovator in pursuit of something that may not be workable within the time cycle allowed for the effort.

Product Distribution. Does the current product distribution system (the means for moving the product to market) meet the requirements of the proposed innovation? Developing a new distribution system involves significant investments in people and capital. This is often forgotten not only by the innovators but also by product development managers. It may be exciting to consider the global possibilities of this new product, but does the required distribution system exist?

Without the right distribution system, even the best product cannot succeed.

Marketing. The input from marketing determines the success for introducing a new product. Innovators must, at a minimum, be conversant with the proposed work effort. Marketing input will be absolutely essential. There is a tendency for innovators to minimize the value of marketing input. Innovators cannot succeed without it. We all know about the negative comments directed toward marketing people when they essentially misread a market requirement, but we need to remember that innovation (from concept to implementation/commercialization) involves a great amount of thought regarding an undefined future. Information relative to market potential, market competitiveness, market share, and market protocol must be investigated early in the innovation process.

Marketing must also recognize its own limitations. Market surveys and focus groups are beneficial. But the marketers need to understand the business and the history of the industry. A person who gained experience when an industry was in its growth stage may be able to bypass most survey work and marketing studies. That person probably has contact with five or six major players in the industry who are keenly aware of where the industry is going. It may take a market researcher six months or more to acquire the information that the person with knowledge of the industry can obtain in a few telephone calls.

Sales. The result of an innovation must be sold. Regardless of the emphasis on e-commerce, someone must usually make an initial sales call, especially for a new product. Products must be sold to provide a benefit to the firm. Without an established, knowledgeable, and well-motivated sales force, a good product development effort will be doomed to failure. Building a new sales force could be a knockout. Recognizing that it could be a knockout defines it as a problem that requires an answer.

Physical Distribution. Unsuccessful innovators too often ignore the physical distribution side of their work effort. Distribution systems involve not only significant capital investment and must be considered early in the process. Yet, the lack of a distribution system can negate years of creative work.

Customer Service. Customer service involves a pre- and a post-sales activity. It begins with an attempt to sell the customer and ends when the product is delivered, working to specification, and meeting the customer's requirements. Customer service is not just about solving a customer's problem. It's also about educating the customer. Customer service does not stop after the product is delivered; it's only the beginning. Society became aware of the need for customer service with the advancement of computer and e-mail technology. The complaints continue about inadequately trained customer service people in all industries.

Market Opportunities, Customer Base, and Other Needs

Market information, or perhaps more appropriate at this stage, "potential customer information" relative to uses and needs, becomes important. That information relates to:

- Product type

- Product uses

- Market opportunities

- Customer base

- Validating need

- Metrics

Integrating this information allows the innovator to begin to realize that innovation involves all the elements from raw idea to implementation/commercialization.

Product Type. How do innovators find the market opportunities? Any idea that is developed into a workable concept usually stems from some knowledge or at least intuition that a market need exists. However, the details of a market need are not always easily recognizable. It is one thing to say that a market exists for Product X. But what are the implementation requirements of Product X? What do the users need? What do the users want? Do they possess the skills and/or competencies required? Are they capable of using the product effectively and efficiently? These types of questions must be asked and answered to gain an understanding about the benefits of the innovation.

Product Uses. Defining the possible uses for the potential product is a given. There must be some initial obvious customer requirement. The needs, however, are not always obvious. It may take a considerable amount of time and effort to determine some specific need. In most cases, early needs are exaggerated and rightly so. It's easy to blue-sky the possibilities. Without some calculated exaggeration of the potential, it may be very difficult to find support, not just financial support but moral support. Somehow discussion of the potential innovation must stir somebody's interest and possible action, if not to fully participate, at least not to outwardly inhibit the effort. At times it may be necessary to work with a potential customer to really define product requirements. However, complete disclosure of the concept may not be feasible for business reasons. If the proposed concept is of significant value, possible disclosure to a competitor could result. The innovator is usually faced with limited resources during this conceptual stage. Sufficient funds for marketing will most likely not be available. Nevertheless, some marketing information is absolutely essential.

Market Opportunities. Market opportunities are often a neglected activity, yet they play a major role in successful innovation. Too often even the innovators are too close to their organization's area of common interest and forget to look beyond the immediate less apparent possibilities. The organization produces nails so it makes more and better nails. Does the organization fully understand the use of nails? Or is it in the fastening business? This is a simple example, but a visit to a Home Depot shows the proliferation of specialized fastening devices.

Customer Base. Innovations usually arise from people who have some understanding of needs in a specific market area. Innovators may have worked in the area, are working in the area, or have some insight into an area that may require the integration of several disciplines. They don't have these ideas and develop them into concepts without some knowledge. But the customer base needs to be defined, and much can be accomplished in the initial stages by reviewing basic demographic data.

Validating Need. At this stage the validation of need will be very preliminary. At times it may be obvious. If it is obvious, preliminary information can be developed from considering the demographics of the potential customer base. But that analysis needs to be done by someone capable of understanding a particular market sector. As an example: I reviewed a business plan for an exciting new product. The market study in the business plan showed a potential market exceeding $5 billion. After reviewing the specific segment in which the product would develop a customer base, using more targeted market and industry data, the figure was reduced to less than $250 million. This was still a substantial market, but the plan now used a more realistic figure with which to consider future opportunities. Overstating market size is not only a common failing of innovators but also a trait of many professional marketers. Most market projections seldom materialize. Overstating leads to unrealistic expectations that eventually need to be defended, and that can also diminish the credibility of the innovator.

Metrics. By whatever means, the innovator must consider an appropriate metric for the proposed investment of resources. That metric can include a single or combination of measures, but it needs to be an appropriate metric for the project. Market projections are usually overstated or understated, seldom very accurate. That's to be expected. But innovators need to keep in mind that when they make projections they are limited to knowledge that is available at the time that the decision is made. Innovators are now at the bottom of the learning curve and need to remember that these customer needs are far more difficult to develop when the innovation involves a new-to-the-market or breakthrough product than when the innovation involves a product enhancement.

Strategic Fit

Is there a strategic fit? This is a relatively simple question to answer. Going too far outside the purposes and objectives of the organization could result in much time and effort being directed in nonproductive activity. The concept must also be compatible with the vision (what the organization wants to be) and values of the organization. Going too far beyond the organization's technology strategy requires additional effort to convince the skeptics. However, if the innovation depends on introducing leading-edge technologies, the innovator has no alternative except to use the new technology. Using existing technology or existing technology platforms minimizes the selling effort. The same holds true for marketing strategy. Straying too far beyond the current approaches only adds to the effort required to justify an investment. The use of the existing technologies and marketing capabilities must be balanced with the scope of the effort regardless of the prevailing attitudes concerning change. If new technologies and marketing capabilities are required, that need should be recognized during the ICI stage.

Linking Organizational Resources, Infrastructure, and Information

Innovation cannot occur if the appropriate resources, infrastructure, and information are not available. Resources without an adequate infrastructure will not foster innovation and a supportive infrastructure without the resources is equally inadequate. Information crosscuts both the resources and infrastructure elements. Why should innovators be concerned about these linkages? The resources and infrastructure requirements can be quite different depending on the type of project. While there are common requirements for most projects, most also differ in scope, complexity, levels of involvement, and organizational impact. While the fundamental process may be the same, the requirements for achieving the objectives can be quite different. A project to develop a new technology would have different requirements than one for integrating the activities of diverse organizational units. A manufacturing process project would be structured differently than an information systems project. Each has their own individual needs even though each may follow a consistent series of process steps.

Organizational Resources. Are the resources available? Resources depend on the type of innovation. Those resources need to be described in specific terms. Organizational resources include people, intellectual property, information, technology, time, customers, suppliers, plant and equipment, facilities, and financial. See Chapter 8 for a full discussion of resources.

Organizational Infrastructure. Does the organizational infrastructure support the innovation? Innovation cannot occur without an adequate and appropriate infrastructure that supports the particular innovation. Organizational infrastructure includes purposes, objectives, strategies, leadership, communication, management attitude, guiding principles, support for innovation, acceptance of risk, organizational structure, and organizational attributes. While most innovators are passionate about their particular activity, there is little point in hoping against hope that the organizational infrastructure will change to accommodate the innovator. See Chapter 9 for a full discussion of infrastructure issues.

Organizational Information. The level of confidence in pursuing an innovation depends on the integration of the resources, infrastructure, and information. Organizations become involved in many different types of projects: business, technology, product and process, information systems, integration, and administrative. Every organization will need to relate project types to their particular requirements. Each project type will exhibit different requirements depending on scope, complexity, duration, and many other factors.

Figure 5-3 illustrates the relationship between resources, infrastructure, and information in achieving the objectives. The three-dimensional model helps innovators and managers consider the impact of the missing links in pursuing an innovation. As Figure 5-3 shows, the ideal situation occurs when the cube—which includes resources, infrastructure, and information— reaches unity. The three axes of the cube—called resources, infrastructure, and information— each have a maximum value of 1. If, as an example, the innovator had only one-half the resources, one-half the supporting infrastructure, and one-half the information required, only 12.5 percent of the cube would be filled. That's not a very good point from which to begin. Even if you had 100 percent of any one of the three dimensions but only some fraction of the other two dimensions, you need to consider whether it is wise to begin.

Don't expect the resources, the infrastructure, and information components to approach 100 percent. That seldom occurs in real life. Obviously, some minimum level of resource availability is essential. The point, however, is not to spend a great deal of time doing quantitative studies, but to evaluate the difficulties that may arise if certain conditions are not met. The level of fullness of the cube in Figure 5-3 provides a measurement of the confidence level for the innovator.

Figure 5-3. Integrating resources, infrastructure, and information.

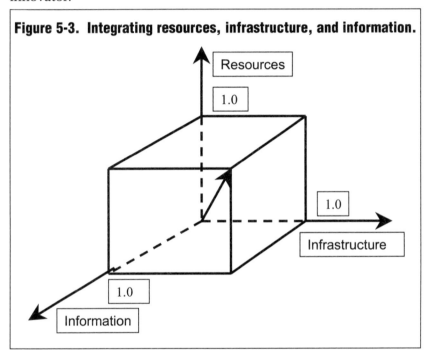

Deliverables of the ICI Stage

The ICI stage ends when the innovator has identified some minimum but acceptable level of feasibility and confidence that allows the innovator to progress to the pre-project stage. Up to this point, the top-down innovation project has probably been adequately funded and staffed. The bottom-up innovator will have bootlegged the resources in order to go through the many iterations needed to take the idea and develop it into a workable concept. In both cases, the innovator should have demonstrated feasibility within the limits of the support. The top-down innovator should have capitalized on the knowledge of colleagues, managers, and external resources. Hopefully, by this time, the bottom-up innovator's immediate supervisor has become sufficiently interested to help move the project to the next stage.

The deliverables for the top-down and bottom-up innovators will be the same. Both provide the same deliverables, although it may be more difficult for the bottom-up innovator. But the deliverables do not include what is normally considered as a formal business plan. There is insufficient information available to develop even a preliminary business plan. The description of the deliverables may be the first formalized request for funding and takes the form of a project plan. It's management's opportunity to get involved.

The deliverables at the end of the ICI stage include:

- A detailed statement of the idea, the concept, and the invention

- Statement of purpose that describes benefits to the organization, impact if not approved, and reasons for management support

- Description of the features, advantages, and benefits to the user

- Some general discussion of the market opportunities

- Impact on manufacturing, pilot plants or prototype departments, and research and development

- The fit with the organization's mission/purposes, objectives, and strategy

- Justification for further investment of resources

- Proprietary position related to patents, copyrights, or trademarks

- Discussion of technologies—old, leading edge, unknown

- Description of any potential knockouts

- Analysis of the major uncertainties—what isn't known that should be known

- Some idea of the financial requirements, the competencies from other functional groups, and a time line for monitoring future progress

The ICI stage may be funded in different ways, depending on the sponsor and the type of innovation. If the project is a top-down project, independent of who conceived the original idea, the ICI stage will generally be officially funded. If the project involves a bottom-up project, the majority of resources will have been bootlegged with some possible support from the innovator's immediate management. Top-down or bottom-up incremental innovation projects generally have no problem being funded as long as the traditional technologies and marketing directions remain the same. A major change in either technologies or how the marketplace is approached will require additional justification.

The ICI stage is an iteration stage. There is no limit to the number of iterations that may be required to complete the deliverables. Innovation is not about pursuing a defined plan. The ICI stage is about working through the myriad of details that are required to define the system and understand the implications of a potential investment. In my own case, these activities usually began with an offer of $25,000 to anyone who had an idea and was willing to pursue it with a serious commitment. Subsequent funding depended on progress and the ability to clearly articulate and demonstrate the status. It was not uncommon to go through four or five such cycles. Even in today's economy, $25,000 can provide the start for demonstrating feasibility. One can argue that not much can be done with $25,000 these days, but this is not about building prototypes; it's about demonstrating feasibility and thinking through the details from a business perspective.

Pre-Project Stage

Management has a choice to fund, not to fund, or ask for more information based on the deliverables of the ICI stage. Regardless of the decision, this experience allows the innovator to gain some valuable insight by listening to management's concerns. If management approves, there is obviously no problem to continue the effort. If management decides not to fund, the innovator has an opportunity to continue to pursue the effort even in the face of instructions not to do so—it depends on the innovator. Real innovators do not take "no" for an answer. They keep coming back with updated proposals. That continued effort may or may not be sanctioned by the innovator's immediate supervisor. If management requests additional information before making a commitment, the innovator has no alternative but to provide it. At least some progress has been made. But the innovator needs to try and find out specifically what additional information is required. If management merely requests more information without being specific, it's a management cop-out. By presenting the concept to management, the innovator has the opportunity to ascertain where the support exists, what are the major management concerns, and the reasons for any opposition.

There may be several pre-project requests for funding support because as new information is acquired in the development process, previously unknown issues are uncovered. Decisions may have to be reevaluated. It is not possible to define all the parameters and their interrelationships in the ICI stage. There are times when the innovator has no alternative except to go to the organizational bank. An astute management will realize that the first funding will not be the last—it's only the beginning of a series of successes and partial failures followed by more partial successes and failures.

Assuming that the concept is gaining some acceptance, a more directed effort is now needed. Although the activity will most likely be led by the innovator, other organizational functions will have to participate. The activity is no longer a one-person show. Marketing and sales, manufacturing, distribution, and the administrative functions must be brought into the project officially for their expertise. There may be specific issues related to safety, environmental, and patent considerations, and there also may be governmental regulations that must be considered. These new people, whose assignments may be temporary, will undoubtedly frustrate the innovator because their input may require changes in approach and design. Also, the innovator's project may not be at the top of their priority list.

The pre-project stage begins to appear more like basic project management. The ICI stage has been basically completed until at some time it becomes necessary to revisit it because of new information. Although market opportunities have not been completely defined, consensus has been reached regarding direction of the major issues. Competencies from other disciplines have been identified. The need for additional resources has been recognized although not necessarily resolved. Technology direction has been ascertained. Knockouts have been rationalized. Redundancies for the moment have been identified. In essence a first cut has been approved recognizing the uncertainties associated with pursuing the challenges relating to new technologies and markets. Some general time lines can now begin to place more control on the project.

Pre-Project Work Effort

The beginning work of the pre-project stage sets the process in motion for developing a project plan and a business plan for the product. The work effort involves taking what is known as a result of the ICI stage investigations, adding new information, further demonstrating technology and market viability, building the workable prototype, and formulating a plan that meets the purposes, objectives, and strategies of the organization. During this pre-project stage, the work effort focuses on:

- Assigning the people resources from the required disciplines

- Developing a project team that focuses attention on the business, not just on technology or markets

- Finalizing a definitive concept with justification

- Validating the invention

- Breaking down the project into its many pieces based on competencies and available skills

- Doing the design work

- Building and testing a workable prototype

- Defining, evaluating, and justifying the business

- Validating that the knockouts have been rationalized

- Investigating the possible proprietary position related to patents, copyrights, or trademarks

- Developing a time line to guide the project's schedule

- Using project reviews to guarantee that all activities are coordinated and that everyone on the team is meeting the assigned responsibilities

Measuring Success

There is no single measure of success for implementing an innovation. However, some criteria need to be established before major investments are approved. Measures of success usually involve a combination of items from the following list:

- Degree of profitability—plus or minus from some acceptable level

- Payback period

- Domestic market share

- Foreign market share

- Relative sales for similar products

- Relative profits for similar products

- Actual sales versus sales projections

- Actual profits versus profit objectives

- Opportunities for spin-off products

- Opportunities for entering new markets

- Use of existing product platforms

- Basis for future technology advancement

These *pre-project stage* activities may require going back to management for additional funding. New problems and inconsistencies will be uncovered. Some assigned people may leave the project. Additional knowledge of competition may become known. Some new technology or market characteristics may have be identified that demand further investigation. A competitor may preempt the introduction of the product. And the list can go on with the reasons why changes in scope and direction may become necessary. Innovators and managers should accept the fact that the pre-project stage may require returning to the organizational bank several times for additional funding.

Project Stage

The pre-project stage activities set the stage for the project stage. The project plan and the business plan have been completed. Now the team needs to practice the fundamental principles of integrated project management. This project stage requires a skilled manager with a successful track record. It cannot be put in the hands of a neophyte without a thorough understanding of the complexities of bringing projects in to specification, on time, and at cost.

The project stage brings together all the necessary disciplines and molds them into a team. Up until this time, the innovator has been the star, but an individual can take an idea only so far without some help and counsel from associates. There comes a time when additional expertise can no longer be bootlegged. This situation often creates difficulties because of the relative independent thinking of innovators—*don't mess with my baby*—but that baby now needs some serious attention from other disciplines. Expertise must be brought into the project at some time if the work effort is to benefit the organization. As noted, timing is important. Creativity now takes second place to doing the nitty-gritty detail work. The innovation activities become very pragmatic. The innovator's role now may be diminished, because the project requires not so much of the innovator but the master project manager—the person who can negotiate with all the different interests in order to deliver a successful product.

Innovation really ends with the successful completion of the pre-project activities. This is not the time to begin reinventing. There have been plenty of opportunities to review and make the necessary changes and improvements. Obviously, there can be some last-minute problems that need to be corrected, but the team should have been tracking potential problems. Innovation requires more than technical talent—it requires those put-it-all-together skills that include leadership, communication, and the necessary people skills.

Innovation involves more than disciplinary knowledge and experience. It requires that those on the team replace their professional discipline hats with their business hats.

Product Launch/Follow-Up Stage

Discussion of product launch goes beyond the scope of this book. Product launch is driven by the industry involved and the product, and is also affected by whether the effort was directed to an incremental, a new-to-the-market, or breakthrough innovation. The expected result from the ICI, pre-project, and project stages is a product, process, service, or introduction of a new administrative benefit. The difficulty in many cases is that this stage, is not integrated with the others. Since it's the last stage, it often does not receive sufficient attention during the idea to implementation cycle. Launch must be integrated no later than the latter part of the ICI stage.

Figure 5-4 shows a generalized innovation time line with only start and finish times. The interval depends on the innovation and the contextual considerations of the environment in which it's being implemented. The dotted lines indicate an overlap of activities. The amount of the overlaps will vary by the type of innovation and the availability of the organization's resources and support of the infrastructure. Product launch costs depend on the type of innovation and the method of distribution. Those costs can be very large. Product launch involves more than providing for the sales effort.

Figure 5-4. Typical innovation time line.

Innovation Stage	Overlapping Activities		
ICI			
Pre-project			
Project			
Launch			
	Start		Finish

At the very least, product launch involves:

- Getting the product to the customer to specification, on time, and at the agreed cost with the required quality and reliability

- Providing customer service—something much better than what exists today via e-mail, telephone, and the Web

- Managing the customer returns

- Meeting the product modification requirements for offshore sales

- Working with the customer to optimize product performance

Summary

- There are significant differences in top-down and bottom-up innovation. Top-down innovation eliminates most of the frustrations faced by the bottom-up innovator. Bottom-up innovation generally requires a high level of ingenuity for co-opting the required resources.

- The innovation process needs to take into account the type of innovation, the timing and time to completion, the sources of innovation, the organizational infrastructure, the organizational resources, and resolution of the unknowns.

- The innovation system process model emphasizes the ICI and pre-project stages. The project and launch stages require primarily project management skills.

- The deliverables from the ICI and pre-project stages are the same whether applied to top-down or bottom-up innovation. Metrics will always be important. Resources will always be limited. But those metrics need to be known before significant resources are provided.

- Introducing new technologies into new products and pursuing new markets simultaneously create additional incongruities and complexity.

- Technology, marketing, sales, distribution, and customer service knockouts must be rationalized in the pre-project stage.

- Resources, infrastructure, and information form a triad that governs the innovation process. All must be merged for successful innovation.

- Incremental innovation can be planned. It must be planned. Prudent management suggests that specifying time for completion of a new-to-the-market or breakthrough innovation prior to completion of the pre-project stage is not advisable.

6

What Is Organizational Culture?

Research on the impact of culture on organizational behavior has not yielded the results that could be used to develop a theory of organizational culture. Yet it is obvious that culture affects business performance. Academics have published many books, the management gurus have pursued their single-issue proposals, and the consultants have attempted to provide their packaged programs. As we enter the new millennium, we have no theory of organizational culture that applies to all organizations under all circumstances. Human behavior probably does not lend itself to broad generalizations.

Backdrop on Culture

What is organizational culture? Organizational culture includes the shared values, the beliefs, the legends, the rituals, the past history, the intellectual and operational traditions, the pride in past accomplishments, the policies and practices, the rules of conduct, the organization's general philosophy of operation, and other artifacts that define an organization. Culture either stimulates or inhibits performance of the organization from meeting its purposes. One point is certain, culture isn't theory, it's practice. Those war stories, embellished with each repetition, do have a purpose. Culture goes beyond the statement that "people are our most important asset." The reality of that statement is measured by how managers act and colleagues respond.

From this practitioner's perspective, what is commonly referred to as organizational culture really doesn't exist in the operational sense. There may be statements that attempt to define the desired culture, but culture cannot be dictated from the top. The people in the organization define the culture. It's almost impossible to conceive of a culture where large groups of individuals display similar behaviors. The only exception may be the military. Although there may be a consensus about the organization's vision, beliefs, and traditions, the culture in the operating units, while adhering to these general norms, will be quite different. Unless an organization clones its managers, each operational unit will reflect a quite different culture while espousing the general organizational culture. Although culture can be defined in simple terms, building a culture to meet specific organizational requirements has been a major challenge over the millennia. Building a culture involves working with people who come together with different interests and often conflicting ethnic, religious, economic, and educational value systems. Culture is about people and all of their skills, competencies, and their foibles and prejudices. Research has not provided any formulas for developing a specific type of culture, but some guidelines emerge that help overcome some of the hazards. There's not much point in waiting for definition of the seven steps to build the ideal culture. Culture is contextual.

Classification of Culture

The results of three researchers have been selected for consideration since they provide in the aggregate a base from which to consider the do's and don'ts. John P. Kotter and James L. Heskett classify cultures as Theory I, II, and III; Judith M. Bardwick classifies cultures as entitlement, earning, and fear; D. R. Denison establishes hypotheses and uses empirical evidence to provide some conclusions; and finally there is a fourth one that I refer to as the no-rules culture.

Kotter and Heskett

What do we know about culture and how do we take a measure of its importance to organizational performance? Kotter and Heskett show that while many shared values and institutionalized practices can promote good performance in some instances, those cultures can also undermine the organization's ability to adapt to change. They classify cultures as Theory I, Theory II, and Theory III.[1]

Theory I Cultures. Firms operating in uninhabited markets where they have almost monopolistic power can become inwardly focused, arrogant, and bureaucratic. These firms are often characterized as having strong cultures, giving the impression that strong cultures create excellent long-term performance. The performance measures used by Kotter and Heskett include average yearly increase in net income, average yearly return on investment, and average yearly increase in stock price. In these strong cultures, which are defined as Theory I cultures, managers operate with a consistent set of values and methods of doing business. New employees are expected to adapt. Changes in management create no change. Managers in essence are clones and a new manager continues where the last one stopped. Normally strong cultures operate with effective and efficient bureaucracies that do not tend to diminish motivation or innovation. Organizations described as having strong cultures are perceived by outsiders as having a particular style for managing their business.

Kotter and Heskett's research shows that a firm can have a strong culture and poor performance or a weak culture and excellent performance. Neither possibility can be explained by the "strong culture" perspectives. The researchers concluded that there's a modest relation between a strong culture and long-term economic performance, but the statement "Strong cultures create excellent performance" appears to be misleading. Theory I cultures can also lead the organization into uncharted areas where they lack the resources and the required infrastructure.

Theory I cultures assume that the world economy is relatively stable and predictable, but such an assumption no longer holds. When certain organizations like Kodak, IBM, and General Motors were considered to have strong cultures, they were successful when they dominated their markets. But then Fuji and other photographic companies began to invade Kodak's markets, Digital Equipment and others took on IBM, and Japan took on General Motors. These strong cultures began to lose market position once the competitors provided improved products and took the lead in applying leading-edge technologies. Kotter and Heskett concluded that Theory I may not be wrong, but it is incomplete and overlooks too many ancillary factors.

Theory II Cultures. Theory II cultures are only beneficial when the patterns of behavior fit the organizational context—its specific needs. There must be a fit with the purposes, objectives, and strategies of the organization. The values and behaviors are probably more important than its strength in its combined resources. One size does not fit all and there are no generic elements that define the optimal culture. Theory II cultures maintain an appropriate fit between culture and context. The same culture would not be appropriate for both Microsoft and the New York Metropolitan Opera Company. The cultures of slow-moving industries are quite different from the cultures of the fast-moving companies. The culture of an entrepreneurial venture is different from that of an established firm. What constitutes a good-fit culture is probably difficult to describe in detail, but there are certain characteristics that will define the culture, such as speed of decisions, levels of approval, the role of technologies, and the presence and influence of the founder. The general conclusion is that the better the fit, the better the performance; the poorer the fit, the poorer the performance.

Theory III Cultures. Theory III postulates that cultures that anticipate and adapt to environmental change will be associated with superior performance. Theory III cultures adapt, focus on creativity, promote a proactive approach, accept risk, and deal with uncertainties. Members are receptive to change and innovation, and there is a shared feeling of confidence and support in identifying problems and implementing solutions. Ralph Kilmann describes an adaptive culture as one that " . . . entails a risk-taking, trusting, and a proactive approach to organizational as well as individual life."[2] Kotter and Heskett cite 3M as an example of a Theory III organization—it tries consciously to adapt culture to a changing world.

Issues Undermining Performance. Kotter and Heskett also conducted research to identify the factors that undermine long-term economic performance. The following sequence of events is an example of making the transition from success to failure:

- Visionary leadership with a bit of luck builds a successful organization.

- A workable strategy is implemented by a committed group of people.

- The organization becomes dominant in the market.

- A strong patent position or confidential processes may exist.

- Market dominance becomes a routine process.

- Growth now begins to create internal challenges.

- People are selected as managers who do not display the necessary leadership.

- These managers become top executives.

- True business leadership somehow begins to evaporate.

- We're successful—"it ain't broke, so why fix it."

The rest of the story tells about the failures of the organization to meet its objectives. The question that remains, What role did leadership play in these early years of success? Kotter and Heskett found that managers who demonstrated leadership were often not promoted. The downsizing of the 1980s, although a history often forgotten, should have taught that arrogance and a self-satisfied approach could devastate an organization. Did too much socialization on the golf course blind executives about the real competencies of their appointments? Did CEOs begin to depend too much on the recommendations from the human resource specialists in advancing people to the management ranks? Would people with leadership characteristics like those of Jack Welch of General Electric or Robert Lutz, the former president of Chrysler Corporation, be turned down today for a management position?

Bardwick

Judith Bardwick classifies cultures as entitlement, fear, and earning.[3] Every classification harbors some anomalies. Bardwick's classification fits this suborganizational level more appropriately than that of the parent organization.

Although we like to speak about a *corporate* culture, it can only be in very general terms. For example, 3M has a culture that focuses on innovation. It also supports a culture that focuses on respect for the individual. Not every manager will comply all the time, but the 1,000 or more managers do not treat innovation in the same way. In most cases, that suborganizational culture is more important because it affects the average employee directly every day. Unless you clone managers, you'll find that teams and other organizational units all have different cultures.

Entitlement Culture. Entitlement cultures demonstrate high levels of apathy and complacency, conformity to rules and procedures, rule checking, bureaucracy, dependence, and risk avoidance. These characteristics then show low levels of innovation, empowerment, accountability, morale, motivation, flexibility, evaluation, and termination. Entitlement cultures emphasize process and procedure. Precedent governs decisions. Incremental innovation is treated as a big deal. Promotion is based on seniority and little distinction is made between high and low performers. Time is not of the essence and there's just a little too much agreement and graciousness. Creating dissonance is not an option.

Fear Culture. Fear cultures are dominated by a lack of security and predictability, an absence of knowledge about just where the organizational unit is going, and little direction from the top in the form of top-down communication. Turf and self-protection, denial, cynicism, and stress are apparent. There's a tendency to overreact and develop a fire-fighting mentality. A great deal of time is consumed in correcting mistakes. Blame dominates the daily scene. The basic philosophy says, "Just do what I tell you to do." The fear culture resembles the typical command and control culture.

Earning Culture. Earning cultures demonstrate high levels of trust, accountability, innovation, leadership, risk taking, teamwork, and excitement. Change is typically thoughtful and logical. Outcome is more important than process. The system rewards performance. The unit is driven to surpass its objectives. Constructive mavericks are respected. A high level of collegiality brings divergent personalities to focus on objectives. The earning culture also looks to the future. Earning cultures push the envelope. The internal rate of change keeps up with the external rate of change and may even drive the rate of change. Earning cultures are proactive.

These three cultures probably do not exist in pure form. Within any organization, pockets of entitlement, fear, and earning will exist simultaneously. In any large organization, there are many different cultures, and operating units may change from one to another culture for short periods of time. The project manager of a major project may have developed a culture that is earning oriented, but when the project schedule begins to lag, some form of fear culture will surface, creating uncertainty and possibly fear of losing one's job. Or, where a parent company's organizational culture is generally perceived as earning based, there may be times when a little bit of fear regarding less than expected performance levels can create the necessary tension that leads to improved performance. In spite of these limitations, Bardwick's classification provides a useful model for examining the characteristics of the three types of culture.

Denison

D. R. Denison considers the relation between culture and effectiveness and has suggested four hypotheses, which he designated as involvement, consistency, adaptability, and mission.[4] He described these hypotheses as follows:

1. The *involvement hypothesis* suggests that high levels of involvement and participation create a sense of ownership and commitment. This ownership generates greater commitment to the organization and provides a means for enhancing autonomy.

2. The *consistency hypothesis* emphasizes the positive impact of culture on effectiveness. It argues that the shared system of beliefs, values, and symbols has a positive effect on the ability

of the organization to reach consensus and carry out coordinated actions.

3. The *adaptability hypothesis* emphasizes that a culture usually consists of behavioral responses that have proven in the past to be adaptive to the organization. This hypothesis focuses on three aspects: the ability to perceive and respond to the external environment, the ability to respond to internal customers, and the capacity to change behaviors and processes that allow an organization to adapt.

4. The *mission hypothesis* provides purpose and meaning by defining a social role for the organization and the importance of individual roles within the organizational role. According to Denison, "behavior is given intrinsic, or even spiritual meaning that transcends functionally defined bureaucratic roles."

Denison tested these four hypotheses by surveying the CEOs of 3,425 organizations (969 responded). His measures of effectiveness included new-product development, sales growth, market share, cash flow, return on assets, and overall performance.

The empirical results support the four hypotheses and provide information for the possible integration of these hypotheses into a general theory of culture. The study did not address the interrelationships among the hypotheses. Denison recognized that his study relied on the responses from CEOs whose comments may need to be validated. From a practitioner's perspective, Denison's hypotheses appear to be self-evident, but the validation adds importance to the hypotheses. We know that when people become involved they become committed. It's obvious that if we have a common set of values, we have a better chance of reaching consensus. Adapting to conditions in all sectors of an organization's arena is essential. That mission statement, if it's real and implemented, sends a clear message as to where the organization is going. Culture can either reduce everyone to some lowest common denominator or raise the bar to use the competencies to the benefit of the individuals and the organization.

The No-Rules Culture

The information age gave birth to the no-rules culture primarily associated with the computer industry. These cultures displayed high levels of innovation, dedication in pursuit of goals, willingness to work around the clock if necessary, lack of bureaucracy, little or no formal organization, and much social interaction. Some such companies have been successful while others were total failures. Apple is probably the best example of this culture, and the ups and downs of Apple are history.

In more recent years, the dot-com culture evolved, featuring long hours, in some cases minimum direct compensation but significant stock options, and exceptional motivation. Unfortunately, many dot-coms disregarded management fundamentals and ended up on the business scrap heap, the obvious lesson being that profits are an absolute requirement for sustaining a business. At some point, the no-rules culture must develop some minimum levels of organizational discipline.

Reconciling Research on Cultures

In summary, Kotter and Heskett provide us with three theories of culture, each with different characteristics. Theory I cultures, defined as strong cultures, tend to remain unchanged over many years, aligning their goals, creating high levels of motivation, and providing the needed structure and controls without inhibiting performance. In Theory II cultures, there must be a fit with the purposes, objectives, and strategies of the organization—the context within which the organization functions. Theory III describes the culture of the adaptive organization—an organization that promotes a culture that can deal with the dynamics of a world economy. The organization alters its purposes, objectives, and strategies as needed, but with thoughtful consideration of the consequences.

Bardwick proposes three types of cultures: entitlement, fear, and earning. These classifications provide a tool for evaluating a culture and determining its direction. Few organizations could be identified as being in just one category. An entitlement culture could not survive without at least some minimal influence from the earning type culture. Likewise, a fear (control) culture will not survive without some influence from an earning culture. An earning culture will also be influenced by components of the entitlement and fear cultures.

Denison's hypotheses appear to be self-evident to a practitioner. He verified that:

- High levels of involvement create a sense of ownership and generate greater commitment.

- Shared system of beliefs, values, and symbols help an organization reach consensus.

- Adaptability emphasizes that a culture consists of the collective behavioral responses to changing conditions.

- The mission defines the social role of the organization and the individual within the organizational role.

The *no-rules culture* can work in entrepreneurial organizations in their formative years. There's nothing wrong with providing freedom but most people cannot accept total freedom. It's possible that colleagues can either influence or coerce other members to fall into line. But there comes a time when schedules must be met, orders must be placed, designs must be completed, and products must be built, tested, manufactured, and shipped. When the organization begins to take shape, there may not be time for the Friday afternoon "Beer Bust." The demise of many dot-coms shows that the basics of management cannot be disregarded.

Which approach does an organization follow in developing an acceptable culture? There is no one right culture that will fit every organization. There are certain minimal requirements for building an innovative culture. There are requirements for understanding the purposes, objectives, and strategies of the organization. There is a need to recognize the different needs of employees and their talents and motivations. There must be levels of operational discipline that allow an organization to move forward. All of these needs must be tailored to the organization.

3M and HP are often cited for having cultures that foster innovation. But not all segments of these organizations are equally innovative nor will all of their managers foster innovation. Cultures vary from one entity to another but at the same time meet the general organizational definition of its culture. Each entity will most likely develop its own culture. The cultures will vary because the needs are different.

The conclusion from the practitioner's perspective is quite simple: The culture must fit the organization's context, and it must adapt to changing requirements. The culture must also adequately meet the needs of all stakeholders. It must provide not only leadership from the top but recognize the leadership that exists throughout the organization—the silent leadership—by listening to and acting on those dissonant voices that often provide the link to the future success of the enterprise.

Cultural Stagnation

What has happened to organizations that at one time developed cultures that fostered innovation? What are the reasons for the cultural changes in these respected firms? First, the changes began to take place long before the impact was noted. The downsizing in the 1980s and the current economic slowdown have not been a major factor. The comfort zone began to expand in the 1970s, continued on through the 1980s, and continues today. There are several reasons for this: the lack of straight talk, the change in the social contract, and the change in management's focus, style, and attitudes.

Straight talk

We like to think of these old paternalistic institutions as cultures where peace and quiet reigned supreme. On the contrary, there was a directness of purpose and communication in the early paternalistic institutions. IBM provides an excellent example. T. A. Wise recaps the arguments and the repercussions of those arguments as IBM considered investing in the development of the IBM 360 computer.[5] This investment caused sweeping organizational changes, with executives rising and falling with the changing tides of the battle. The IBM 360 project was jokingly described as the "You bet your company" project. IBM was viewed as a model of rationality. Project leaders were described as being impatient with staff reports and meetings and committees. Executives who hadn't done their homework when presenting proposals were sent back to the drawing board. As Wise notes, meetings were more like inquisitions.

This IBM example as presented by Wise does not suggest that arguments should be encouraged, but when differences of opinion exist, they need to be resolved. In most cases, if the facts are available, a decision can be reached that is acceptable to all the concerned entities even though everyone did not receive 100 percent of what they considered they needed. But there comes a time when straight talk may be absolutely essential. When facts are replaced by wishful thinking, someone needs to raise a flag. When the immediate quick-fix takes precedence over meeting the organization's purposes, objectives, and strategies, someone must speak up. When employees become passionate about what they consider the right track and when managers disregard their comments, someone must act. The problem is that too few people have the courage or the resolve to question those that are in charge. But those challenges are essential for the good of the organization. That's how those innovative organizations became the innovators. They didn't achieve that status as the most innovative by promoting a yes mentality.

Whether the comfort zone has grown because of relaxation of the codes of dress and conduct, and the proliferation of e-mail, Web sites, and cubicles, is really not clear. But all these conditions probably have had some influence. Many organizations appear to be dominated by certain nonchalance, an acceptance of work effort below standard without questioning, and an attitude that excuses missing commitments. When management tolerates nonperformance at all levels, there is no mystery as to why low levels of performance exist.

The Social Contract

The contract between employers and employees began to change in the early 1980s when major downsizing began in many U.S. organizations. Executives, managers, and professionals became the targets for significant reductions in staff for the first time in history. The tradition of lifetime employment began to erode significantly. Organizational loyalty, according to some management observers, was relegated to the trash can. The business press proclaimed that the social contract had been broken and that loyalty to the organization no longer existed. According to Amanda Bennet, middle managers thought they had a contract with their employers, even though it was unwritten and unspoken.[6] All they had to do was take care of business, be faithful, obedient, and only modestly competent, and they'd have lifelong employment with all the perks. What was top management thinking when all they expected was faithfulness, obedience, and modest levels of competency? That attitude bred complacency and a lack of realism in evaluating performance. It lost sight of competitive realities and created a form of management gridlock.

The supposed loyalty probably never existed as proclaimed. Organizations bought this loyalty to a certain extent through expanded employee benefits. Educational benefits were offered, vacation periods were extended, medical and insurance benefits were expanded, recreation activities were sponsored, and profit sharing and pension plans became more inclusive. There is no argument that these benefits were good for society. But in the process, organizations became less disciplined in their operations. There was a time when executives and managers were involved and were part of the process. They did more than sit in judgment of the actions of others. They knew what was going on. The professionals recognized their responsibility in meeting commitments. If the work required extra time, they gave it freely.

Realigned Protocols

With the demise of the social contract, the modus operandi changed, from the chief executive officer down to those performing routine and repetitive activities. Executives and managers began to accept excuses for nonperformance. They had no alternative because, in the process of relaxing performance requirements, they became disengaged from the real work of the organization.

In Abraham Zaleznik's discussion of the *Real Work* of the manager, he proposes the need for positively directed aggression: "Aggressive energy channeled into real work is the one sure route to a sense of mastery, to the pleasure that comes from using one's talents to accomplish things. When managers avoid aggression (to the extent that they have little desire to offer constructive criticism) they suppress valuable emotion that is essential for being a productive contributor."[7] According to Zaleznik, management leadership includes both task and social leadership, which requires maturity not only to tolerate others' aggressiveness but also to direct it to substantive issues. His concern is that managing by indirection develops subordinates who are less autonomous, more psychologically dependent, and more concerned with avoiding identity-threatening episodes than engaging in real work. Whatever else real work involves, it involves thinking. When leaders substitute ritual for thought, they do not fulfill the need for thinking that must precede action in order to inform and direct it.

From years of experience and observations in a consulting practice, I found a significant change in management attitudes and priorities since the mid-1970s. In many instances, executive ego began to replace concern for the business. Management style often ignored the constituencies that it served. Managers at all levels became reactive, and too many managers and professionals worked far below their levels of competency and compensation. Executives and managers lost sight of their priorities. They functioned more as administrators than as leaders.

Changing a Culture

Can cultures change and how long does it take? An excellent example of changing a narrow reactive culture to a proactive one is the Silverlake Project,[8] which describes the cultural transition at IBM Rochester (Minnesota). Tony Furey arrived at IBM Rochester as the hand-picked director of the development lab, with 2,500 engineers and programmers involved in designing computers. Furey, age 45 and a 24-year IBM veteran, had been sent to Rochester to transform the laboratory and manage it as a real business, with the same disciplines as any commercial enterprise. The Rochester staff considered Furey to be in way over his head—he didn't have the kind of experience they thought the new boss should have. They were looking for the business equivalent of a Winston Churchill, and now here comes this unknown quantity. As one staff member observed, "To top it off he was an outsider, an IBM East Coast smoothie coming to the prairie." He didn't exactly endear himself to the staff when one of his first actions involved redecorating his office and the adjoining conference room because he thought it was below the requirements for someone of his status.

At the time of his arrival, the IBM Rochester lab, in spite of its impressive output over the years, was ranked—on measures of "technical vitality"—in the lower third of fifteen IBM development sites. They published fewer papers, filed fewer patent applications, and could boast only one IBM Fellow. The question was, Why? IBM Rochester in conjunction with its headquarters had become a bureaucratic organization. It had become filled with people responsible for something even though the actual work did not require a full-time assignment. There had always been difficulties in obtaining the necessary resources. The staff became involved and suggested that if Silverlake was to be successful that managers would need to lead more and manage less. Don't manage people but manage the process, manage the risks, make sure the project stays on track, and keep the goals in focus. Managers were not expected to abdicate control. After all, they were accountable for results. How could IBM Rochester be so oblivious to these simple fundamentals of management? Describing the expectations is the number one commandment of management.

Furey began by asking questions and seldom received satisfactory answers from the staff. Their job was to design, build, and program computers. Customers, market share, and related business issues were none of their concern. Since they didn't have the answers, Furey put them to working in multidisciplinary teams to find the answers. When they finished their research, they found out just who they were. They had 220,000 customers worldwide, of which 60 percent were in the United States. From this study, Furey came to a decision as to what IBM Rochester would be: "the undisputed leaders of the global mid-range market." IBM Rochester would be fashioned into the corporate exemplar of the market-driven organization. Instead of being the nice small business for IBM, they would become a major player in IBM's product portfolio.

In twenty-eight months, IBM Rochester went through a metamorphosis, changing from a laboratory to a market-driven organization. Silverlake gave birth to the AS/400 mid-range family of computers. Two years later, the company added the prestigious Baldrige Quality Award to its impressive gains in market share and profitability.

Culture Histories

Where does culture begin and how can it be sustained in order to meet changing global economic conditions? In recent years, firms that once were admired for their innovation seemed to be losing ground. How did these cultures begin and how did they manage to maintain the momentum? What happened to these cultures that served the stakeholders so well? Although many factors affect culture, innovation cultures were usually driven by the founder or founders. It was their philosophy that guided managers to provide the environment.

IBM

In its prime, IBM was an example of a strong culture. It had a reputation for loyalty, high levels of motivation, respect for dignity and the rights of each person in the firm, and a general consensus on how to conduct its business. IBM employees dedicated themselves to pursuing the organization's objectives, and customer service was always a top priority. As the dominant player in the computer market, IBM also had adopted policies that led to it becoming a paternalistic organization.

But something happened at IBM during its growth into one of the most prominent and well-managed industrial organizations. IBM had always been identified by the word THINK. Did IBM executives, managers, and professionals stop thinking during the 1980s? IBM reached a peak employment of over 450,000 people in 1985. By 1993 that workforce was reduced to 256,000 people. The Silverlake Project also took the reader behind the scenes and tells much about IBM's executive level management. Minnesota was too far west to receive attention from New York. As the authors noted, "We were out of sight and out of mind. They left us alone and we kept to ourselves. We met our sales and profit targets for the year." Is this the type of THINK that at one time pushed IBM to the forefront of the computer industry? Obviously not. IBM had achieved its prestigious status because many people had contributed to that thinking process, but along the way far too many became comfortable, put on the blinders, and went into mental hibernation. Only in recent years IBM is once again challenging all its competitors with innovative approaches.

3M

3M was founded on a serious mistake. The mistake occurred in 1902 when 3M, then known as Minnesota Mining and Manufacturing, began mining corundum in Crystal Bay, Minnesota. Corundum was considered to be an excellent material for making the grit used for sandpaper. 3M's founders thought that corundum could be mined and then sold to manufacturers of grinding wheels. They soon discovered that they were not mining corundum but some other material not fit for abrasive applications. By the end of 1904, a share of 3M stock would not buy a shot of whiskey at the local bars.

William McKnight, 3M's chairman of the board and president, defined the company's culture of 1948 when he challenged management with the following statement:

> As our business grows, it becomes increasingly necessary to delegate responsibility and to encourage men and women to exercise their initiative. This requires considerable tolerance. Those men and women to whom we delegate authority and responsibility, if they are good people, are going to want to do their jobs in their own way. These are characteristics we want, and people should be encouraged as long as their way conforms to our general pattern of operations. Mistakes will be made, but if a person is essentially right, the mistakes he or she makes are not to tell those under its authority exactly how they must do their job. Management that is destructively critical when mistakes are made kills initiative, and it is essential that we have many people with initiative if we are to continue to grow.[9]

That statement defines the 3M culture. The emphasis was on people. It's interesting to note that McKnight included men and women. In 1948, the U.S. management ranks and professional groups were almost 100 percent male dominated.

Lew Lehr, 3M's CEO from 1978 to 1986, commented on one of 3M's cultural mandates at the University of Pennsylvania in 1979:

> As befits a company that was founded on a mistake, we have continued to accept mistakes as a normal part of running a business. Every single one of my colleagues in senior management has backed a few losers along the way. It's important to add, however, we expect our mistakes to have originality. We can afford almost any mistake once.[10]

These were powerful statements and made at the right time. The history of 3M's innovation activities is well known. The 3M culture provides the freedom to propose new initiatives, the opportunity to function as an entrepreneur, and to upset the status quo when necessary. It allows for the practical bootlegging of knowledge and resources in order to promote innovation. At the same time it has its share of internal intransigence that forces the innovators to fight for their causes. That's not all bad. It keeps technical and marketing people focused. But today there may be too few employees willing to take on the charge and move the organization into new technologies and new markets. 3M's comfort zone expanded in recent years. The last breakthrough innovation, Post-it Notes, occurred about twenty years ago.

Xerox

Xerox is an example of an organization making a transition from success to failure. Was it executive arrogance that developed when Xerox dominated the market and when top management became indifferent to its constituencies? Xerox was founded in 1906 as the Haloid Corporation, and it manufactured photographic papers in a city dominated by Kodak. In 1946—after Chester Carlson was turned down for his concept of electrophotography by companies such as IBM, RCA, A. B. Dick, and others—Haloid negotiated limited rights to Carlson's patents. Fourteen years later, the first Xerox machine appeared on the market. In the late 1950s, Haloid became Haloid-Xerox. In February 1960, Xerox introduced the 914 model, which generated sales of $393 million by 1965. By the end of 1968, Xerox's revenues were $1.125 billion, with a net income of $138 million. The 1960s were years of tremendous growth for Xerox.

What happened to Xerox? *Business Week* describes Xerox as a history of highs and lows. "Once synonymous with corporate success and technological innovation, Xerox is now struggling with losses and a leaden stock—not to mention a reputation for fumbling high-tech opportunities."[11] Xerox lost its market lead in copiers. Its stock price of over 60 in 1990 plummeted to 7 in December 2000. The research results of the Xerox Palo Alto Research Center, where the personal computer, the mouse, and Ethernet software were invented, were never exploited. Also, Xerox was slow to respond to competitors like Canon, Minolta, Ricoh, and Sharp. Why did Xerox management allow this to happen? Did Xerox managers succumb to the comfort culture and forget that world dynamics were changing? Kotter and Heskett suggest that Xerox did not adapt to the changes taking place in the global economy.[12] Information relevant to their continued success was disregarded and they clung to strategies that were no longer viable. There was a reluctance to change. In essence, managers were living in the past and did not provide the necessary leadership. They most likely disregarded the suggestions of the productive mavericks and in the process stifled individual initiative. The win culture had lost to the bureaucratic culture.

Summary

- The comfort zone can undermine performance and destroy the capacity for innovation.

- The response to organizational culture is limited—suborganizational culture takes precedence.

- Cultures can be changed.

- Kotter and Heskett's Theory III culture focuses on the future where adapting to changing business dynamics is essential.

- Bardwick's earning culture represents an ideal but will be influenced by those people who expect entitlement and live in fear.

- Denison links high levels of involvement, ownership, shared values and beliefs, adaptability, and mission as a base for developing an appropriate culture.

- There are no right or wrong cultures; there are only cultures that allow the organization to sustain itself.

Notes

1. John P. Kotter, William McKnight, and James L. Heskett, *Corporate Culture and Performance* (New York: The Free Press, 1992).

2. R. H. Kilmann, *Beyond the Quick Fix* (San Francisco: Jossey-Bass, 1984).

3. Judith M. Bardwick, *Danger in the Comfort Zone* (New York: AMACOM, 1991).

4. D. R. Denison, "Organizational Culture and Organizational Effectiveness: A Theory and Some Empirical Evidence," *Proceedings of the Academy of Management* (1989): 168–172 (Best Paper).

5. T. A. Wise, "IBM's 5,000,000,000 Gamble" *Fortune*, September 1996. Reprinted in *Readings in the Management of Innovation*, Michael L. Tushman and William L. Moore, editors (New York: HarperBusiness, 1988), pp. 45–54.

6. Amanda Bennett, "Broken Bonds," *The Wall Street Journal*, December 8, 1989, p. R 21.

7. Abraham Zaleznik, "Real Work," *Harvard Business Review*, January–February 1989, Reprint 97611.

8. R. A. Bauer, E. Collar, and V. Tang, *The Silverlake Project* (New York: Oxford University Press, 1992).

9. Ernest Gundling, *The 3M Way to Innovation* (Tokyo: Kodansha International, 2000), p. 58.

10. Lou Lehr, dinner speech at the Wharton Entrepreneurial Center, University of Pennsylvania, 1979.

11. Anthony Bianco and Pamela L. Moore, "Downfall," *Business Week*, March 5, 2001, pp. 82–92.

12. Kotter, McKnight, and Heskett, *Corporate Culture and Performance.*

7

Culture: From Theory to Practice

Developing a culture that fosters innovation often generates high levels of frustration. Building that innovative culture involves practicing the fundamentals of management: the competency to design a culture that fosters innovation. Culture is about people, how they perform their work, and how they interact. If people are the most important asset, then managers must follow through with appropriate actions. At the same time, both employers and employees must recognize that we live in a dynamic global economy of ever increasing competition. As organizations consider developing a culture that fosters innovation, they need to keep in mind that there is no single issue that will make innovation happen. An organization that makes a decision to improve its level of innovation or become innovative needs to focus on three major areas, all of equal importance:

1. *People*—optimizing people involvement

2. *Management*—guiding management practices

3. *Attitude*—encouraging professional attitudes

As you consider these three areas that determine culture, you may conclude that it's impossible to take all of them into account.

There is no choice but to understand that these three areas must at least meet some minimum requirements related to the organization's business context. Every action contributes to building the innovative organization and cannot be disregarded. Management sets the pace, people at all levels contribute their competencies and skills, and the collective attitudes determine the culture.

Optimizing People Involvement

No one will contest that people are the organization's most important asset. But those are words that need to be turned into actions that demonstrate the full meaning of the statement. Words alone are insufficient. Those words need to be practiced. The following considerations apply to building realistic people relations.

Stressing the Importance of People

The distribution of any group of people shows different levels of interest, motivation, aptitude, and performance. Why does a person who was hired because of specific and desired competencies fail to meet the job requirements? Either he faked the competencies or the immediate manager failed to provide the proper guidance. Perhaps he really didn't have the qualifications. This may be an oversimplification of the issue (there may be family issues, health issues, etc.), but barring these, there is only one solution: provide him with the additional education or training to improve the level of competency. If he responds negatively, admit the mistake and either move him to a new position or terminate him. If you accept years of nonperformance, provide annual increases, and then decide to terminate, you will have destroyed that person's career. This is really a case of management malpractice. Difficult decision, yes, but you cannot accept below-par performance. If the situation is not resolved, the organization and the individual eventually pay the price.

Identifying the Critical Mass

Every activity requires a critical mass of talent. Project success does not come from numbers of bodies. It comes from having the right mix of people with the required competencies, whether available inside or outside of the organization. It also comes from making sure that the talent has the necessary people skills. People skills are not the fuzzies, but having respect for the individual and the ability to communicate with other disciplines. Professionals must be working at or above their level of capability. Without a challenge and without stretch targets, good contributors become poor contributors. The critical mass also means having the right talent at the appropriate competence and skill levels.

Working with a Lean Staff

You have probably heard managers invoke the phrase "lean and mean" as good management practice. But "lean and mean" is not a very good strategy. The lean is okay but certainly not the mean. Lean, competent, and motivated are the more appropriate terms.

• Hiring practices often fail to provide for a lean organization. Managers fail to ask the difficult questions. Why is this person needed? What are the alternatives to adding staff? What is the value added to the organization by hiring this person? Can other lower priority projects be eliminated?

• Inflated staff services decrease overall organizational effectiveness. Too often staff people are assigned as coordinators. Assigning coordinators implies that some group or groups are not meeting their performance requirements. Staff services often become the dumping ground for people who should undergo training, counseling, or be terminated. Staff services can also be the scapegoats for managerial nonperformance.

• The *responsible-for approach* makes assignments for an activity without sufficient investigation as to whether that activity is a full-time responsibility. Once the assignment is made, it becomes difficult to de-assign. Human nature, being what it is, affords managers to build fiefdoms that are difficult to penetrate. Expansion always seems to be justified.

Building Trust

It's not necessary to climb mountains or shoot rapids to build trust; these ways may be nonconventional and some may even be considered innovative, but they are hardly essential. There is little doubt that trust is essential in any dealings between individuals and organizations. Although the days of sealing a contract with a handshake are probably gone forever, trust continues to be an essential part of business operations. Lack of trust breeds cynicism and cynicism is more contagious than trust. Negotiations, at all levels, both in and outside the organization, must be carried on in good faith. Mergers too often create cynicism, such as the newly appointed CEO saying that employees will not be terminated and that the family will stay together—and then layoffs begin two weeks later. With events like this becoming increasingly common, it is not surprising that trust is hard to find.

Trust is essential, not just for innovation to flourish but for the organization to survive. But it is easily destroyed. These are some trust destroyers:

1. Allowing the co-opting or appropriating of ideas from others

2. Managers not keeping promises or commitments

3. Changing the rules of the game once it has started without considering the players

4. Lack of open communication

Establishing and Maintaining Integrity

Integrity goes beyond telling the truth. Integrity involves adhering uncompromisingly to a set of moral and ethical principles in all relations—personal and business. In our fast-paced competitive economy, moral and ethical principles are often placed out of sight and out of mind. If everybody is doing it, why shouldn't we? That philosophy has led to the courts on many occasions. Integrity encompasses the way people interact in any organizational setting. It's not so much about what integrity does for an organization but how a lack of integrity begins the downward spiral of what once reinforced positive attitudes. It may take years to build integrity, but it can be destroyed by a single incident. Integrity is very difficult to describe, but it includes all of the following qualities: candor, character, conscientiousness, credibility, decency, fidelity, frankness, high principles, loyalty, reliability, responsibility, accountability, and sincerity.

Expecting Involvement

For managers, professionals, and hopefully for all those support people who make an organization function, involvement in the organization's business is not a choice, but an expectation. The level of involvement, however, depends on how managers manage. The gurus took over empowerment but didn't tell the whole story. Empowerment doesn't occur without management involvement. It's not possible to empower people who are not involved. People were told they should take charge, take the initiative, make decisions, make an impact, seek significant work, and create value, but they didn't have the preparation to empower themselves.

Empowerment has consequences. You make the decision, not someone up the organizational ladder. Although it's very easy to criticize the decisions of others, it's much more difficult to have to make those decisions yourself and suffer the consequences if they turn out to be the wrong decisions. It takes courage to accept responsibility for one's decisions when they may be scrutinized by colleagues or managers.

Promoting Teamwork

Turf building and protection will probably never go away. Both are destructive forces within organizations that limit communication and destroy interaction. Also, destructive is the "stay out of my sandbox" approach, which is the attitude of people who stay in their cubicles and focus solely on their own work without consideration of how it relates to the other parts of the organization. The question is not whether to opt for team or individual performance, but how to do both. It's impossible to build a successful team if individual performance is not recognized.

There are no valid reasons for not promoting teamwork as long as the contributions of individuals are not compromised. Although teamwork continues to be a highly recommended approach to managing, it is only recently that it has been applied to other than the technology areas. But teamwork doesn't come about from teaching teamwork. It comes from a culture that has developed high levels of collegiality. Building that collegiality begins with managers having full knowledge not only of the competencies of the team members but of their personal attitudes related to developing working relationships.

Promoting Lifelong Learning

Lifelong learning is not a choice; it's a requirement. The increasing complexity of societal interactions demands more intellectual effort today than what was required during the early days of the industrial revolution. Intellectual curiosity cannot die at the end of the university commencement exercise. About 50 percent of the learning that any professional possesses at the time of graduation will decrease in value unless updated continually. The fundamentals remain the same, but the new application knowledge requires new learning. Lifelong learning involves high degrees of curiosity. The consequences of disregarding lifelong learning can be disastrous.

For example, should a manager terminate a 50-year-old professional with twenty years' experience and replace her with a new graduate that can be hired for half the amount? After all, the twenty-year veteran should be able to provide a greater valued-added component than the new person should. But what if the long-tenured employee didn't have twenty years of experience but rather just one year of experience twenty times? There's a significant difference.

Insisting on Accountability

Accountability implies obligation to do something. There are no statistics to tell us whether there was greater accountability in the past. Demonstration of accountability begins at the top of the organization. Innovation depends on accountability from all the participants for their contribution to the final effort. Failure is part of the innovation process. There's a distinct difference between failure that occurs as a result of experimental activities and failure due to negligence. Negligence cannot be accepted. Failure from trying the new will always exist, and lessons can be learned from those failures. Innovators are accountable for those failures and they accept responsibility. Accountability is a two-way street: Innovators are accountable and their managers are accountable for the actions of the innovators.

Pursuing Excellence

There is a difference between excellence and perfection. Excellence involves doing the best that can be done with available knowledge and resources. Perfection considers some ultimate state that can no longer be improved with the available knowledge and resources. A student can write an excellent paper, but chances are it will not be perfect in every way. But anything less than excellent should not be accepted.

Excellence, which implies outstanding quality or superior merit, is not difficult to define, but it must be described in the context in which it is being used. For example, excellence for a symphony orchestra is quite different from excellence for a baseball team. Orchestra conductors would not last very long if their performance were rated .325. Yet in baseball a batting average of .325 is considered to be an excellent performance.

A design may be considered excellent but certainly not perfect. Most of the time insufficient information prevents reaching perfection. Emphasizing the pursuit of excellence applies to daily work, even the minutiae. There is little doubt that too often mediocrity is the goal and accepted. Such an attitude only breeds more mediocrity. Life has become more complex, and people often lack the necessary skills and competencies to meet new requirements

Guiding Management Practices

Management practices determine culture. Building a culture starts at the top. Although a culture can be built from the bottom of the organization, it is questionable whether in this day of ever-increasing competition an organization has the luxury of using this strategy. The following actions need to be revisited and acted upon when trying to develop a culture that fosters innovation.

Defining Purposes, Objectives, and Strategies

In spite of all the efforts to direct organizational activities, executives find it difficult to adequately define the organization's purposes, objectives, and strategies. These are three simple words—purposes, objectives, and strategies—but they are so difficult to develop and communicate. Is there some secret as to where the organization is heading, how it plans to get there, and how employees need to respond? What may appear to be clear and concise at the executive level needs to be translated into meaningful terms as it flows down through the organization.

Management needs to answer these questions: Why does this organization exist? What are the short- and long-term objectives of the organization? What are the objectives of the many organizational units to achieve that corporate objective? Finally, what is the organization's strategy to achieve its objectives and meet the purposes for which it exists? A strategy that suggests that the organization will be the greatest something or other in the future is not specific enough and has no meaning for the design engineer, the laboratory technician, or the support personnel.

Communicating and Communicating More

Lack of adequate communication is the precursor to project and organizational contentiousness. An organization that intends to operate effectively and efficiently cannot disregard the importance of communication. The organization's purposes, objectives, and strategies must be communicated effectively.

With today's e-mail mentality, too much discussion involves speaking in 60-second shorthand, ignoring the requirements of effective communication. Communication is a two-way street. Unfortunately, too much communication begins at the top of the organization or unit and somehow works its way down without any feedback. The dialogue is missing, yet that dialogue is essential for understanding. Most project failures begin with a lack of two-way communication.

Providing Leadership

There is little doubt that many employees, including some high-level executives, prefer the status quo. So where does leadership enter? Society generally views leadership as taking place at the top of the organization. Corporate executives, members of congress, university presidents, union executives, and other people at the top are generally recognized as leaders. But do they provide leadership? Some do; many do not. But leadership is not about where one sits in the organizational hierarchy. People display leadership throughout the organization, at all levels, and in all disciplines. That's because leadership is about doing; it's not about being in charge or winning a popularity contest. Leadership is about making the difficult decisions that impact not only the lives of the organization's constituents but also society. There's also that invisible leadership in the bowels of the organization that may have a significant impact on the future of the organization. That often not recognized leadership comes from all disciplines and from all levels. Not every manager or every professional is able to provide leadership, but there must be a sufficient number of leaders at all levels. Taking a leadership position usually involves going against the status quo. Leaders put their reputations on the line

Establishing Operational Discipline

It is not necessary to set policies and then insist on blind obedience. It is not necessary to "tighten the screws." It is not necessary to treat people as automatons. It *is* important, however, to set guidelines, set appropriate rules of conduct, insist on meeting commitments, and adopt a "no excuses" approach to meeting those commitments. Yes, there will be failures along the way, but those failures cannot be failures caused by a lack of concern and a lack of dedication in meeting commitments. Three other issues relate to operational discipline:

1. Lack of understanding of how objectives are achieved

2. Removal of the word "think" from the organization's vocabulary

3. Disregard for just what it takes to accomplish some specific objective

Too many projects begin without sufficient thought given to the required up-front work—the period where hasty decisions create later delays and rework. Target dates are important but resources must be available. Setting impossible expectations or failing to recognize the lack of resources leads to chaos and only raises questions about management's ability to deal with realities.

Focusing on Outcomes

Many organizations believe that if you follow the process, you can't go wrong. In recent years, this attitude has become contagious. Many consulting firms focus on process. The theory is that if you follow the prescribed process with its fixed methodologies you will be successful. Not so, at least not always. There is no doubt that following some applicable process helps meet goals. But not every problem or opportunity can be resolved with the same process. Process tools must be applicable to the problem. All the charts that fill the war room will not guarantee success. Those charts can often hinder progress because they don't tell the whole story yet consume countless hours of discussion over minutiae. General Eisenhower said about the Normandy invasion that before the battle, plans are everything, but that as soon as the battle is joined, plans are worthless.[1]

Focusing solely on outcomes can be equally dangerous if the effort only considers short-term impact. For example, reducing investment in innovation can provide immediate financial benefits but have a negative impact on the flow of new products. Cutting back on investments in manufacturing equipment will provide short-term benefits but lead to future problems. Not bringing in that new group of graduates can reduce short-term costs but create a long-term shortfall in essential competencies.

Seeking Breakthrough Opportunities

Organizations need to direct attention to breakthrough improvements and/or opportunities in performance. Incremental improvements alone cannot provide a competitive advantage except in an industry that suffers from levels of paralysis. Breakthroughs are normally associated with products and processes. The breakthrough products provide significant growth opportunities. Breakthrough processes can destroy competitors. Breakthroughs obviously involve greater risks and resolution of greater uncertainties but also provide significantly greater benefits. That last incremental improvement may not have added value. Because of competitive pressures, the improved product may not have recovered the added cost. There are also significant opportunities for administrative breakthroughs— breakthroughs that involve simplifying routine jobs that consume resources. These administrative breakthroughs are not quite as glamorous as the new products or processes, but they can provide significant savings.

Taking Acceptable Risks

Focusing on innovation involves taking risks. There is no guarantee that the product will be timely or that it will fully meet the customers' requirements. So there are risks involved. But risks are not a role of the dice. Evaluating risk is not yet a science. The gut reaction of an experienced manager may be preferable to an extensive study by someone who does not know the industry. A person who has a sense of the industry's history, who knows the related technologies, who is familiar with the market requirements, and who has developed a client list of industry leaders can easily appraise the viability of going in new directions. This industry knowledge minimizes the risk. Most business risks can be managed with some thought and a willingness to face facts. But consider the innovation that requires a billion-dollar investment in production equipment. The decision is not a simple one, and just reading the predictions by the economists about economic conditions five years into the future doesn't necessarily offer sufficient guarantees.

Introducing Change

Change obviously creates levels of discomfort. It makes little difference whether the change involves bringing in a new CEO or making some lower level management changes. The same applies when organizations attempt to introduce new technologies, enter new markets, consolidate operations, make organizational changes, or introduce minor changes in administrative procedures. Change automatically creates various levels of discomfort. The change from alphabetical telephone dialing to number dialing, a relatively minor change, created significant amounts of discontent. The change to electronic banking was met with distrust of the system. But change is absolutely essential for survival. Society would not give up the automobile, the airplane, the highway system, and the infrastructures that allow society to function. Society accepts these changes in lifestyle. They provide higher levels of comfort. People fall someplace on a continuum from those who resist change to those who can't live without change. Innovation will not take place when those who resist change dominate an organization's direction.

Making Timely Decisions

Managers who delay decisions create levels of frustration that decrease motivation. We have all heard statements like this when proposals are submitted: the timing isn't right, we need to expand the study, or they'll never buy it the way it's structured. Such actions not only decrease motivation but also demonstrate that managers aren't minding the store. These are costly misadventures. Professionals who delay decisions in their operations create a form of chaos that flows through many functions. Delays in any function—product development, manufacturing, marketing, accounting—can result in losing significant market revenue. The decisions made by the professionals or their entities most likely will be required by others in the workflow chain and must be accommodated.

Disregarding the Management Gurus

Management gurus have their place, but too many have taken organizations down the wrong track. Although some have had worthwhile programs, most deal with single issues. Focusing solely on a single issue even if that issue is innovation will not guarantee business success. Not too long ago, organizations were sending all their managers to various training programs on quality management. Recall those quality circles that were awarded various prizes even though there was no way of measuring performance. Counting the number of quality circles became the game. Did American industry need these gurus to convince them that they had quality problems and that poor quality was robbing them of profits? These problems required management's attention. Why do organizations wait until a downturn in the economy occurs to review how many people are consumed with details that are no longer necessary, how many people are added to the staff without a critical analysis of the need, what is being done that no longer needs to be done, or how much of the work effort adds value? Executives shouldn't need consultants to tell them that they have problems.

Starting to Think About Systems

Few organizations have adopted the systems approach as a management philosophy. What is the systems approach? A simple example demonstrates what is meant by a system: You're planning a dinner party. Just think of all the elements that you need to consider for having a successful dinner party. The system will include everything from developing the guest list, finding a suitable date, selecting an appropriate menu, defining the cooking cycle, planning the table settings, selecting the beverages, planning the topics of conversation, through all the activities after the party, including washing the dishes and doing the general cleanup. So from a business perspective the systems approach is the process-oriented discipline of problem solving. It includes the integration of people, products, processes, and procedures in order to translate user needs into design requirements and then into an operational system that includes the complete life cycle. Can you imagine a dinner party where no consideration was given to the menu, or no arrangements were made for the cleanup?

Although industry is not a dinner party, activities allocated to functions cannot be accomplished independently or irrespective of the needs of associated disciplines. This lack of coordination of the functional activities leads to a situation where priorities often lack consistency. Even when teams are assigned to projects, the unity so essential to effective project performance is often missing. The logic is disconcerting: How can a product development group not take into account the need for new manufacturing facilities until the product is developed? How can that same development group disregard the needs of the marketplace? How can executive management tolerate this lack of integration between functions and disciplines?

Anticipating Future Events

Ignore the future and it may be necessary to turn out the lights. There are not many organizations that can ignore the events that will shape their future. The future relates to issues affecting their business, their technologies, their markets, their resources, and the technologies that they use to optimize their output. IBM didn't anticipate the PC. U.S. automobile and electronic companies did not anticipate Japan's emergence as a dominant competitor in the 1980s. The networks didn't anticipate CNN, and CNN didn't anticipate Fox. The statement made many years ago that the "future belongs to those who prepare for it" was not an idle statement. Changes take place over time, not in step-by-step functions that go from A to B in essentially zero time. But anticipating the future is not restricted to the executives and managers. Whether an organization is able to anticipate the future depends on the people they have hired over the years. The professional people in all disciplines cannot disregard the importance of future needs and directions.

Making Time for Innovation

I often hear comments like, "All we do is put out fires; we don't even have time to think" or "I'm overworked since all this downsizing has taken place." We really must evaluate where we're spending our time. We need to ask continuously, Why are we doing what we're doing? Is what we're doing adding value or is it busywork? If a high percentage of time is allocated to putting out fires, managers may need to reappraise the organization's work habits. Allocating more time to *setting opportunity fires* provides a far better payoff. It's time to get out of the box and the cubicle and look for those opportunities.

There certainly is no shortage of tools to improve effectiveness and efficiency. Telephones, cell phones, voice mail, all kinds of beepers, laptops, e-mail, the Web, all types of computer-aided programs and a multitude of software programs—all improve opportunities for saving time when used judiciously. These tools cannot be allowed to become obstacles, a burden, or an end unto themselves, rather than the means. Perhaps too much time is spent clicking and dragging. In the process, we've developed a mentality where everything is urgent. That beeper sounds, there's an e-mail, time to go into action—just another disruption. Innovation must be on the organizational priority list. It means making time available for thinking, and thinking is hard work. Time can be found for innovation by examining work methods and eliminating the non–value-adding activities

Encouraging Professional Attitudes

The attitude with which we approach any activity makes a significant difference in the outcome. Whether the attitude relates to a child doing some unpleasant task, a football team attempting to become the national champions, or an orchestra conductor working with a group of musicians, attitude affects the performance. No organization can progress and meet its purposes without taking initiatives to develop positive attitudes. Unconcerned, dispassionate, or perfunctory performance of duty militates against developing a successful conclusion. Negativism is not an acceptable behavior. This section considers some of the essential attitudes for developing a culture that fosters innovation.

Creating a Sense of Excitement

A sense of excitement about work can easily be identified. Walk into a laboratory, a product development group, or any organizational setting and the sense of excitement becomes immediately apparent. Apathy on the other hand seems to be a common disease that inhibits not only organizational growth but destroys careers in the process. Apathy kills careers because education ceases to be important. It seems to disengage people from reality. Living in the past becomes more comfortable for them than experiencing the future.

Excitement should not be limited to fun and games, although they do help to develop higher levels of camaraderie. Creating excitement needs to be directed toward the intellectual levels of discovery. Excitement is contagious and enthusiasm can be contagious, although it is true that not every person can become excited about their work or remain in a constant state of intellectual challenge.

A real sense of excitement can make the difference in the organization's future, even though there are many routine tasks to be accomplished that seldom generate excitement. Innovation needs access to that sense of excitement—access to those units that demonstrate high-spirited intellectual curiosity and that are willing to put their jobs on the line.

Fostering Creativity

Why is there so little creativity when organizations spend a significant percentage of their training and education budgets promoting creativity? After a three-day creativity session, participants are expected to return to their organizations and be creative. The problem is not likely to be a lack of creativity but the fact that creativity requires more than playing the usual games. There is no ten-easy-lessons plan on how to become creative. Perhaps more resources need to be dedicated to teaching managers how to a manage creativity.

Creativity involves more than instituting a company-wide suggestion program and hoping that some great revelation will come out of that box. Although suggestions can be useful and are an important part of organizational success, creativity goes beyond generating suggestions and ideas. Creativity requires action. Innovation dies without creativity. Although everyone has the opportunity to be creative in some venue, not all will take up the banner.

Taking Initiative

How does an organization convince its employees to take initiative on their own? First, those who take initiative on their own display certain characteristics such as courage, prefer to look for problems than to be assigned problems, and possess significant levels of security. The initiators know where they want to go and they go there quickly. They like to rock the boat to its limits. The majority who work with the initiators will consider them to be workaholics dedicated to the organization. But these same people have little difficulty exhibiting some of the same characteristics outside the work environment. The organization needs to reward the initiators in both tangible and emotional ways, similar to the primarily emotional rewards they receive outside the organization—from family, friends, and colleagues.

Innovators take the initiative and don't ask for the next project. They *are* the next project.

Providing Flexibility

Conforming to patterns of behavior provides security but destroys initiative. There always seems to be the company way: We've done it this way for decades. It is time to change. The comfort zone has grown too wide and too deep. Conformity in thinking can devastate an organization. General Motors may be a prime example of groupthink gone astray. If flexibility in thought and action provides benefits, then the question becomes, how much flexibility should the organization provide? Some people require norms of conformity in order to function effectively. A project composed solely of nonconformists will not accomplish its goals, since it's unlikely that they could reach agreement on critical issues. But those people who think differently and ask the difficult questions are essential. Flexibility and conformity must be balanced—enough to raise the critical and controversial issues but not so much that it hampers meeting the objectives. Flexibility needs to be dispensed to those who can manage it.

Motivating Through Example

There is little doubt that self-motivation transcends any program that may be used to motivate an organization. Unfortunately, not all people are self-motivated when it comes to their work life. The self-

motivated individuals are usually those whose avocation and vocation are compatible. If Monday morning begins with a recap of the
weekend activities and Friday is spent thinking about weekend activities, then there is most likely a mismatch between vocation and avocation. But motivation through action begins at the top of the
organization and at least at the first levels of management. It will be
exceedingly difficult to motivate a group if the immediate manager
seems to lack interest and approaches the unit's work in a lackadaisical manner. Managers need to recognize that motivation depends on
them. That's why they were supposedly selected as managers. They
need to show high levels of motivation through their actions.

Giving Freedom to Act

Giving freedom to act provides a real challenge to many managers.
Anyone questioning the rules and procedures immediately is looked
upon with certain suspicions. Freedom to act goes beyond conforming to behavioral patterns. Innovators need freedom to act. Without
some fairly high level of freedom, not much innovation will occur.
Innovators cannot be locked in a box and told what to do. But that
freedom must be guided by some operational discipline. There are
some expectations that must be met.

Acting With Confidence

It is easy to sense whether a person speaks and acts with confidence.
Right or wrong, a person who speaks and acts with confidence immediately gains credibility. That credibility can be misdirected because the person could be a charlatan. However, confident people
are generally given the benefit of the doubt. An individual who lacks
confidence and attempts to gain management backing to promote a
concept will find it difficult to obtain that backing. Management usually relies on the display of confidence. That confidence must be
grounded in knowledge and facts. As a newly minted graduate presenting a paper at a physics conference, I received great advice from
a physics professor at the University of Chicago. He suggested:
"When you get up to make your presentation, take a good look at
your audience, take three deep breaths, and remember you know
more about your topic than anyone else in the audience." The
clincher was "know more about your topic than anyone in the audi-

ence." If you know your topic, it's easy to demonstrate confidence. Innovators must know their topic.

Promoting on Performance

If the majority of your professional employees prefer the automatic progression method of rewarding exceptional work, it may be advisable to forget about innovation or find a way of removing those people who consider longevity as a measure of success. Longevity in many situations is only a measure of the ability to outlast the previous managers who were either deposed for some reason or decided the environment was not conducive to their career advancement. Over the past two decades, what at one time was considered a merit increase has lost favor with many human resource professionals. Giving a one or two percent increase as merit pay for exceptional performance is not merit pay: It's bringing everyone down to the lowest common denominator. Merit pay must include at least a minimum increase of 5 percent (not a magic number—100 percent could be more appropriate in certain circumstances) over and above the annual increase. Managers should be given the authority to decide how available funds should be distributed within their group. The innovator's criterion for success may not be money, but money needs to be there.

Defining Job Security

What is job security? It's not about longevity. It's not about whom you know in the organization. Job security is what you have in your head—your knowledge, your many skills, your integrative skills. You own them and no one can take them away from you. Assuming that management operates from a set of ethical and fair-minded principles, the only security is the knowledge and experience of the individual. All the learning that has taken place resides with the individual. Job security gained through bureaucratic policies related to longevity or social association provides no real long-term security. Routine jobs that involve following the rules provide little opportunity for advancement. But advancement will most likely come to those who have prepared for it. At the professional level, job security depends on performance. Peers, colleagues, management, external professionals, and professional societies must recognize that performance.

Reducing Dependence on the Organization

The entitlement culture has grown over the last three decades. The entitlement mentality transcends all disciplines, the complete social spectrum, business and industry, academia, and government. Society continues to expect more and more from industry and government. People have become dependent on the organization for services. At times it appears that society would like to return to the days where, for example, textile mills or mining companies owned everything and provided all the services—grocery stores, elementary schools, the service providers, and maybe even housing or religious services.

Education, which is a personal matter, is an example. Industry began supporting education for its professional people after World War II, and soon it became the responsibility of industry to not only pay for the education but provide for time off. Professionals began to hold industry responsible for their professional development. Such actions could be expected and justified if new knowledge was required because of some actions taken by the organization, but not when the courses served a strictly personal benefit. I'm always reminded about the $100,000-a-year professional who expected the organization to pay for a personal subscription to *The Wall Street Journal*. What were executives thinking when they began offering such perks? Certainly not motivation for the people who keep the wheels turning.

Managing Inadequate Performance

Accepting inadequate levels of performance tends to erode a culture. The difficulties occur when too many managers lack the knowledge and courage to evaluate performance against objectives. Over the years I have served on many corporate committees that reviewed methods of evaluating employee performance. My suggestion that a performance appraisal begin with a blank sheet of paper with the person's name at the top was always summarily rejected with the proviso that managers were not capable of following such a simple method, which made me question how such people could have been appointed as managers.

My approach may appear idealistic, but isn't the immediate manager the only one who can resolve inadequate performance? A culture that tolerates inadequate performance not only begins to destroy motivation but too often destroys careers. Positive performance appraisal is easy. Negative appraisals become difficult and require honesty and integrity from both the reviewer and the person being reviewed. Innovation depends on excellent performance by many people of different disciplines, and managers cannot shirk their responsibility of making the difficult decisions.

Summary

- People, management, and attitude form the culture triad.

- People are the most important asset but only when reflected in management actions.

- Attitude can transcend many of the difficulties encountered in developing an innovative culture.

- Managers are not administrators: They are leaders and teachers.

- Building culture begins with management at all levels in the organization.

- The process is complex and at the same time simple: It involves those unknowns about how groups of people interact.

Note

1. Quoted in Stephen E. Ambrose, *D-Day June 6, 1944: The Climactic Battle of World War II* (New York: Simon & Schuster, 1994), p. 125.

CHAPTER 8

Dimensions of Organizational Resources

This chapter looks at the spectrum of resources that are critical to innovation, beginning with people and ending with money. This spectrum is broad in scope, so it will also be broken down into subcategories, depending on the specific requirements of the business. As an example, intellectual property, time, and input from customers and suppliers are all vital resources. Innovative organizations try to build on what is already known—their intellectual property—and avoid reinventing the wheel. Time is certainly a vital resource: It cannot be replaced. Those and other essential resources exist both within and outside the organization and in any global geographical area. The list of organizational resources is shown in Figure 8-1.

People

People are the most important organizational resource/asset! At the same time, people may be the most difficult resource to manage. Participants in the innovation process can come from different disciplines and from different ethnic backgrounds, and may also have

---

Figure 8.1. Organizational resources.

Intellectual property
Access to information
Technology
Marketing and sales
Time
Distribution
Customers
Suppliers
Production capability
Operating facilities
Finance

---

different philosophies of life and living, different aspirations, different talents, and a lot more. The objective is not to develop a melting pot that's guided by the lowest common denominator, but the more appropriate goal is to create a salad bowl in which people with various characteristics and competencies can be blended into a functioning unit.

Managing people resources often degenerates into a numbers game. Unfortunately, upper management often knowingly or unknowingly not only accedes to such practices but also promotes them through their actions. A manager's next promotion may be based on the number of employees reporting to him, and not necessarily on the manager's performance. In recent years hiring practices have often resulted in excess personnel. Hiring for the immediate need may be a necessity at times, but it should not become policy. Those particular skills that appear to be so urgent may not be required at some time in the near future. Hiring practices that disregard future assignments create additional human resource management problems.

It also doesn't take research to determine that people who work below their competency level soon become a burden on the organization. Often these people may be shuffled from job to job in the organization and eventually terminated. Such situations have a negative impact on motivation, and managers have a responsibility for not allowing them to occur.

There was a time when some organizations were driven by headcount. I remember that at one time during my career at 3M I had to make my case for adding staff to the vice president of engineering, and at another time to the president. Is this micromanagement that should not concern executive management? An argument can be made pro and con, and the answer depends on the circumstances. Unfortunately, too many managers feel that all problems can be resolved by adding staff. Perhaps many organizations could have avoided some of the 1980s and more recent downsizing had someone paid attention to the rate at which headcount was being increased. Part of the difficulty in controlling by headcount lies in the fact that organizations have all these good programs and they keep adding more, but they never cut those that may no longer add value.

Intellectual Property

Organizations develop intellectual property in every facet of their operations. Unfortunately, much of the experience and knowledge is seldom documented in such a way as to be of use in the future. In recent years, concepts such as knowledge management, data mining, and the learning organization have not received a great deal of practical attention. Dumping all types of data into a database doesn't provide a lot of benefit. We haven't yet learned how to extract the data that's necessary. Any search through key words generates lists that are almost incomprehensible. Those lists have multiple references to the same information. It's a painful process to find the nuggets of information.

The intellectual property includes more than memos, formal engineering drawings, laboratory results, test data, customer concerns, and all the other formalized documentation. Intellectual property also includes all those models used to demonstrate feasibility, the notebook data, the hand sketches that are usually discarded, and the working models. Chemical companies are probably the best at managing their laboratory data. As an example, in a laboratory doing polymer research and development, not only are details of the experiments documented, samples are also stored appropriately for future investigation and possible use. Most chemically oriented functions also use a formalized notebook process for entering all experimental data. This notebook approach is seldom implemented in the design of electromechanical equipment because of the size and scope.

However, any experimental work in reference to proof-of-concept should be fully documented. There needs to be a way of tracing why a technical decision was made.

While intellectual property is an organizational resource, the not-invented-here (NIH) syndrome continues to flourish. Organizations cannot justify starting every project and every employee at the bottom of the learning curve. That learning curve is too long and too difficult.

Knowledge gained through daily work must be viewed as an organizational asset. The questions to be answered are: How does an organization make use of that knowledge? How does an organization communicate and implement, as an example, the best practices from one unit to all other units? How does management force the adoption of a best practice when necessary? There are no simple answers. But management does have certain prerogatives and that includes managing effectively, efficiently, and with the economic use of resources. Whether a subunit accepts a best practice should not be a matter of choice. It may be necessary in some situations to direct the use of a best practice. Organizational/intellectual knowledge is an organizational asset and needs to be actively protected and disseminated throughout the organization.

Access to Information

Organizations have not been reluctant to invest in information systems. However, even after the installation of all those computers, the development of massive databases, and the extension of the use of the Internet and intranets, the inability to communicate adequate information at the appropriate level continues to limit performance. Perhaps there's too much information. Do the top-level executives really need to know the output of a plant in real time? Do they need to know the sales per hour in real time? If they have this information, how do they use it? Before computers became ubiquitous, the same questions were asked but in reference to paper. What was the result of that report or that study that may have taken months to compile? What happened to the consultant's recommendations? How many file cabinets could be emptied? Our databases have essentially replaced the filing cabinets and often require the same effort to retrieve information. But the tragedy is that much information required by workers is not easily available.

There is no doubt that certain information must of necessity be limited to those who have a need to know. Communicating details about future directions of the organization may be not only unwise but also counterproductive. Competitors also have antennae. I'm reminded of a case in which a division vice president would not allow his engineering manager access to the division's strategic plan. The document was restricted not by the company but at the whim of the division vice president—an excellent example of management malpractice, because that information was essential for the engineering manager to perform his job effectively and efficiently.

At the same time employees often think they need information that is totally irrelevant to the work at hand. My personal studies have shown that although employees often complain about a lack of information, when asked whether at any time the lack of information created any problems in their daily work, the answer was a resounding no. There was just a desire to know more.

Very few innovations begin without some information/knowledge base. Capturing the required and often available information may be more difficult. That organizational database should be of some value in providing information related to corporate markets, customer demographics, and historical records. But that database must contain more than data. It must provide *information*, and that means that someone has organized the data into a useful form. Until organizations transform their databases to information bases, innovators will need to continue to tap the body of knowledge that resides in the minds of coworkers.

Technology

What do we mean when we speak of technology? There are many descriptions: Technology is a means for accomplishing a task; technology is what it takes to convert resources into products and services; technology is the knowledge and resources needed to achieve a goal; technology is a body of scientific and engineering knowledge that can be applied to the design of new products; technology represents the artifacts developed from applying the principles of science and engineering. I prefer to describe technology as the knowledge embedded in products and processes, and the knowledge of creating, producing, reproducing, and using these products and processes.

Technology drives most innovative organizations. The innovator needs to understand the level of technological knowledge and expertise available by discipline both within and outside the organization. This appears to be a given but experience shows that too often innovators spend considerable effort reinventing the wheel. Although "understand the level of technical knowledge and expertise" may be a simple statement, it requires more than cursory knowledge. Innovators need to understand the range of technologies within the organization and the level of expertise available to them. That expertise also includes experience with the technology. Having knowledge without experience is insufficient.

Knowledge of the technologies involves more than the technologies required for developing a product that meets certain specific requirements. Production technologies must also be known—they determine the scope of work required to produce the product. If new production facilities are required, there will also be new production technologies.

Technologies are an organizational resource. Knowing how to use those technologies is also a resource. But the technologies must be identified as to their value to the organization. As new technologies are introduced, the old need to be abandoned unless they can be updated to meet new requirements. There appears to be a consensus that technologies are advancing very rapidly. But there's a need to look beyond the computer-related areas. Many industries operate with relatively stable technologies. Improvements are certainly made, but they are often not radical departures from the traditional.

Marketing and Sales

If innovation = invention + implementation/commercialization, then something must be sold or some action must take place for innovation to occur. The innovator may or may not be knowledgeable in marketing and sales, but the innovator needs to understand the role that marketing and sales will play in the success of the innovation. It may seem unreasonable to discuss marketing and sales issues at the beginning of the innovation process, but although no decisions may be made at that time, the consequences of an inadequate match with the organization's purposes, objectives, and strategies may prove to create a misallocation of critical resources.

The type of innovation will largely determine the marketing and sales issues. If the new effort involves incremental innovation, there should be little difficulty in identifying the critical issues. But the scope of the incremental innovation must be kept in perspective. As defined in Chapter 2, incremental innovation can vary from minor to major improvements. Those critical issues may include the impact on current products, the need to create awareness, the degree of acceptance among the current customer base, the possible expansion of the customer base because of new features and advantages, and the effort necessary to retrain users as well as maintenance and customer service personnel. In some cases the enhancements that do provide benefits may involve substantial costs. The innovator needs to be sensitive to the impact on the customer's bottom-line performance.

New-to-the-market innovations present a more complex problem. Top-down projects will not present a major problem because the resources will be provided. Many of the decisions related to marketing and sales will probably go through traditional channels. The Canon case discussed in Chapter 2 is a good example of an innovation driven from the top; even the project manager was a high-level executive. The bottom-up innovator faces more serious problems— specialized knowledge and experience in a single discipline, general problems with introducing a new idea, probably minimal if any support from immediate management in the initial stages, and a need to find support in many disciplines. Engineers and scientists will most likely lack knowledge in marketing, sales, distribution, customer service, and a host of related areas. Marketing and salespeople will lack understanding in the technology-related issues, manufacturing, and other functions. Acquiring that information is absolutely essential for timely innovation.

Time

Time is a vital resource in today's competitive global marketplace. It cannot be replaced. A major issue that innovators face is the time-to-decision. Most organizations are guided by a timetable, and innovators are not necessarily sensitive to the policies and procedures generally required in most organizations. The phrase "time is of the essence" has little meaning today. Managing cycle time provides a better approach when dealing with innovation. Cycle time includes three distinct interacting elements: time, timing, cycle duration. These three elements work interactively, collectively, and concurrently.

Time is a commodity and a business resource. It cannot be reclaimed or recycled. There are a limited number of hours in a day. A great many books have been written about time and how to use it more effectively, all with the hope of making more time available for real work. There are prescriptions for making to-do lists, and suggested shortcuts to various standardized activities and general work processes. We have been "electronicized" with cell phones, beepers, and hand-held computers, but questions still remain as to how effectively we use time. The penchant for doing before thinking generates much wasted effort.

No one will probably question the need for timing new product introductions. Timing requires a very positive response from all organizational functions. Realistic timing begins at the top of the organization. While timing is one aspect of planning, some degree of flexibility is essential. A McKinsey & Co. study[1] showed that a product six months late to the market misses out on one-third of the potential profit over the lifetime of the product. One can argue with such statistics, but whether the fractional loss is one-third, one-fourth, or one-tenth is of little importance. The simple fact is that there is a loss in profitability. Time is an important issue.

Cycle duration includes the time required to accomplish a task independent of its size or scope. In its simplest form, cycle duration can be described as the length of time it takes to meet some objective that begins at point "A" and ends at point "N." Managing cycle time involves defining point "A" and point "N." An organization manages time when managers broaden their perspective of the business beyond their immediate functional responsibilities and focus on the business objectives. Time becomes an effectively managed resource when organizations learn to integrate time, timing, and cycle duration to work interactively, collectively, and concurrently.

Distribution

The distribution system involves three distinct functions: 1) the means by which the organization sells its products, 2) the physical plant and equipment that move the product from the warehouse to the customer, and 3) customer service. Too often organizations fail to recognize the costs associated with developing and maintaining these three distribution functions. Booz-Allen and Hamilton reported in 1982 that 46 percent of business resources was devoted to product development and commercialization of unsuccessful products.[2] Robert Cooper and U. de Brentani also reported that 35 percent of projects fail commercially.[3] Not a very good track record. Lack of an adequate distribution system plays a significant role in these less than impressive figures.

Organizations sell their products through a direct sales force, independent representatives, various dealer organizations, distributors, and all of these in various combinations. These sources require an investment of organizational resources—time, energy, and money. These selling organizations undergo changes just like any other organizational entity. Salespeople leave the organization. Independent representatives may reorganize product lines and may no longer service all previous clients. Distributors may lose personnel.

Physical facilities and equipment to move the product to the customer represent a major resource. Physical distribution presents managers with many challenges. The physical distribution functions includes receiving incoming orders and processing them, determining availability, scheduling product movement, and making sure that the right products are shipped, in the right packaging with the appropriate documentation. Too often bottom-up innovators disregard the effort that it takes to develop and maintain these functions. These operations require continual upgrading to meet customers' requirements for more rapid and efficient delivery.

As technology continues to play a greater role in all business operations, customer service will take on more importance. There was a time when customer service was given little visibility. I recall an incident when a controller presented the potential "savings" that could be achieved by eliminating the customer service department. While organizations now consider customer service an absolute essential, most organizations have a long road ahead in meeting customer requirements. Those automated services definitely do not pass the test. Those customer service representatives who can only work by the book do not meet the requirements. Most organizations have a long way to go before their customer service departments meet their customers' expectations. Innovators need to be sensitive to the customer service requirements during their design activities. Providing customer service in real time is an organizational resource that requires continuous attention and often is the deciding factor in vendor selection.

Customers

Customers can provide valuable input, but primarily for improving products and processes that already exist. Don't expect a breakthrough innovation from a customer. Contrary to some academic research, these breakthrough concepts seldom come from customers. Any need expressed by a customer must be more than, hey, that's a great idea or that's something we could really use. There must be some in-depth understanding of both the need and the potential benefit to both the customer and the innovator. Customers' suggestions and interpretations must be validated. Customers can be a valuable resource when the organization knows the customer; the customer's needs, and understands how the customer uses the equipment or service.

Knowing the customer includes more than recognizing that a good relationship exists and the customer pays the bills on time. Some in-depth questions need to be answered. What is the customer's business? What segment of an industry does the customer serve? Is the specific customer a leader in the industry? What is the history of the customer in adopting the new and untried? Does the customer provide a local, national, or international view? Is the customer's business growing or stagnant? This list can be as short or as long as the particular situation requires, but the purpose is solely to be able to validate the information. Recommendations from a customer who is losing volume in an industry that's expanding must be viewed with caution.

Defining customer needs involves a more complex process than normally expected. Who in the customer's organization is capable of defining any improvements, enhancements, or new-product ideas—people in purchasing, engineering, customer service, manufacturing, or in some obscure unit of the organization? These needs must be validated through some method of cross-checking information. In some cases, it may be necessary to contact several people.

How does the customer actually use the equipment? This can become a difficult question if there are multiple users. Not every person uses equipment in the same manner and with the same care. One person can be very positive and another very negative under the same conditions. If a customer's use of the equipment can be viewed in an operational mode with an operator, the bias—except for that of the observer—can be removed.

To fully use a customer as an additional organizational resource, you must know the customer, the customer needs, and understand how the customer uses the equipment. Although it sounds very simple, it requires a specific type of competence in investigation, combined with patience and tact.

Suppliers

Suppliers have provided a major resource long before downsizing and outsourcing became popular. When outsourcing became the flavor of the month, there were scenarios written that all a corporation needed was a CEO. Everything could be outsourced: research, development, engineering, manufacturing, marketing and sales, distribution, and all the related administrative activities. This is not a very realistic scenario for a major corporation, but there is no doubt that many activities can be outsourced with a very positive impact on the organization. No single organization can maintain competencies in all disciplines and employ those disciplines effectively. Regardless of any intervening facts, suppliers in all business areas provide a valuable resource. Innovators have a tendency to discount the potential benefit of working with suppliers. A particular component may not be commercially available so the innovator begins to delve into areas outside his personal knowledge or experience instead of working with organizations that already have the required basic knowledge.

In today's economy, many organizations have become assembly

operations. In the past, Ford manufactured its steel and glass, cast its engine blocks, and made its own bodies and many other component parts within its own facilities. But today Ford and many other automobile manufacturers are primarily assembly operations. The major emphasis is on design and the negotiation of contracts to produce components to specification, combined with very efficient assembly and distribution systems. These organizations use the many technologies in which other organizations not only have expertise but also are the leaders in their industry.

Many smaller firms provide expertise that may not be present in major organizations. Operations such as heat treating, machining of components, designing of tools of manufacture, designing of automation and robotic systems, creating new products, providing education and training, and managing many specialized administrative functions are invaluable resources that if used effectively and efficiently allow an organization to multiply the value of its people resources.

Tapping these external resources requires a significant amount of management skill. Managers will always be told that the work can be done more effectively within the organization, and that it's just too hard to work with outside vendors. Not really; all it takes is dedication to the activities as though they were performed internally. Using outside resources is a joint effort, and the effort does not consist of writing a purchase order and then resurrecting it five days before the delivery date. The process requires continuous follow-up. In today's multidisciplinary project world, all of the competence and expertise cannot reside within any one organization. Managing these external resources as partners amplifies the organization's capabilities.

Production Capability

The organization's resources include the production facilities and production know-how, which may or may not be a resource for this particular innovation. Innovators need to understand the availability of both the facilities and the process know-how. Both will eventually be important. Several questions must be considered and answered within the scope of the innovation. Discovering late in the game that major capital investments are required for production will only exacerbate the innovator's frustration level. Will the proposed product be produced on existing equipment, or will new equipment be needed? If existing equipment is used, will it lengthen the development time? If new production equipment is necessary, what level of investment may be necessary? Are the pilot plant or experimental facilities available? These are questions that must be considered before embarking on a major investment of resources. Production facilities are only a resource if they can be utilized in the manufacture of the new product. Likewise, the production know-how will only be valuable if the same processes are used.

Opportunities for innovation may be limited if products must be produced on existing equipment. Extra development time may be required that could not only delay product introduction but also significantly reduce the financial reward to the organization. I'm reminded of a program that remained in the laboratory for almost an additional three years because the team thought that the product had to be produced on existing equipment. New equipment would not only have reduced the development time but provided a greater return to the organization. This type of decision must be made early in the innovation process.

The capability and limitation of production equipment and processes in any organization should be a known as a matter of good business practice. Innovators need to be knowledgeable about this resource. Most production facilities include many different types of production equipment and processes and each must be investigated as to its relevance to the current task. Some processes may be applicable and others may not. If a breakthrough innovation is under consideration, many of the production facilities may require significant modification or even replacement, and totally new capabilities may in fact be needed.

People competencies also enter the production capability equation. Since many production operations are routine, managers often decide that upper-level process engineering is no longer required. The process is working, so why change it? Such thinking usually creates major difficulties when new processes are introduced. During this somewhat stagnant period, the plant has become comfortable with meeting its production targets with little attention to future activities. If the process engineering effort is reduced substantially, the breadth of process knowledge required for introducing new products that require new processes will not be available.

Operational Facilities

There was a time where the office included only a typewriter that, compared to present writing equipment, presented few problems: Clean the keys on occasion and schedule an annual alignment. Today's office includes computers, copying machines with many additional advanced features, fax machines, and all the other electronic gadgets deemed necessary. Research departments require not just computers but a whole range of sophisticated analytical equipment. The drafting board has been replaced with computer-aided-design (CAD) software. The slide rule has become a relic of the past and also has been replaced by various electronic devices. Not many secretaries remain, and professionals making $100,000 or more per year hunt and peck and click and drag their way to the next piece of correspondence. Offices have become personalized printing plants since the advent of the computer printers. The old-style bullpens have given way to isolation booths where people prefer to communicate by e-mail with colleagues in adjacent cubicles rather than stand up and talk face-to-face over the cubicle wall. Many people do not even answer their phones; they prefer several e-mail exchanges to a single phone call that might end with a decision.

All of these new tools should provide significant benefits but will not do so until we learn how to use them effectively and efficiently. Correspondence should not be limited to e-mail that now contains grammatical and spelling mistakes that in the past would not have been tolerated. There is some more appropriate office design between the extremes of the hundred-person bullpen and the individual cubicle. Face-to-face contact continues to be a necessity. Conference calls can be productive as long as the people have had some prior contact. Virtual meetings using the Internet also provide opportunities for improving productivity.

The organization's operational facilities are an essential resource for innovators and help reduce the time from concept to implementation/commercialization. The innovator requires adequate tools to perform at a high performance level, especially now that innovation cycle times must be reduced. Taking time to find and organize those facilities only detracts from the effort devoted to the innovation. Computer capability using the best of available search engines provides the means for simplifying the acquisition of required data. Basic computational computing capability with the appropriate level of sophistication needs to be available 24/7. Communication facilities must meet the needs of the innovation. Innovation that involves support from non-USA organizational units must be built on similar platforms. All of these tools—used both individually and synergistically—allow the innovator and the team to reduce the time from idea to implementation.

Finance

There comes a time where a financial investment will be required and innovators need to recognize the limitations of the organization's financial resources. I have intentionally placed the financial requirements as the last item in this group of resource dimensions because too often money is used as a reason for not promoting innovation. Investments will vary significantly, depending on the scope of the innovation. Financial requirements for incremental innovation are generally not a problem. But most likely the new-to-the-market and breakthrough innovations will require significant funding. Major financial investments will eventually be required but attempting to determine those figures in the concept and pre-project stages with any significant level of confidence is a mistake. There just isn't enough quantifiable information available to make any kind of rational judgment. Mixing these financial requirements with the technology and marketing issues in the concept stage is a mistake, as discussed in Chapter 5. This does not suggest that the issue of potential financial resources should be ignored but is unnecessary at this time unless the potential investment completely exceeds the means of the organization.

The ability to finance an innovation in the pre-project, project, and project/product launch stages needs to be assessed in relation to the organization's ability to provide the financial resources. Financial resources may also be required to fund additional people with new competencies and skills; information resources may need to be upgraded; imported technologies may require royalty payments; and marketing, sales, and distribution may require new resources. These additional resources do not come without some drain on the organization's financial resources.

Summary

- Innovation cannot occur without adequate resources.

- People are the most important asset, but the objective is to optimize their use for the organization and their professional development.

- Intellectual property provides opportunities for not reinventing the wheel.

- Access to information allows innovators to speed the innovation to a conclusion.

- Technology does drive the innovative organization, but only in relation to providing a business opportunity.

- Marketing and sales drive the innovation into the marketplace and determine its viability.

- Time, timing, and cycle time must work interactively, collectively, and concurrently to achieve market dominance.

- Distribution activities determine whether the customer will return.

- Customers are the ultimate judges of the innovation.

- Suppliers provide those specialized skills and resources that supplement the organization's resources.

- Production capability involves more than plant and equipment and process knowledge for products; it also includes the resources required for service industries.

- Operating facilities for all organizational entities involve significant expenditures. They need to provide productivity benefits in relation to their investment.

- Finance eventually becomes the ultimate broker in sponsoring innovation. The financial justification for the innovation cannot be disregarded.

Notes

1. T. Vessey, "The New Competitors: They Think in Terms of 'Speed-to-Market'," *The Academy of Management Executive* V, 2 (1991): 23–33.

2. Booz-Allen and Hamilton, *New Product Management for the 1980s* (New York: Booz-Allen and Hamilton, Inc., 1982).

3. R. G. Cooper and U. de Brentani, "Criteria for Screening New Industrial Products," *Industrial Marketing Management* 13 (1984): 149–156.

CHAPTER

9

Dimensions of Organizational Infrastructure

Resources provide the raw material, but organizational infrastructure provides the catalyst that allows innovation to occur. People individually and in groups promote innovation based on how the infrastructure responds to those new, troubling, and sometimes off-the-wall ideas. While innovators generally become passionate about pursuing a particular activity, some minimum level of infrastructure support is absolutely essential for them to move forward. The infrastructure must find a way to accommodate the innovation process, or innovation will not take place. There comes a time when the innovator must be recognized as a participant in the business of the organization. As Tom Peters once noted, "You innovate or die."

New demands are placed on management and the innovators as organizations seek to move from the relatively stable set of management principles that have been in use since the start of the industrial age to those necessary for a global competitive age, a period in which knowledge is taking precedence over physical attributes. The social structure has changed in recent years, which places new demands on all organizations and their employees, whether in academia, government, or industry. Organizations now need to carefully assess where they invest their limited resources—in new technologies, in new markets, and in what kinds of products, services, and processes. Billion-dollar organizations need to develop some algorithm by which to judge value-adding investments.

Managers define the organizational infrastructure through their daily activities. Too often the impact of that infrastructure on performance is disregarded. The organizational infrastructure issues are shown in Figure 9-1.

The manner and extent to which these twelve issues affect organizational performance depends both on the recognition of their importance and on the emphasis on their implementation. These infrastructure issues determine the level of success achieved when organizations sponsor innovators. The simple format lays down the fundamentals. Purposes need to be understood. The organization needs to know where it wants to go and how it plans to get there. Some objectives must be defined and a strategy developed to accomplish them. Astute management is essential and must know how to live with uncertainties and risks. Those policies and procedures and practices cannot hinder progress in any way. Partnerships need to be developed with external resources. And two imperatives cannot be disregarded: leadership in the truest sense of the word must exist and the leaders must communicate in a meaningful way. Leadership is more than proposing that everyone charge the gates and communication is more than sending memos and e-mails, hoping that everyone will read and respond. The infrastructure issues cannot be disregarded, and if innovation is essential for future growth, then the infrastructure must allow it to happen.

Figure 9.1. Organizational infrastructure.

Purposes
Organizational vision
Organizational objectives
Strategic planning or strategy
Organizational structure
Management attributes
Uncertainties and risks
Support for innovation
Role of policies, procedures, and practices
Essential partnerships
Leadership
Communicating

Purposes

Organizational purpose must be described within the context of the business. The questions might seem elementary, because logic would indicate that an organization should not only understand its purposes but also clearly communicate why it exists and what purposes it serves. That statement must go beyond stating that it will meet the needs of the stakeholders, optimize stockholders' returns, or make a profit. Such statements do little to motivate the participants to go the extra mile.

The needs of stakeholders, stockholders, and making a profit are important. While making a profit is absolutely vital for sustaining operations, there may be better ways of making money than investing in people and equipment and facing all the associated problems. A greater return may come from other investment strategies with reduced risk. The fact remains that most organizations exist for something more than just making money. Making money is a result of effectively using resources and comes from pursuing the purposes for which the organization exists.

Organizations usually exist to provide products, services, or both. The industrial revolution was built around supplying products and building the nation's infrastructure. The expansion of information systems products now presents new opportunities for growth. But we haven't as yet learned how to use information systems effectively and efficiently. We have a long journey ahead before we transform all that data to easily searchable useful information. So, as our organizations become more complex, their purposes must be defined more appropriately. Executives need to determine what business they're in and its purposes and support innovation that furthers those purposes.

In *In Search of Excellence* Tom Peters identified eight attributes that characterized excellent and innovative firms. One was *they stick to their knitting*. It's important that organizations stay fairly close to the business they understand and have the resources to follow through successfully. As an absurd case, McDonald's is probably not thinking of designing and building airplanes and Boeing is most likely not thinking about going into the fast-food business. The range of the *allowable knitting* must be defined for the organization at all levels. Setting some limits on an organization's interests should not in any way diminish opportunities for innovation. Those limits will provide direction. That innovator's dream at some time in the future will require a major investment and the organization needs to reflect such issues in its statement of purpose.

So although that *statement of purpose* is important, it requires expansion and a more directed explanation of what that statement means. Purposes involve more than a statement of why the organization exists. Those statements represent the skeleton upon which to build a reality into the statement. Likewise, the statement of purpose of every organizational subgroup should link it to the organization's purposes.

Organizational Vision

The concept of the organizational vision has been overworked and under-implemented to the point where the concept of vision has little if any meaning. Not too long ago every organization was visioning in some manner. Even elementary school teachers were visioning. Visions without actions and without resources to accomplish them build expectations that are not realized. After all, what could be more important than discussing the organization's vision? That is high-powered stuff. But visioning joined the ranks of other single-issue mandates such as strategic planning. Visioning exercises have not been very productive in changing behavioral patterns. Jack Welch, former CEO of General Electric, enunciated a very simple vision statement: "We'll be number 1 or number 2 in the markets we serve." Not much room for argument. Welch supplied the resources, built the infrastructure, and provided the leadership to fulfill the vision.

In Chapter 6, I mentioned that 3M began with a mistake. 3M ended the year 2000 with sales of approximately $16 billion and profits of $1.86 billion. 3M has a typical vision statement that involves providing quality products and services based on product and technology platforms, reducing pollution to the extent possible, building an environment that fosters innovation, treating employees fairly, and providing opportunities for employee growth. Providing leadership in the company and the community and fulfilling duties as a good citizen are essential. This statement is not the official one, but the unwritten one that is implemented at the operational levels. Vision statements must include more than being the greatest this or that. Organizations need to define what they want to be and then communicate the message. Doing what is needed to make the organization what it wants to be requires focus and management competence.

Organizational Objectives

Objectives define what the organization hopes to achieve in the short and long term and by what means in relation to growth, products, technologies, and markets. There is no doubt that both the short- and long-term objectives need to be satisfied. The persistent arguments that the organization considers only the short term and only pays attention to the quarterly bottom line may or may not be true. Development of new products or services involves a significant investment and that investment is only possible if the short-term revenue streams meet their targets. Does Wall Street demand quarterly results? Definitely. This simple fact remains true: An organization that does not meet its short-term goals seldom meets its long-term goals. A similar situation exists when a project fails to meet its milestones. It's very difficult to recover the lost time even if additional resources are provided.

Defining corporate objectives doesn't guarantee performance. Those corporate objectives must be broken down into objectives for every operational unit and for the functions within the operational units. The development of a new product must be broken down into meaningful objectives for each of the many involved functions and then integrated into the project. Too often this integration effort is disregarded. Perhaps that's the reason less than 10 percent of projects meet requirements, come in on time, and meet the original cost projections.

Setting objectives for introducing new technologies and obsoleting some of the old seldom receive the desired attention. New technologies need to be introduced long before they can be applied in new products. It takes time to evaluate the pros and cons of going with the new and often requires evaluation to eliminate some of the uncertainties. It is too late to evaluate those new technologies when the product is ready to ship. In some situations prototyping, modeling, and simulation may be necessary to understand the limits of the new technology. Some of the old proven technologies that may no longer meet the operational, reliability, and cost parameters need to be eliminated.

Dealing with the marketing issues also poses problems that can determine success or failure in the marketplace. An organization dealing primarily with industrial customers will find many new issues to deal with as it tries to enter the consumer markets. The needs and discipline are totally different. Many years ago a Fortune 500 company primarily involved in industrial products attempted to go to the consumer market with a truly innovative product. For years it tried to get the product on the grocery store shelves with little success. Originally, the company refused to go through brokers, which at the time was how most products would reach the grocery shelves. In addition, they used their industrial sales force, who knew nothing about the commercial market. Eventually, the company did go through the brokers and the product generated better sales than projected. Marketing objectives must be clearly stated and people with the required competencies assigned to meet the objectives.

Strategic Planning or Strategy

Very little strategic planning evolves into strategy. In the past year, I've participated in many industry and not-for-profit organizational meetings where the results of strategic planning sessions were presented. I expected to hear something about strategy or strategic direction but instead listened to a listing of operational objectives without any discussion of the strategy to achieve the objectives. Also, very little was said about just where the organization wanted to go or what it wanted to be. It is not possible to develop a strategy if an organization doesn't know what it wants to be and how it plans to get there.

Research on the benefits of strategic planning is limited. The gurus promoted it and executives bought it. From personal experience, I have concluded that much of strategic planning is based on seven questionable assumptions:

1. Assumes steady-state conditions for the economy, technology, and markets

2. Disregards the dynamic issues that affect strategy

3. Operates on a twelve-month cycle

4. Deals with data rather than knowledge

5. Ignores leading-edge technologies

6. Focuses on incremental improvements

7. Uses planners who are not the implementers

Any one of these seven assumptions diminishes the value of the effort to create an organizational strategy. The dynamics of global competition make a twelve-month strategy irrelevant. How can an organization assume steady-state conditions for the economy, technology, and the marketplace? How can an organization develop a strategy without an emphasis on new-to-the-market and breakthrough products and processes? Strategy must be real.

Over the years strategic planning became an effort that required considerable time and effort, concluding with binders full of numbers and charts, results that occur only in the fourth or fifth year, and plans that are neither strategic nor operational. Corporate executives review and approve the plan, and then it goes onto the shelf until next year's cycle. It's difficult to understand why managers have not recognized that we live in a dynamic world. A strategy or a strategic direction statement should require no more than a single page, and its validity needs to be challenged as new information is uncovered.

Mintzberg on Strategy

Henry Mintzberg brings the practitioner's approach to strategy. His thoughts should force managers to rethink their approach to strategy. He has continued to be vocal about many management issues and considers strategic planning performed in the traditional sense as an oxymoron. Mintzberg presents two scenarios, one the traditional and the other using the crafting metaphor.[1]

> *Scenario 1.* Senior managers with selected colleagues formulate strategy by some orderly process that others will implement on some defined schedule. The approach stresses rational control, systematic analysis of competition and markets, and a typical review of strengths, weaknesses, opportunities, and threats that produce explicit strategies. Information is accepted from many sources and usually without adequate validation.

> *Scenario 2.* Mintzberg suggests that the crafting metaphor with the image of the potter turning a lump of clay into a piece of

art more appropriately captures the process by which strategy comes into being. The executive or manager as a craftsman working as an organization of one resolves the greatest challenges an organization faces while knowing the organization's capabilities well enough to think about its strategic directions.

The potter begins with a lump of clay and eventually fashions it into a work of art. The potter with knowledge and experience and competence blends thought with action followed by more thought and action. Action drives thinking. Through the thought-to-action process, a strategy emerges that can be implemented. Strategy looks at the past but focuses on future opportunities. Mintzberg's metaphor promotes the concept that managers are the craftsmen and strategy is their clay. Strategy involves more than collecting data, manipulating it, and making statistical analyses of the non-validated numbers. Mintzberg considers strategy to be more like managing stability than change: It is not so much a matter of managing change as knowing when to introduce it. He proposes that strategic planning does not create strategy, but is a means for programming an existing strategy. Strategic planning focuses on analysis while strategy focuses on synthesis.

Organizational Structure

The idealized organizational structure may not provide opportunities for innovation; on the other hand, what may be considered an unmanageable organizational structure may produce great numbers of innovations. Management research has not provided much insight and guidance regarding organizational structure because of the inherent difficulty in identifying the real-life structure that lies behind how the organization functions. Those boxes with the solid and dotted lines do not tell how the business is managed or how people communicate. Filling in the white space on the organizational chart may define the structure more clearly, but that may be an impossible task since the structure of necessity must adapt to changing organizational dynamics.

Structure depends on people. People come to the organization from different disciplines, with different levels of education and professional experience, from different geographical areas, with different business experience and orientation, different physical and emotional needs, different purposes and goals, and all of the different characteristics that make them unique human beings. But their performance often depends on how the organizational power structures function. Right or wrong, power centers exist. Integrating a group of people into a functioning project team presents a complex problem; consider what it takes to integrate a management team at the corporate level. So organizational structures need to be designed taking into account the available people with all of their talents, foibles, prejudices, and interests. Those power centers must be managed by someone at the executive level to reduce and possibly eliminate any negative impact.

There is no doubt that structures may require changes periodically at all organizational levels. Structure depends on the context in which it operates. If the business context changes, the structure probably requires some changes. In a dynamic economy an organization may choose to organize across product lines, market sectors, or geographically, or in any appropriate manner to meet its objectives in a dynamically changing economy. There is no ideal organizational structure. But before changes are implemented, thought should precede action.

I am reminded of a situation in which a consultant was hired to assist in the restructuring of a research facility of a major corporation. In preliminary discussions the consultant asked about previous reorganizations. The research director responded that the previous restructuring took place within the last two years. The consultant followed up with, "Why wasn't the old one successful and what are the problems with the current organizational structure?" No one, including the CEO, the research director, and senior staff, had bothered to identify the problems that another new structure might resolve. The consultant terminated his relationship because he quickly discovered that the organization was not searching for resolution of a problem but looking for a cursory rearrangement of the boxes on the organization chart. Organization charts do not tell how an organization functions. The interactions and the interplay between people and functions are too complex to be identified by interconnecting boxes. Those relationships may change significantly as new people are brought into the organization and others leave.

There is also no doubt that structure is important, but structure begins and ends with people involved in the structure. Corporate executives who protect their fiefdoms at the expense of corporate performance need to be replaced. Managers, in all disciplines, who focus on developing their own fiefdoms at the expense of total organizational performance shirk their responsibility and need to be replaced. A group of professionals in any discipline who build an impenetrable wall for their function at the expense of organizational performance also need to be replaced. Organizations cannot optimize their performance by tolerating destructive fiefdoms.

Management Attributes

Every organization possesses certain operational attributes based on its value system. Attributes are the glue that keeps the organization together and moves it forward. It's the invisible. It's the vitality. It's the motivation to succeed. It's the desire to pursue excellence in all activities. But excellence should not be confused with perfection. Management attributes include management astuteness, management attitude, acceptance of risk, living with uncertainties, support for innovation, and attitude toward policies and practices.

Management Astuteness

I use astuteness instead of expertise because it's more encompassing. Astuteness implies having a breadth of knowledge, understanding interlocking relationships, contributing to the innovative needs of the organization, being mentally alert and discerning, being comprehensive but within realistic limitations, and just being believable and creditable. Managers cannot focus on single issues: They need some breadth of knowledge related to the business. Business school educators who promote the idea that "if one can manage, one can manage anything" have probably never worked for one of these managers. The quick learners don't learn that quickly. They don't understand the company, the products, the markets, or the technologies.

Witness the number of CEOs who have moved to new positions and after reorganizations one, two, and three continue to perform below expectations. Managers need to understand and manage many, often conflicting interfaces. Mental alertness to surroundings and issues related to the business needs continuous attention and cannot be supplied by some staff member with a written report. This all makes managers believable and creditable.

Management Attitude

Competence is only part of the business success equation. Attitude drives performance. Attitude plays a major role in all dealings, and management's attitude is doubly important when innovation becomes a top priority. If managers demonstrate a can-do attitude, what needs to be done will probably get done. If managers, on the other hand, demonstrate a lackadaisical attitude, that attitude will radiate a lackadaisical response throughout the organization. If managers tolerate late arrivals at a meeting, the sub-groups will follow suit. If managers accept below-par performance, below-par performance will follow throughout the organizational unit. Managers really need to be role models in every aspect of their activities. It's a tough job, but essential. That's why they're managers.

Attitudes, both good and bad, are contagious. If managers categorically reject new ideas as interruptions, that attitude will communicate a strong negative message. If, on the other hand, the manager suggests, "Let's talk about it," even though the idea may not be pursued, at least there was an opportunity to discuss it. While ideas must fit the business purposes and objectives, some of those unrelated ideas could often introduce some new thinking. The idea may not be of any significance, but managers need to listen and then probe and contribute their own thinking rather than just reject—they need to challenge the idea and themselves.

Unfortunately, too many managers have become bureaucratic administrators. If managers spend all their time in the office and deal solely from the paperwork (now e-mail) that goes through the in and out basket, they demonstrate a particular attitude—all I need is the report. Employees will respond in the same manner. If managers focus on themselves rather than on contributing directly in some way to the organization's productivity, they send a destructive message to their colleagues. Project managers who work only from the reports without continual personal contact with the team members will eventually have to face up to the surprises. A negative attitude breeds more negative attitudes, which will flow throughout the whole organization. A positive attitude even in the face of great difficulties often brings the best from all those involved. When everyone is doing more than his or her fair share of the effort, it's difficult for a slacker to survive.

Uncertainties and Risks

There is a difference between uncertainties and risks. Uncertainties include the entire list of the unknown and unpredictable issues and events at the time that decisions are made. All of the answers related to technologies, markets, and the firm's business will seldom be available at the time that decisions must be made. The level of these uncertainties determines the risk. The risk must be evaluated in relation to the organization's capability to accept the risk. Small organizations usually will accept greater risks than the billion-dollar global organizations.

3M is an example. From 1902 to 1925, 3M was basically in the sandpaper business. Scotch masking tape was developed in 1925 and was the first nonabrasive product. To enter this market, management basically pledged all the company's assets, a decision that turned out to be the right one. But as a $16 billion-plus company today, it would not possibly pledge any large percentage of its assets to enter a new field.

Managing the Uncertainties

Every project begins with what's known, what isn't known, and those troublesome uncertainties. Research, development, manufacturing, and marketing all experience these three categories of information. The known factors usually present no problems as long as there's a full understanding of the *known* and the appraisal conforms to a rigorous evaluation process. What is *not known* can usually be identified and measures can be taken to put the unknowns in the known column after some investigation, leave them in the unknown column, or eliminate them from further consideration. After some investigation these *not known* items may continue to be listed with the uncertainties. The uncertainties now need to be evaluated as to their possible use. Not all of the uncertainties will be resolved. But a judgment must be made regarding the extent to which a particular uncertainty will be introduced.

The major uncertainties relate to technologies and markets. Introducing a new technology that has not been fully field-tested represents an uncertainty and a risk. Introducing a new manufacturing process that allows higher output, improved quality, and lower cost also involves uncertainties that will not be determined until production begins. Regardless of the modeling and simulation and testing, there is a scale-up period in which output will be lower than predicted, quality may be less than expected, and cost considerably higher. As the scale-up continues the problems will be resolved. Eventually, all the parameters that determined the initial decision to go ahead with the new process may exceed the original performance standards. However, until at least the basic product parameters meet the requirements, some level of uncertainty will exist and the uncertainty will increase significantly from those doing the hands-on work through the various levels of management.

The marketplace presents many uncertainties, especially if the new product includes new technologies, a new market segment, a new distribution system, and a new or reeducated sales force. This combination of newness requires careful evaluation. Each additional uncertainty compounds the difficulty in reducing the negative impact. An in-depth effort should be made to examine these uncertainties before embarking on such a project.

The process begins with evaluating the product concept. Product specifications require validation against customer requirements. The importance of educating customers about the benefits and limitations of the new product concept should not be underestimated. The market segment must be identified. Any uncertainties about customer acceptance need to be rationalized. Was that market size of billions of dollars reduced to reflect the size of the market segment in which the new product will actually be salable?

Accepting Risks

The sum of all the uncertainties involved in any business defines the risk exposure. Innovation is subject to various degrees of risk, but business always involves taking calculated risks. Managers must support some level of risk if innovation is to take place. Technology, production, marketing, sales, and distribution all present some level of risk that needs to be understood in terms of the systems needs. None of these risks can be ignored. A significant amount of risk can be avoided or at least minimized if the organizational purposes, objectives, and strategies are aligned. Knowledge minimizes the risk. Although all the knowledge may not be available, a sufficient amount must be available to justify some level of risk.

Much of what we call "risk" can be minimized if there's a commitment by those involved in taking the risk. Commitment really means do or die. It doesn't stop at 5:00 P.M. and begin the following morning at 8:00 A.M. Commitment says we will do it, no matter the obstacles. Obviously, there are times when the risk is not fully evaluated. Implementing a new technology without adequate testing may be suicide. But new technologies should not be implemented without testing applicability to the product. Going into new markets also needs full consideration of the market testing that may be required if the process is new or unknown.

Support for Innovation

It takes an astute executive or manager to support innovation. Those bean counters who only look at today's results would probably not support innovation. There are bean counters who support innovation when they become part of the process. Support involves providing not only the physical resources but also the emotional support that every innovator needs at times during the innovation process. Executives and managers who do not understand the issues that face the innovator may find it difficult to support innovation. They need to know what it takes to be an innovator. If innovation was such a simple and ordered process, we could expect it to happen more often.

Role of Policies, Procedures, and Practices

How long is the shelf that holds the policies, procedures, and practices manuals? Or how many CDs does it take to document them? Innovation is inversely proportional to the length of the shelves that store these documents. There is no doubt that this information plays a major role in maintaining some level of organizational discipline. Discipline as used here refers to maintaining some level of order. However, how those policies, procedures, and practices are interpreted and employed in the management of the organization has a significant impact on the amount of innovation.

Organizations need to be flexible in applying rules and regulations that inhibit the innovators. Innovation cannot occur within a strict interpretation of rules and regulations. Innovators need to be given some slack, but their own judgment determines how far they can go without creating unnecessary problems. Ethical conduct cannot be compromised.

Essential Partnerships

Organizations do not exist without the support from many other entities. Good relations with external sources are based on mutual interest. Customers are an absolute essential, not only as buyers of the organization's products and services but also as sources of information regarding future needs. Suppliers contribute their specialized expertise in providing some of the organization's needs. Regulatory bodies of many different types, whether the industry watchdogs or those seeking to work with industry to provide for community needs, both interact with the organization and have an impact on performance. Finally, the organization has some social responsibility to the community. Each of these entities affects the organization's performance and in turn is affected by the organization.

Customers

Organizations cannot exist without customers. The proponents of the "customer is king" philosophy have developed all kinds of programs to recognize the contributions of customers. The management literature in both the trade and the academic press pitch the view that it's necessary to stay close to the customer. Granted, the customer is important. But staying close to the customer in order to obtain customer input for next-generation products requires staying close to a particular kind of customer—the customer who really understands the industry and knows where the industry wants to direct its attention. The 3M marketing department listened to customers and concluded that there was no market for Post-it Notes. The innovation team responded by distributing pads throughout the organization until Post-it Notes became addictive. Customers are not always right, and their information must be validated across a spectrum of customers who would actually use the product. Refer to Chapter 8 for additional comments regarding customers.

Suppliers

In recent years outsourcing has become more prevalent in most organizations. Suppliers now play a greater role in meeting organizational commitments and need to be managed to provide a benefit. Sending a purchase order or signing a contract for a major piece of work of any type and then forgetting about the supplier until the delivery date is suicide. Suppliers need to be treated as partners rather than adversaries. Refer to Chapter 8 for additional comments regarding suppliers.

Regulatory Bodies

Although many executives regard regulatory bodies at all levels of government as simply interference with the organization's activities, they have no alternative except to work with these groups to reach agreement on the possible. While these regulatory bodies are often considered a waste of time and effort, organizations also use them to gain approval of specifications written around their product. Executives willingly provide assistance in preparing these specifications. Getting the government to write the purchase specification around an organization's product specification that others may not be able to meet may be the ultimate prize.

Why are these interactions with regulatory bodies so important? As an example, it is too late to consider environmental and safety issues as the innovation is about to enter the marketplace. These issues must be managed during the design process and not during the product launch. Most innovators will not be familiar with these ancillary issues, so knowledgeable professionals must be brought in during the design phase. When a product is about to leave the distribution center, it is too late to consider the safety, environmental, or weights and measures requirements. In recent years product recalls for safety reasons alone have seriously affected the profitability of many organizations.

Social Responsibility

An organization's social responsibility is reflected in its internal responsibility to the stakeholders. There can be too much and too little.

Beware of the managers who always willingly volunteer to take on some external activity but seldom manage their own operations at an acceptable level. A problem is brewing. Some level of dissatisfaction most likely exists. When there's more interest in external activities than the work at hand, the person may have reached a level of incompetence. The purpose of a business organization is not to become the number one nominee for social responsibility. Although social responsibility requires organizational support, most of it must come from the personal time of its employees. Social responsibility involves two major activities: those sponsored by the organization and those that occur when promoted by the organization through employee volunteerism. The organization's social responsibility involves providing safe products at the required quality and minimizing any negative impact on the environment. Organizations through their foundations contribute by promoting education and assisting the community in times of some catastrophic event. Employee volunteerism when integrated with the organizational business effort provides a community where the organization and the community become one.

Leadership

Leadership is one of the most critical dimensions of the organizational infrastructure. Leadership needs to exist at all levels: individual, functional, subbusiness unit, business unit, and organizational. Leadership continues to receive a significant amount of attention in both the academic and business press. There was a time when the word *leadership* meant Leadership, and that leadership involved going above and beyond what was expected. Leadership involved taking risks and managing them, and it meant sticking your neck out because you were committed to accomplishing something. With the volume of literature on leadership in recent years promoting the idea that everyone can be a leader, the word *leadership* and what is expected of leaders has lost some of its significance and has been considerably diminished.

Leaders are often classified as visionary, strategic, or managerial. But if someone is considered to be an industry or organizational leader, that person focuses on vision, strategy, and management. It is difficult to be a leader in today's global economy without fulfilling all three of these requirements. Vision (what does the organization want to be), strategy, and management are absolute precursors of leadership. Otherwise, leadership does not exist. A strategy cannot be developed without some defined vision.

There is a tendency to equate leadership with level in the hierarchy. There is also a tendency to equate leadership with credentials. But hierarchy and credentials do not necessarily relate to leadership. Leadership in the proactive and innovative sense seldom exists at the top of the hierarchy. There are exceptions, but not many. There are many people in academia, government, and industry who have reached the top in their organizations but are not necessarily leaders. They managed to go with the flow and reached the top of the organizational ladder. They may have been excellent administrators, but they are not managers or leaders. Likewise, credentials do not automatically bestow leadership qualities. There are many people with a Ph.D. in the technical and social disciplines that do not even take on a leadership position in their own discipline. They may be knowledgeable about what goes on in their discipline, but they're not the leaders—they're not the people working on the edge of their discipline. They may be good workers but they play it safe. There's a significant difference in obtaining the credentials and then taking a position in leading the discipline into new territories. Refer to Chapter 10 for additional comments on leadership.

Communicating

Communicating involves not only the sender but also the receiver. Too often what seems adequate to the sender is totally inadequate to the receiver. Some suggest that there can never be too much communication. That may be true but we can't spend all of our time communicating. Communicating nonessential information can hinder rather than help. The difficulty lies in choosing what should be communicated.

The issues related to communicating are complex. I use the word communicating rather than communication intentionally—communicating a communication. Too often the communication cycle ends when a message has been sent. Communicating involves some form of acknowledgment or feedback. There are different types of communicating in relation to innovation. Communicating can come from the top of the organization down to the subunits and most likely will not request any feedback. Innovators and their colleagues basically accept or reject the importance.

Communicating where innovation takes place involves exchanging thoughts. Those thoughtful comments that provide constructive critiquing whether positive or negative need to be heard and acted upon. Innovators need to be forthright in communicating their thoughts and listen to those responses. These opportunities for dialogue often lead to better understanding. Most innovations are not clearly understood in the early stages, and the input from colleagues in other disciplines often opens new areas for consideration. So it's necessary that innovators vacate their cubicles and recognize the benefit of occasionally meeting at the water cooler.

Listening is hard work and perhaps especially for the innovator. We know or think we know what the other person is going to say so the cutoff switch is activated. That may be necessary under certain circumstances. Feedback needs to be relevant to the issue under discussion. It takes discipline to listen without making a judgment. At the same time beware of the time killers—people who bring in extraneous and unrelated topics. Questions shouldn't turn into lectures. Refer to Chapter 10 for additional comments on communicating.

Summary

- A supportive infrastructure fosters innovation.

- Executives own the infrastructure responsibility.

- Purposes, objectives, and strategy form an inseparable triad.

- The infrastructure develops capability toward extraordinary achievement.

- Managers do not manage people: They lead people and manage activities.

Note

1. Henry Mintzberg, "Crafting Strategy," *Harvard Business Review,* July–August 1987, Reprint 87407.

CHAPTER 10

What It Takes to Be an Innovator

So, what does it take to be an innovator? Do innovators possess any particular personal characteristics that provide an advantage? This chapter focuses on the issues commonly referred to as *soft skills, characteristics,* and *attitudes,* which in most situations are just as important as if not more important than discipline knowledge. There is nothing soft about these skills. They determine performance. These soft skills can be more appropriately referred to as integrating skills, or collaborative business skills. They are the skills that allow the implementation of discipline knowledge to achieve an objective. In the final analysis the innovator needs what I refer to as the *put-it-all-together competence* that includes skills, characteristics, and attitudes. The bottom-up innovator will need an abundance of this competence.

The business climate has changed in recent years as new factors and characteristics have appeared, such as:

- Shortened technology and product life cycles

- Business globalization

- Increasing demands for accountability

- Emphasis on the bottom line

- Growing potential of the virtual organization

The mantra of faster, better, and cheaper will continue. New skill sets are needed to meet these requirements, and the career paths of the next generation will change. Innovation will take on greater significance and require a new kind of professional employee. The new skill sets include systems and knowledge integration as well as the abilities to manage complexity and uncertainty and to work in a multicultural environment—all of these skills are the essence of innovation. The new career paths will include formation of new enterprises, greater emphasis on product and process development, infrastructure renewal, and more consideration of material and energy utilization and conservation. These factors all create opportunities for the innovator. Joseph Bordogna, then acting Deputy Director of the National Science Foundation, said:

> The future belongs to those who can make sense of the complex, to those who can take an idea from conception through the functional integration of many complex technologies and disciplines to product realization, to those who can put complex products out the door.[1]

That statement has significant implications for the innovator. It requires building a put-it-all-together competence.

Figure 10-1 shows the skills, characteristics, attitudes, and knowledge required of the innovator. First, there are three principal *skills* that innovators need to develop: leadership, communication, and project management. Second, innovators also display certain personal *characteristics* that allow them to take a broader perspective of their responsibilities. They think strategically. They may be engineers or scientists or marketers, but they can wear the business hat when necessary. They are masters in some discipline but knowledgeable across many other disciplines, and they learn to do and do to learn. The need for these characteristics depends on the scope and type of innovation. The bottom-up innovator will require an oversupply of these characteristics.

Third, there are *attitudes* that allow the innovator to manage the

Figure 10.1. Put-it-all-together competence.

Skills	Characteristics	Attitudes	Knowledge
Leadership	Opportunity finders	Flexibility	Major field of interest
Communications	Problem solvers	Agility	Related technical fields
Project management	Powers of observation	Reliability	Manufacturing
	Ability to conceptualize	Integrity	Marketing
	Analyzers	Respect	Evaluation
	Synthesizers	Anticipation	Gaining support
	Inventive	Environmental cues	Sponsor
	Self-motivated	Accuracy	Peers and colleagues
	Strategic thinkers	Toward colleagues	Decision processes
	Tacticians	Divergent thinking	Business practice
	Business orientation	Other cultures	Make the complex simple
	Strong work ethic	Continuous learning	Managing time
	Integrating knowledge and practice	Proactive	Setting priorities
	Polite aggressiveness	Commitment	Project management
			Concept to commercialization process
			Product development process
			Systems thinking

innovation process. And the fourth element is *knowledge*, which is the essence of innovation. The ability to observe the environment and uncover opportunities depends on the breadth of knowledge. These four elements are interrelated and define the put-it-all-together competence. The innovator needs to possess some minimum level of each.

Skills

Leadership, communication, and project management skills give the innovators a head start in gaining acceptance of their ideas. People who can be pathfinders and look to the future, communicate that vision, and manage their projects from a strategic perspective reduce the obstacles in gaining support from management and their colleagues and peers. Communication skills are a necessary element of leadership and project management. Leadership demands high levels of competence in communicating at all levels of the organization. Project management skills provide the tools.

Leadership in Innovation

Leadership is often classified into three categories: strategic, visionary, and managerial. Where does leadership in innovation fit into this classification? What kind of leadership does the innovator demonstrate? Innovative entrepreneurs usually demonstrate all three types. Vision (what do you want to be), strategy (how will you get there), and management (providing the resources and the infrastructure) describe innovation leadership in the three subclasses of technology, marketing, and business.

Management researchers and consultants attempt to differentiate between leadership and management and treat the two as independent functions. The act of managing can be divided into three interlocking components: leadership, direction, and administration. The innovator, by the very essence of the actions required of the innovator, fulfills the role of the manager. Leadership is one component of the management triad. It involves pathfinding and determining how to travel that path; it is not some esoteric management activity that results in a vision statement. Without the leadership component, managing becomes the domain of the caretaker or the bureaucrat. Leadership is a state of mind and makes demands on the person who provides it. Leadership involves going beyond the accepted facts, opinions, processes, rituals, and the chosen flavor of the day. Academic research on leadership usually deals with management. No known research studies relate to the leadership role of the innovator. Experience tells us that innovation depends on the leadership displayed by the innovator.

There are two types of leadership that the innovator provides: leadership in innovation and leadership in the business of the firm. Leadership in innovation doesn't require being a multidisciplinary specialist. It does require a knowledge base and the skills and competencies to promote innovation. It requires the ability to separate from the pack, think independently, and often take a position contrary to the consensus. This takes a high level of maturity, a modicum of diplomacy, the ability to accept criticism as well as possible mental abuse, and the courage to disregard the naysayers. The following quotation from an unknown source applies to innovators and leadership: "The bird that never learns to get around in its environment, that is to fly, will never go far."

Innovators also have an opportunity to provide business leadership. Successful innovation that is adequately rewarded motivates others to pursue the same pattern of accomplishment. While providing leadership in the business may not be the goal of the innovator, it can be an added benefit. Innovators bring a set of special skills to the table. Successful innovators have the ability to take an idea, turn it inside out, turn it upside down, rotate it, and manipulate it until the idea makes sense. This type of thinking can be contagious if allowed to grow, but it cannot be micromanaged. That talent can also be used to search out those opportunities disregarded by the rank and file. As a colleague of mine once remarked, "Too many managers pull up the plants every morning to see how the roots are growing."

Developing leadership skills in innovation and being that pathfinder requires that innovators do less clicking and dragging, exit their cubicles, and gain an understanding of the world in which they operate. Managers suggest that everyone should "think outside the box," but before anyone can think outside the box they need to get out of the box. Innovation does not take place in isolation. Knowledge of what is going on in those other cubicles cannot be disregarded. Innovation leadership requires listening to what others are saying.

Leadership has little to do with position in the organization or society. The September 11, 2001 terrorist attacks have led to countless acts of leadership and heroism by "ordinary" people. One does not decide to become a leader at any one point in time. Leadership takes on many different forms and depends on being able to take advantage of the opportunities when presented. But leaders do possess certain attributes and traits that allow them to take that opportunity to lead. The following list of attributes applies generally to all leaders in industry. These same attributes apply to innovators.

1. *Accept responsibility and accountability.* The rose must be pinned on someone.

2. *Don't kill the messenger.* While bad news is difficult to accept, if it is accepted immediately, it creates a minimum negative impact. Time really is of the essence.

3. *Make judgments based on acceptable facts.* Leaders can't wait until all the facts have been accumulated. Some minimum level is required. The rest is judgment even with the support of a host of sophisticated models, simulations, and computer programs.

4. *Make the complex simple.* Make the complex easy to understand. The essence needs to be communicated.

5. *Follow through with clear decisions.* Eliminate any hidden meanings. The decision may not be acceptable, but it must be understood. Acceptance involves understanding the implications.

6. *Challenge the so-called experts.* Experts have their place, but they also have agendas. They may be experts of the past and not focused on the future.

7. *Understand that the devil is in the details.* Attending to details is boring but essential. Poor project performance often results from a lack of follow-through on details.

8. *Develop a proactive philosophy.* Leaders exhibit a proactive stance. It is too late to become proactive when an emergency

arises. That emergency might have been avoided if someone had been proactive.

9. *Obsolete the present before its time.* It's difficult to obsolete products, processes, and activities that at one time provided significant benefit. Timely obsolescence prevents future crises.

10. *Promote a positive attitude.* Look for solutions, not scapegoats. Blame only creates discord and destroys relationships. Those responsible must be held accountable, but the problem requires a solution. Focus on the resolving the problem.

How do innovators develop these leadership skills? They learn by trying and doing. Not everyone has the capacity to take on a leadership role. People satisfied with the status quo should probably recognize their limitations in providing leadership and become constructive followers who fully understand the goals of the leaders. Developing leadership qualities requires what I call a *pay-as-you-go-plan.* It begins with minor efforts that look to the future. The plan often begins early in life—some children have a penchant for doing more than is expected, show the courage to go against the mainstream, and display a sense of curiosity about the world and how it functions. As an adult, it's time to propose some ideas that might change the name of the game in some aspect of the business and see what happens. But know the limitations. Everybody in the chain of command cannot be alienated. A Ph.D. in leadership is not the answer. The mind-set and the challenge provide the stimulus to continue in spite of the odds.

Bob Lutz, former chairman and president of Chrysler Corporation, stated, "Chrysler's return to prosperity was engineering driven."[2] He could just as well have said that Chrysler's return to prosperity was innovation driven. The engineering effort took leadership to drastically alter those traditional and embedded work methods of doing engineering, meet the highest standards of innovation, and counter the opposition. The Chrysler effort was a display of innovation leadership by the innovators.

Communication Skills

If an idea cannot be communicated, it is of little value. Someone somehow must be able to clearly articulate not just the idea but also its importance to the organization. Communication involves more than being able to draft a simple letter. As Norm Augustine, retired Lockheed Martin Corporation CEO, reminded engineers, "In my career, I've seen engineers do a beautiful piece of work, and then make it sound like garbage when they write it up."[3] While this statement was directed to engineers in relation to written reports, it applies across the board to all professions and to all segments of the population. CEOs, executives, and managers are not excluded. Every profession seems to have its own language and its preferred list of acronyms. How many different things do those same acronyms suggest? Readers often must simply guess what the author means. In one form or another, innovators need to communicate their idea and that communication cannot be the same for every listener. There's not much point in discussing technology or marketing if the listener has no background with which to make a judgment. Communication is a two-way street, and the interests of the communicator and the listener need to be aligned.

But communication involves more than the written word. The ability to communicate effectively in many different formats cannot be overemphasized. There are five basic types of communication:

1. Oral

2. Written

3. Graphic

4. Listening

5. Reading

Oral. Oral communication is probably the most important. We spend a great deal of time in face-to-face communication. Whether the content of the communication passes on information, gives specific instructions as to how to perform a particular task, or attempts to sell an idea, listeners must understand the message. Effective oral communication is not learned from reading; it requires practice. It requires attention to the choice of words. It requires feedback from the listener.

Oral communication often lacks the required specificity. Too often what should take one sentence goes into extended and unrelated commentary. Too often more information is being provided than what is necessary. Too often the important part of the communication gets lost in detailed minutiae. Too often the original comment is repeated without adding any additional information.

How and where do people learn to improve their oral communication? The first rule is to just answer the question that was asked. All the background isn't required unless essential. If the question was vague, ask for a clarification. Many educational organizations provide instruction in effective oral speaking. It only takes practice.

Written. Written communication takes many different forms. It includes general correspondence, documentation of various types, reports, proposals, operating instructions, manuals, specifications, and formal presentations. While clear writing is a requirement, the format, scope, and amount of detail may be quite different. Writing for the audience usually creates the major problem for innovators. The innovator's audience will most likely include people whose needs are different and whose level of comprehension may also be quite different. The objective should be to deliver the message with the least amount of professional jargon. If it's impossible to circumvent the jargon, the innovator probably has not reduced the concept to its essentials. The communication must meet the needs of the receiver. The extensive use of e-mail has destroyed much of the clarity in the written word. The writer has failed if the receiver does not comprehend what was written.

Graphic. Graphics communicate ideas without the use of extensive verbiage. However, it is becoming a lost art among technical professionals—sketching an idea on a napkin during lunch is no longer in fashion. Many years ago those paper napkins at lunch were a source of ideas. Those involved were engaged. Today, it appears that the napkin has been replaced with a computer and software packages, and results in statements like "We'll have to delay that thought until we return to the office." Using graphical language can often provide a more effective medium for explaining a concept. The adage, a picture is worth a thousand words, cannot be disputed. New tools to simplify the work are essential, but we shouldn't forget what can be communicated using that proverbial napkin and a simple pencil with an eraser.

Listening. Let's face it; it's difficult to listen when we have so much to say. Listening is more difficult if the speaker doesn't cut to the chase or we've heard the message before, maybe even several times. However, listening is a necessary skill for the innovator. The nonessential can be filtered but even the innovator should listen to those often irritating messages; there might just be a kernel of truth that stirs the imagination.

Reading. Reading continues to provide us with one of the best methods of generating relationships and creating ideas. Reading is just another means for acquiring information. Not everything that's printed is worth reading and choices must be made. Each of us can name a number of publications that force us to think. Those publications may not be related to our professions, but they still provide the stimulus for creative thought. Scanning that periodical or that newspaper often provides new information for the innovator. That simple act of scanning may lead the innovator to sources of information related to a specific innovation. Those sources may even provide information relative to the innovator's work. Remember the Tylenol incident some years ago when Johnson & Johnson removed Tylenol from the shelves to prevent any further deaths? Consider the innovation that occurred as a result of new regulations for preventing tampering with products before being opened by the purchaser. Anyone who read about the incident and had any sense of the potential market for new safety packaging couldn't help thinking about how to improve product safety.

Is All This Necessary?

You may wonder, how can I innovate with all of these communication requirements? If you haven't learned to communicate effectively in each of these modes, chances are you'll need to find someone who can be your surrogate communicator. I stress the communication aspects of innovation because the innovator's success depends on good communication. Ideas require making explanations to many people who come from different disciplines. The typical high school or college educational program does not include significant requirements in science and mathematics, so a large percentage of people lack sensitivity to the technology issues. At the same time, the technically educated lack the ability to bypass the jargon. The idea or concept must must hit someone's hot button. You have your personal examples of the impact of miscommunication. Innovators are not expected to be orators, literary giants, or artists—they need basic communication skills to tell their story to many different types of people.

Project Management

Project management principles that include only meeting specifications and providing on-time delivery within estimated costs will not be sufficient in the twenty-first century. Dr. Aaron J. Shenhar suggests that today's dynamic business environment requires taking a strategic approach to project management.[4] The strategic framework focuses attention on creating competitive advantage in the marketplace rather than just getting the job done.

Strategic project management is based on six principles:

1. *Leadership.* Turn project managers into project leaders. Make them totally responsible for business results—not just the typical results relating to meeting the agreed-upon deliverables, on time, and at estimated cost.

2. *Strategy.* Define the competitive advantage of your product and articulate a detailed project strategy to win in the marketplace.

3. *Spirit.* Articulate a meaningful and exciting product vision. Develop a project spirit to support the vision and create energy and motivation.

4. *Adaptation.* Assess the environment in relation to economic, competitive, political, geographic, and other variables as required. Classify your project as to market uncertainty, technological uncertainty, project complexity, and pace.

5. *Integration.* Create a strategic hierarchical plan that is driven by the strategy and includes spirit, organization, processes, and tools. Integration involves consideration of cost, time, quality, and risk, as well as product design, systems engineering, customer connection, testing, manufacturing, and customer acceptance.

6. *Learning.* Create a project-learning organization. Every monitoring and controlling activity includes lessons learned.

Even though most projects begin with a project plan, strategy seldom receives any consideration. Projects are executed in a competitive environment. Typically, the project outcome—whether a product, process, or service—faces some level of competition in the marketplace. So the question becomes how to differentiate between competitive products and then decide on the approach that provides the greatest benefit based on the organization's resources, infrastructure, and competencies. How do you gain a competitive advantage? This involves strategic thinking.

Developing a strategy is about winning in the marketplace. It's about being successful. Every project requires a plan. But the plan is not the strategy. Project strategy occurs at a higher level than the project plan. Project plans include decisions about activities, and statements about the resources, the timing, the deliverables, and all those details that must be integrated to meet the requirements. Project strategy drives the project plan. It involves defining the critical elements for developing a competitive advantage and establishing the pattern of behavior that is needed for winning in the marketplace. A good strategy focuses on both effectiveness and efficiency. Effectiveness comes from making the right choices, and efficiency is achieved during the execution of the many activities involved in the project. Strategic project management involves four distinct elements of project strategy: product definition/competitive advantage, business perspective, project/scope definition, and strategic focus.

• *Product Definition/Competitive Advantage.* At this stage it's necessary to identify the objectives, the competitive advantage and value added, the product vision, the product type, the functional requirements, cost-effectiveness, and product specifications.

• *Business Perspective.* What are the expectations of the project when completed? This statement specifies what is to be achieved in the marketplace. Yes, technology is important but success lives in the province of the marketplace.

• *Project/Scope Definition.* Projects need to have established boundaries to be successful. The boundaries cannot be left to chance. Scope describes the work that is to be accomplished as well as what will not be included. Typically, this involves developing a statement of work (SOW) and a work breakdown structure (WBS).

Uncertainties related to market, project complexity, and technology must be identified. The project pace depends on the competition.

  • *Strategic Focus.* The last part of project strategy creates a set of behavioral guidelines to achieve the competitive advantage. Strategic focus involves four components: position, policy, behavior, and processes.

Although many companies and project managers are employing strategic thinking in the project management process, making it an explicit part of the process involves challenging many current assumptions. Project strategy that is linked to business strategy contributes to improved business results. This change in perspective enhances the role of project managers and provides them with opportunities to have a greater impact on business performance. Managing projects strategically provides a challenge, but the payoff is the potential of significantly better results.

Characteristics

Innovators, like all humans, do possess certain characteristics. Obviously, the degree to which each innovator possesses each of these characteristics will vary. Some talent, a bit of luck, and a lot of hard work are required to reach the top of any profession. It is true that some get there through nepotism or who know how to play the political game to their advantage, but innovators seldom fall into either of these categories. Figure 10-1 lists the desirable innovator characteristics that I have identified through my years as a 3M executive and in consulting practice.

Opportunity Finders and Problem Solvers

Professionals in all fields generally meet the requirements in problem solving. These professionals do the job they're asked to do. Doing what you're asked to do is certainly the easy way out. A nine-to-five workday with only occasional unpaid overtime allows for a comfortable lifestyle. But that philosophy hardly fits that of the innovator. This dynamic and technologically oriented world economy needs more than problem solvers. It needs the opportunity and problem finders, who then also participate as the problem solvers.

Problem solvers are essential to the innovation process. A large cadre of people is needed to solve the problems, and they come from the middle hump of the normal distribution curve. They perform a valuable and essential service, but the organization requires more than these problem solvers. The problem solvers are often referred to, disparagingly, as plodders, but they keep the organization from spinning out of orbit. An organization could not survive without them, but at the same time it will not progress if they are the only source of energy.

The future of the organization depends on the opportunity finders, regardless of their discipline or level in the organization. Finding those new opportunities whether related to products and their processes, markets, and management requires people who have the ability to question intelligently. Not many people think about the future or about defining some new activity. The problem and opportunity finders demonstrate critical powers of observation, conceptualization, and information-synthesizing skills.

Powers of Observation

Why powers of observation? New ideas come from the ability to observe relationships in many different environments. For experimenters, observation becomes the key for future developments. Innovation occurs when observations are finally integrated into an idea. Observation involves more than looking around; it involves looking around and seeing something different than what most people see. Some years ago researchers thought they would be more effective if they allowed technicians to perform and monitor their experimental work. Most programs were less than successful. Yes, the technicians could follow through all the routine steps and record the data, but technicians in observing their experiments did not really know what to look for—they lacked prior knowledge to give them a base from which to observe. Innovation involves knowledge and synthesis of information in its many forms (visual, graphic, written, spoken) from many different sources that eventually are integrated into some definable idea. The process does not lend itself to some mechanistic approach. Those observations may have taken place over many years and at some point in time germinate into an idea.

Ability to Conceptualize

Innovation begins with an idea or a group of ideas, but another critical step is translating an idea into a concept. The idea must be visualized as meeting some set of requirements. Someone may have had an idea for a new widget, but until that idea is conceptualized in relation to usefulness, the technologies, the marketing and distribution issues, and the financial requirements, it continues to remain an idea. The transition from idea to concept represents a tremendous amount of detail that must be organized according to some scheme and scrutinized for validity. The transition involves a combination of creativity and attention to detail that cannot be disregarded.

The Thomas Edison Laboratories provide an excellent example of converting ideas to concepts to inventions. The laboratory is a good example of innovation by design. The methods were relatively unsophisticated and involved a great deal of cut-and-dry activity. If one experiment failed to meet the requirements, another followed and each provided an additional piece of information. Even the negative results proved that there was one less experiment to run. The tools were primitive compared to today's computer-aided design programs that have eliminated much of the drudgery in proving a concept. But the ideas flowed. Some of the inventions that came from the Edison Laboratories include the carbon button telephone transmitter, the incandescent lamp, the phonograph, motion picture devices, and the dictating machine.

Not everyone has the ability to conceptualize. To establish your own ability to conceptualize, think of an idea and then develop it into a concept that would lead to an invention. Invention consists of putting the known into a new form—a way of packaging the known into something new.

Analysis and Synthesis

There certainly is no shortage of analysts in any of the professional disciplines. The problem occurs when we look for people who can synthesize information from many diverse sources. Examples of a lack of ability to synthesize appear in all disciplines. How about the engineer who cannot synthesize the requirements from different engineering disciplines into a workable specification? Consider the product manager who cannot convert the technical and marketing analyses into a coherent business plan, or the scientist who conceives a brilliant technical solution that no one would buy.

Analysis is essential but synthesis of facts into a workable program demands a particular type of talent. Analysts are plentiful, but synthesizers are in short supply. Synthesizers require breadth of knowledge as contrasted to depth. The most capable technical or marketing person may not be able to integrate the needs of both groups. Each looks at personal priorities rather than the requirements to meet the needs of both groups. Every organization can document the wasted effort because of the conflicts that occur between the technology and marketing sides of the organization. While such conflicts can be managed by directive, someone with knowledge of the technology and marketing issues could make a more appropriate decision. The question will not be resolved by consensus within the appropriate time limits; the question will be answered when the needs of those involved are met satisfactorily.

Inventive

Are inventors creative or are creative people inventors? The resolution to this issue goes well beyond the scope of this book. Innovation has been described as a process that goes from an idea to a concept to an invention and finally to an innovation. Many different attributes can be ascribed to inventors. Inventors are intuitive thinkers in their particular area of interest, a trait that stems from a sense of inquisitiveness. Inventors are problem oriented; they not only look for problems, they look for solutions. They like to discuss ideas for the simple sake of discussing ideas. The notes on those luncheon napkins provide a source of energy.

Self-Motivated

Motivation drives innovation. Self-motivation drives innovators, and they demonstrate that motivation in different ways. They seldom require being pushed to make progress, but a watchful eye from an immediate supervisor with an interest in the potential innovation can help keep the self-motivation clock running. Innovation is an uphill struggle toward a goal and innovators have their moments when the end seems out of sight. This self-motivation helps them pursue their goal in spite of setbacks. It takes a lot of setbacks to make innovators give up the chase for a new product or something else that they have decided to pursue. Self-motivated innovators possess self-confidence, a sense of passion that they have the answer to some major breakthrough, and a basic philosophy of going beyond what is expected.

Business Orientation

Innovation by definition is about the future of the firm. Innovators wear many different hats, but the business hat differentiates the innovators from other organizational professionals. While some marketing people will choose to wear the business hat, not all are prepared for it by education or interest. Engineers tend to shy away from the business hat; they prefer to focus on technology. But innovation is about implementation and commercialization. There is an end result that must somehow provide a benefit.

What does putting on the business hat mean? Very simply, it means keeping the end result in mind from a system perspective. Each piece of the puzzle may stand alone, but it also interacts with others so those interfaces must be rationalized. If one of the pieces of the puzzle is missing, the total effort may have been in vain.

Strategic Thinkers

Strategic thinking is not normally associated with innovators. Strategic thinking is not strategic planning. Strategic thinking clarifies and points the direction; it charts the course and makes allowances for deviation in that course. Strategic thinking also describes the process. Charting the course without describing the process by which to proceed on that course leads to undertaking many false starts. A new product innovation must fit into the strategic direction as described by the organization. The marketing and technology expectations must also fit the organization's strategic direction. Why the organization should pursue this particular innovation is a strategic decision. If some level of strategic thinking takes place in the idea to concept stage, the organization can more easily determine its feasibility. Strategic decisions cannot wait until the innovation reaches the project or launch stages.

Tactician

What does it mean to be a tactician? It means deciding how the job will be accomplished. Innovators need to know how to bootleg resources—all of those resources discussed in Chapter 8. They also need to know how to use the organization's infrastructure system, as discussed in Chapter 9. Resources will not be provided on a silver platter. The infrastructure may inhibit the innovator, but that's just one more challenge. Much of what the innovator requires can be obtained through networks, but those networks need to be identified and cultivated. Strategy is essential, but tactics drive the innovation process to a conclusion.

Strong Work Ethic

Innovation is not for the weak in spirit. A strong work ethic is essential but doesn't necessarily mean working around the clock for months or even years. Innovators are often described as being tenacious, committed, and resolute in their pursuit of their goal. These qualities are essential. But a good work ethic also involves capitalizing on the talents of other people. The innovator does not have all the answers, so the sooner other knowledgeable sources are brought into the process the sooner that idea can lead to an innovation. Working under adverse conditions may be necessary. Diligent and persistent acquisition of new knowledge, expertise, and resources is not an option—it's a must. Recognizing personal limitations regarding knowledge and skills allows the innovator to provide for those limitations through others. Such actions allow the innovator to drive to conclusions rather than become frustrated from lack of understanding.

Integrating Knowledge and Practice

Innovation is a practitioner's art—it's not theory. Knowledge and expertise come from practice. While knowledge of innovation can provide the basic understanding, doing innovation takes practice. Like any activity, acquiring the facts is only the beginning. Knowledge and practice follow an exponential curve. Knowledge accrues from doing and learning and doing and learning and so on.

Polite Aggressiveness

Aggressive is a word that appears on many personal appraisal forms. Human resource professionals don't really like the word. Comments usually relate to overaggressiveness rather than insufficient aggressiveness. How strange that someone would complain about an employee being too aggressive. Aggressiveness doesn't compromise respect for people, and it doesn't constitute a breach of acceptable behavior. Was anything ever accomplished without some individual being aggressive? Wouldn't it be more exciting if more people demonstrated higher degrees of aggressiveness?

Innovators by their very nature display some level of aggressiveness. If they were not aggressive, they probably would not be innovators. Anyone who proposes change of any kind will most likely be considered aggressive—and that should be considered a compliment. To be aggressive does not imply being discourteous, disrespectful, impolite, rude, divisive, or disparaging. An innovator may disagree with a colleague or a manager, perhaps even violently disagree, but that disagreement cannot become personal. Significant differences in thinking cannot become personal vendettas. Innovators need to practice a kind of polite aggressiveness. Those who do not understand or support the innovator cannot be considered as unintelligent, unthinking, unreceptive, unreasoning, or irrational people. Innovation involves something new—something not proposed previously. If that proposed innovation affects the status quo, objections will be raised.

Attitudes

Attitude describes the manner in which we approach any activity, whether at home, in the workplace, or in any group of people. Attitudes usually lie on a continuum from positive to negative, from cheerful to moody, from inactive to proactive, and the like. These attitudes determine the success or failure of any innovation. Negative, moody, or reactive attitudes will not generate any support. Attitude defines our personalities and determines relations with colleagues and peers. Moderate discipline competence with the right attitude can often accomplish the impossible. All the knowledge and experience without an appropriate attitude often leads to failure.

Any innovation effort spans a continuum that includes the individual at one end and the group or project team at the other end. Ideas come from individuals; innovation depends on people working together—the team. Innovators need to demonstrate positive attitudes to gain support.

Attitudes include some of the following actions:

- *Adopt a flexible attitude.* You need to show sufficient flexibility, but not so much as to get away from the basic principles.

- *Develop an agile approach.* The times require meeting commitments even in the face of frequent changes.

- *Make reliability your mantra.* You can't build a track record without it, because others need to be able to depend on you.

- *Practice absolute integrity in dealing with people.* Tell the whole story and stick to the facts. The future of the innovator depends on it.

- *Treat colleagues with respect.* Shoddy behavior will return to haunt you.

- *Anticipate needs and events.* This is not about predicting the future, but it involves keeping the senses open.

- *Observe the environment and take the cues.* The internal and external environments provide cues as to direction and business philosophy. You need to know how they affect your performance.

- *Focus on accuracy.* Your signature is on everything you do. Accuracy builds or destroys your credibility.

- *Create opportunities for others.* You may be the innovator, but bring others along and give them credit where due.

- *Accept divergent thinking.* You may or may not be right, and you may learn something of value from others.

- *Accept and understand other cultures.* If working across national boundaries, understand the culture you're working with.

- *Be open to continuous learning.* Innovation should be a continuous learning experience for the innovator.

- *Adopt a proactive stance.* Take the lead; the words *inactive* and *reactive* should not be in your vocabulary.

- *Meet commitments.* If you make a commitment, keep it. Results are the way to demonstrate commitment.

The Innovator's Knowledge Base

The innovation success equation requires acceptable multidiscipline knowledge related to organizational functions, management processes of innovation, and general business practices. Innovators do need some acceptable level of competence, and the level depends on the specific organization, its objectives, its infrastructure, and the innovation under consideration. Not all innovations require the same knowledge base. Most are unique in some sense. An innovation like Post-it Notes in an industrial environment like 3M required quite a different knowledge base than the successful launch of the robotic explorer Sojourner for the Mars Pathfinder Mission. Innovation in the petroleum process industries will be quite different from innovation in chip manufacturing, whether computer chips or potato chips.

Knowledge is more than book learning. But knowledge solely in a specific discipline is insufficient to bring an idea to the marketplace. Knowledge from many disciplines will be required. The innovator need not be a master of all things, but needs to be totally aware of the knowledge associated with purposeful and effective innovation. This knowledge base includes:

- *Major field of interest.* Knowledge in some field of major interest—whether learned formally or informally—is key.

- *Related technical fields.* The complex interrelationship of technologies that go into even the simplest of products requires some understanding of related disciplines.

- *Manufacturing.* Some minimal understanding of the manufacturing requirements, or relying on someone who can raise the issues in the early innovation stages is needed.

- *Marketing.* Markets and marketing drive innovation. Market size, customer requirements, and distribution channel issues require attention.

- *Evaluation or justification.* Substitute evaluation for justification. Innovation involves risks that are not amenable to simple justification criteria.

- *Gaining support.* Some minimum level of understanding of human behavior can ease the road to success. The innovator cannot do it alone.

- *Sponsor.* Innovators need to know how to work with a sponsor. A consistent track record, coupled with total honesty and integrity, is the entry price of admission.

- *Peers and colleagues.* Innovators need to know the competencies of their peers and colleagues, whose level of knowledge is important.

- *Decision processes.* Decision process tools, though helpful, are often insufficient. Compromises among disciplines require judgment.

- *General business practices.* Know where the organization is going and how it plans to get there—its purposes, objectives, strategies, and operations.

- *Making the complex simple.* Simplification—in all activities—tests the competency of the innovator and the organization. Ignore the nonessential.

- *Managing time.* Too often emphasis is placed on the tools of time management. Although time management is important, the use of time, total time, and timing of new product introductions require greater attention.

- *Setting priorities.* Not all aspects of an innovation have the same priority. Resolve those unresolved issues now.

- *Project management.* Successful innovation depends on employing the fundamentals of project management, especially the front-end effort. It's not tools and techniques, but thinking.

- *Product concept to commercialization process.* This process is contextual. Innovators need to understand the working of that process.

- *Product development process.* For guidance, use the lists that suggest details about developing the purposes, objectives, and strategies; developing the framework; doing the up-front work; and managing project reviews.

- *Systems thinking.* Innovation takes place within an organizational system. Innovators must also take a systems approach to innovation. Single-issue emphasis doesn't work.

Managers continually search for the appropriate combination of skills, characteristics, attitudes, and knowledge that define innovator competence. Balancing these elements of innovator competence presents a significant challenge. The role of the innovator is a difficult but rewarding one for the right person. We can see from the requirements that not many people will subject themselves to the rigors of being an innovator. Even though the requirements are difficult to meet, that's not a reason to fear becoming an innovator.

Innovator as a Career Option

Is innovation a career option? The answer can by yes, no, or maybe. It depends on the individual. It depends on what the individual brings to the table and the people who are sitting at the table. We do know that innovators possess a particular kind of drive and a passion for pursuing some type of effort. We don't know the when, how, or where innovators come up with that idea that leads to innovation. We do know that coming up with an idea usually requires a significant gestation period—it's generally not a "Eureka!"

Innovators like all other people go through career stages. A professional from any discipline begins a career with knowledge and not much experience. There are those few who from birth, it seems, pursued some endeavor that led to invention or innovation. There are those few who had work opportunities either prior or during their college years that gave them a head start. Although innovation is not related to any specific time in a career, it usually occurs after some years of experience. Knowledge by itself is usually insufficient in some professions. Knowledge must be coupled with real-world experiences and that requires acquiring a different kind of knowledge. This is what is commonly known as street smarts. It's knowledge that is gained through experience, through learning about the linkages that a particular profession has to other professions.

For example, take the case of the newly minted engineer—four years in engineering college, good academic record, personable, ambitious, and ready to get involved in new product development. It's probably difficult for this person to be the innovator. Some breadth of knowledge of the organization and the industry is probably essential. However, this does not imply that this neophyte cannot make a major technical contribution. This is where the action begins—gaining an understanding of the system in which the work is performed. How management nurtures this early career period usually governs the future of the individual's contribution to innovation.

Opportunity to Innovate

Having the competencies to be an innovator and having the opportunity are quite different. The following survey questions allow potential innovators to assess the opportunities for innovation that exist within their organization. The survey is provided as a guide.

Innovation Survey

1. How important is innovation to your organization? (*Very important? Important? Not important?*)

2. Is the word *innovation* in your organization's mission or vision statement?

                                                          YES   NO

3. Does your organization focus on technical innovation?

                                                          YES   NO

4. Does your organization focus on market innovation?

                                                          YES   NO

5. Does your organization focus on manufacturing process innovation?

                                                          YES   NO

6. Does your organization focus on business operations innovation?

                                                          YES   NO

7. Does your organization view innovation from a systems perspective?

                                                          YES   NO

8. Is innovation in any form one of your organization's top priorities?

        YES   NO

9. Does innovation play a critical role in your organization's competitive advantage?

        YES   NO

10. Is the CEO driving innovation?

        YES   NO

11. Are managers driving innovation?

        YES   NO

12. Is there sufficient innovation to maintain a sustainable and profitable organization?

        YES   NO

13. What are the sources of innovation in your organization? (*Check all that apply.*)
__ Research
__ Development
__ Marketing
__ Other technical staff
__ Executive management
__ Other management

14. Does anyone in the organization have specific responsibility for promoting innovation?

        YES   NO

If YES, what is the professional background of this person?

15. What does the majority of innovation focus on?
a) Current lines of products
b) New products

16. Is the organization pursuing leading-edge technologies?

        YES   NO

17. Are investments in innovation based on short-term or long-term opportunities?
    a) Short term
    b) Long term

18. Is the organization's management knowledgeable about what it takes to develop an environment that supports innovation?

    YES   NO

19. Where is the major emphasis placed on innovation in your organization?
    a) Technology
    b) Markets
    c) Business operations
    d) Products
    e) Processes
    f) Other

20. Does the organization have a set of metrics for measuring innovation?

    YES   NO

21. Are these metrics used to improve future innovation management issues?

    YES   NO

22. Does your organization consider number of patents issued annually as a metric for innovation?

    YES   NO

23. How does the organization promote innovation? (*Check all that apply.*)
    __ Ad hoc sponsorship
    __ Formal programs
    __ Scheduled sessions on innovation
    __ Recapping the innovation successes
    __ Individual recognition
    __ Team recognition

24. Does the organization have any formal programs to educate the employees about innovation?

    YES   NO

25. If YES, which of the following topics are included? (*Check all that apply.*)
    ___ Fundamentals of innovation
    ___ What it takes to be an innovator
    ___ Innovation history of the organization
    ___ How innovations occur
    ___ Review of internal case history
    ___ Lessons learned
    ___ What innovation has done for the organization
    X ___ Your future depends on innovation

26. Are innovators recognized in the organization?

    YES   NO

27. Do your company policies support the innovator—the constructive maverick, the pathfinder, the one who thinks outside the box?

    YES   NO

28. Does your management spend sufficient time on innovation related to:

Technology	YES	NO
Marketing	YES	NO
Business	YES	NO
Human resources	YES	NO

29. Does your management take a single-issue or systems approach to innovation?
    a) Single-issue approach
    b) Systems approach

30. Does the organization focus on incremental innovation or the breakthrough innovation?
    a) Incremental innovation
    b) Breakthrough innovation

The Innovator's Challenge

Imagine for a moment that you're an employee of 3M. You've been successful as an innovator at the incremental level and even had a new-to-the-market product that exceeded expectations. You have a good track record within your own division and you're no stranger to the executive suites; they know who you are and what you've accomplished. You have always focused on the future. You're well respected by 3M management and your peers and colleagues.

Imagine now that you have come up with an idea for a new product that could replace Post-it Notes. What will you do? You have this innovation in mind that eventually electronic media will completely eliminate the use of paper. 3M doesn't publish sales figures of Post-it Notes but industry rumors suggest that annual sales are someplace around a billion dollars. What are your chances of gaining support at any level? Probably not very good at the first encounter. Your immediate manager probably wouldn't want to touch it. What are your chances of gaining support? Should you drop the innovation or pursue it?

If you're really an innovator, you probably will not be discouraged. You keep thinking about it. It keeps you awake at night. So you continue to look for ways to pursue your innovation. You realize that the technologies you need may not be available for some time. Past history tells you that products do have a limited life. Popular products are constantly being replaced. New technologies obsolete old ones. The question you ponder: How can I introduce the new product innovation that could conceivably be a much bigger market than Post-it Notes without destroying the current product line? Do you try to make a case for pursuing this effort incrementally or do you make a decision to suggest that you have a replacement for Post-it Notes?

Even at a company as supportive of innovations as 3M, it would take a very secure person with a great deal of courage to pursue this effort, and you realize that you will need to think in the box, outside the box, and outside the cubicle. As you think about your innovation, you recall a panorama of other innovative ideas that have been scoffed at by management in the past. Can you show that your innovation will exceed the current sales and profits of Post-it Notes? Can you make a good argument to allow you to at least take the next steps in pursuing the innovation?

You happen to believe that at some time in the future all paper products will be eliminated. Although you've preached this gospel for many years, you haven't made very many converts. The nonbelievers remind you of how paper consumption has increased since the birth of the computer industry and related information technologies. You are positive of one thing, however: At some time in the future, a replacement for Post-it Notes will hit the marketplace and the time to begin the work effort is now.

Summary

Innovators need to know the risks of entering the innovation arena. It may be impossible to contemplate all the requirements to qualify as an innovator. Like all humans, innovators grow as they go through various stages of a career. The innovator's first project will not involve the equivalent of putting man on the moon. Those who choose to exercise their creativity in pushing toward the leading edge of whatever profession must keep focusing on developing the necessary skills, characteristics, and attitudes throughout their career.

Notes

1. Joseph Bordogna, "The President's Column," Institute of Electrical and Electronics Engineers (IEEE), *The Institute*, August 1997.

2. Peter M. Tobia, "Robert Lutz Gives Engineers the Nod," Institute of Electrical and Electronics Engineers (IEEE), *Today's Engineer* 2, 1 (1999): 6–11.

3. P. M. McCarter, "Norm Augustine: Pathfinder Extraordinaire," *Today's Engineer* 1, 3 (1998).

4. Aaron Shenhar, "Project Management: A Strategic Approach," Institute of Electrical and Electronics Engineers (IEEE), *Engineering Management Society Newsletter* 50, 4 (1999): 6–11.

11

The Virtual Innovation Prevention Department

Somewhere in every organizational setting exists the virtual innovation prevention department, although it may be hidden from view. It is dominated by an eclectic group of people that might include the organization's CEO, other top-level executives, managers from all functions and disciplines, and other colleagues and peers. Yes, CEOs and executives can be found in the innovation prevention department, but a bigger surprise is that innovators themselves may be there as well. It may appear strange that innovators participate in this department's activities, but often innovators can be their own worst enemies. As shown in Chapter 10, innovators need to build certain relationships, and if those relationships are not built, the innovators will find it very difficult to move forward.

The department also houses all the practices that prevent innovation. These practices not only affect innovation but also the organization's ability to meet its obligations to its stakeholders. Innovation killers include:

Innovation problems

- Undetermined or vague strategies
- Conflicting priorities
- Leadership style that is too top-down or too laissez-faire
- Ineffective executive management team
- Undeveloped middle management
- Absence of business-oriented professionals in all disciplines
- Lack of trust
- Inadequate open communication

The impact of these organizational deficiencies on performance is self-evident—they occur within all organizations to greater or lesser degrees. But there are other more subtle innovation killers in this virtual department. Figure 11-1 lists some of the more troublesome roles of the virtual innovation prevention department. The following sections discuss the effect those roles have in an organization, and how an innovator can overcome them.

M

Resist Change

People, from the top of the organization to the bottom, generally fall someplace on a continuum between two extreme categories: those who cannot accept change and those who find it very difficult to live without change. Most people resist change unless the change benefits them in some way. Their immediate reaction to change may be to ask: Why mess up a good thing? Why take on any new work? Why create problems? They react without any regard for future implications of such thinking on the organization or the person. Fortunately or unfortunately, depending on your point of view, the future will not be the same as yesterday or today.

Successful organizations are prone to resist change and be complacent. After all, sales and profits are meeting projections, so why become concerned? There's money in the bank, employees are loyal, and the organization is respected internationally. But the days of continuous well-being seldom continue. Customers may continue to praise the organization and its products. The organization may be in the top ten on every survey that really counts. The executives may

Mngt. can't manage R & D staff

Figure 11-1. The roles of the virtual innovation prevention department.

Resist change
Refuse to obsolete new products
Reject new thinking
Focus on single issues
Disregard the blind spots
Be uninformed
Don't tolerate mavericks
Focus only on the next quarter results
Institutionalize traditions
Use inflexible hiring practices
Make it hard to find the decision makers
Use corporate accounting practices at all levels
Keep decision processes secret
Have an ineffective bureaucracy
Maintain a nonsupportive infrastructure
Keep organizational structures rigid
Don't allow anyone to break the rules
Don't integrate organizational capability
Refuse to buy innovation
Allow organizational politics to drive decisions
Organize infrastructure

---

not only be collegial business partners but also have common social commitments that in the past smoothed the way for congenial business relations—sociability superimposed on decision processes. But anything that begins at the top of the organization usually flows down throughout all levels of the organization. That attitude of self-satisfaction becomes contagious and too often indicates that the organization has hung up the "gone fishing" sign. In the meantime, the competition has not been hibernating, and, if anything, the jockeying for market share has become more aggressive.

Refuse to Obsolete Products

Not many organizations attempt to obsolete their own products when sales and profits are exceeding expectations. By obsoleting, I mean replacing an existing product with a new product that will increase revenue as well as profit—in other words, a product that makes the potential revenue pie much larger overall, rather than just slicing the same pie another way. Today's business headlines make us aware that a small downturn in the economy coupled with negative currency translations can create unexpected negative consequences in some organizations.

What happened to innovation during the last decade at Corning, Hewlett-Packard, 3M, Kodak, Motorola, Polaroid, Procter & Gamble, and Xerox? In essence, it appears that the flow of new-to-the-market products that generate new business and increase sales and profits dried up. In some cases the market approached saturation with the old products. Any product line, even though it has a long list of enhancements, has a limited life and eventually becomes a commodity in a market with low profit margins. The return on low-margin products cannot provide the return necessary to carry on the research required for the next generation of products. When Kodak introduced a new 35mm amateur film, the revenue pie remained about the same size—it was basically a replacement product. When Motorola introduces new cell phone models, the total pie remains about the same size.

3M is certainly considered one of the most innovative organizations. At one time the target was to achieve 25 percent of sales from products that were not available in the previous five years. This figure was eventually raised to 30 percent in four years. But many of these products were merely substitute products—line extensions that did not create new income streams. Including substitute products in such targets leads to a false sense of security. Also, many of these products produced sales levels too low for an organization of 3M's size. While such targets are good public relations material, they do little for the bottom line. Innovation needs to bring something new to the market, and that something new must be related to the organization's size. Those products approaching commodity status must be replaced, and that replacement process has to begin years before the product becomes obsolete.

Reject New Thinking

Do executives and managers (referred to hereafter as managers) accept new thinking? How much effort is required to convince managers of a new idea or concept? Are managers sufficiently open-minded to know how to handle new ideas? Do managers investigate ideas or arbitrarily make a judgment in the negative? Do managers ever think outside the traditional box? Do managers have firsthand knowledge of what is really going on in their area of responsibility? Do managers make major decisions from reports or from firsthand knowledge of the topic? These are serious questions that require thoughtful responses. Answering no to any one of these questions spells trouble for the innovator and the future of the organization. While it may not be necessary to throw out the old, the old has a limited life.

If managers are not open-minded about new thinking, the innovator must respond in a positive way. It is not sufficient to say that management doesn't understand what I want to do or doesn't accept new thinking, therefore there's no use in proposing anything new. One of the roles of the innovator is to overcome such an obstacle. Just about anything that is presented as new will be challenged in some way and for some reason. Accept that as a given. If the objection doesn't occur, then the innovator will be ahead of the game.

Although there may be resistance on the part of managers to pursue new ideas, it is necessary to understand why. Knowledge about the organization helps in making the decision to remain in the organization or look elsewhere. Even in the best of innovative organizations not every idea, regardless of its high potential for generating profits or new markets, will be funded.

Managers need to recognize that innovators can be a source of irritation—especially those who feel passionate about their idea or cause. They're evangelists. At every step, they push their cause. So, some people just object to their aggressiveness. But these irritants are necessary for the organization's survival. Call these people mavericks if you wish, but if they're productive mavericks, they must be accommodated for the good of the organization. The people who cherish the status quo will not grow the organization; they will not create the revenue that will pay tomorrow's payroll and guarantee a viable future for the organization.

Focus on Single Issues

Innovation involves more than conceiving a product and building a demo model or a prototype. Keep in mind that innovation = invention + implementation/commercialization. So a whole spectrum of issues arises that need to be resolved. Focusing on the product only as a single issue is insufficient. Most innovations are multidisciplinary and require many competencies and skills. So, managers need to think in terms of the system of disciplines the innovation will need for successful implementation and the environment in which the product will operate.

The system of disciplines includes all those disciplines that are essential to commercializing an invention. That invention does not necessarily involve a patent, although most major innovations include some level of patent protection. The system of disciplines includes all of the technical disciplines, the process disciplines associated with the product through manufacturing and production, the disciplines associated with the distribution of the product, and all the other administrative disciplines without which the product could never be produced or reach a customer. Managers need to be sensitive to the need for the expertise of other professionals. That critical mass of talent is essential.

Products perform some benefit or usefulness within a system, and so an innovator who only focuses on any single issue involved in the innovation process is bound to be disappointed. The product will require some applicable warranty or meantime between failure. The product will require maintenance. The product may require technical support. The product may involve certain specific safety requirements. The product may require meeting stricter standards, depending on global geographical location. The product may create environmental problems. The product at some time will most likely require disposal. The development of nuclear power plants provides an example of the importance of system considerations. The power industry decided to build nuclear plants, but it ignored the environment in which those plants would function. The system design never considered the issues related to the transportation or storage of spent fuel, a major oversight in making the plants a successful innovation.

Technology is of little value without marketing. Both are dependent on manufacturing capability. The customer becomes the ultimate judge of the product. The customer determines the future of the organization. Managers who ignore the system requirements pay a high price for their narrow focus and eventually are forced to meet the system requirements. It's not enough to make the bread dough. The bread dough needs an oven, a source of energy, and all its controls to make it a loaf of bread.

Disregard the Blind Spots

Disregarding personal blind spots can be as disastrous as disregarding a red light at the intersection, even for innovators. But managers' blind spots do more harm because they demotivate the people who are expected to be the innovators. The impact on the organization's output can be curtailed significantly if managers are unresponsive to new ideas and concepts. Regardless of which innovation you wish to consider, someone fought the management blind spots.

These blind spots also reflect on how organizations manage the innovation process. Peters and Waterman provide an example of a product innovation that required 223 reviews and approvals from seventeen different standing committees in order to develop it from an agreed-upon concept and bring it to the marketplace. Each of these 223 linkages taken individually probably made good sense but collectively created macro nonsense. Such actions not only create loss of market share but also defy logic.[1]

Think of the 1980s when some management decisions provided decidedly negative results. Electronic masters like RCA, Sylvania, and GE, once the leaders in vacuum tube technology, lost out on the transition to solid-state devices. Celanese replaced DuPont as a major supplier of polyester tire cord. AT&T lost over a billion dollars a year in computers. Eastman Kodak ignored the instant film market and later introduced the disk camera system that fell short of meeting expectations. It is now fighting for a share in digital photography. Polaroid invested millions in research for instant movies, and then the home movie was being replaced by video. General Motors invested billions in a redesigned product line and automated factories that resulted in the highest manufacturing cost in the industry. What happened to the original electronic masters like Farnsworth, Philco, Magnavox, RCA, and Sylvania? Where were these corporate executives? What were the executives at steel companies thinking when they ignored new process technologies coming onstream from abroad? In all of these situations, the warning signs of significant changes in technologies and markets were disregarded. Blind spots are a common executive and organizational malady that have crippled industries or transferred the business to foreign corporations.

Contrast the approaches of the corporate executives who disregarded the warning signs with Steve Jobs of Apple Computer. Apple Computer has had its ups and downs, but doesn't lack in innovation.

Steve Jobs has also received his share of criticism from Wall Street and some former Apple executives.

Jobs could be referred to as a management libertarian. Have a vision and try to fulfill it. Don't worry too much about objectives; just pursue the vision. Use your particular idiosyncrasies and biases toward fulfilling the vision. Don't fret over the false starts, the mistakes, but become the final arbiter and decision maker. Success will come as long as you persevere. For Jobs, bureaucracy is the death of innovation. Comparing traditional corporate executives with some one like Steve Jobs presents us with two management styles at opposite poles of the management spectrum, neither of which can optimize the use of organizational resources. Autocratic management doesn't optimize the creative input of the organization.

Predicting the future may be difficult, but knowing where the future lies just takes a lot of concentrated effort. There are no simple answers. Founders of new organizations often make interesting projections about the future. Here are some examples:

> I think there is a world market for maybe five computers.
> *(Thomas Watson, IBM Chairman, 1958)*

> They will never try to steal the phonograph—it is not of any commercial value.
> *(Thomas Edison, 1915)*

> X-rays will prove to be a hoax.
> *(Lord Kelvin, President of the Royal Society, 1903)*

Many people are thankful that predictors of the future of technologies were wrong. Managers do not have all the answers. All too often they are just too far away from the real world.

Innovators also have their blind spots that often tend to alienate potential supporters and extend the time required to reach the launch stage. Innovators need support, not only from their peers and colleagues but also from anyone who in some way may be affected by the innovation. Granted that it may be difficult to accept criticism of what you think is the greatest idea of the century, but that criticism may be just another piece of information required to force the resolution of some major problem. Right or wrong, accept it and think about it. If it's discarded as inappropriate, reconsider it in the future and determine its applicability. Its usefulness may be rediscovered.

Be Uninformed

Managers come to their positions not only with many different backgrounds but also with many different perspectives. As an innovator, you may be totally knowledgeable about what you're proposing, but you need to consider what the manager needs to know to make the decision.

Some managers prefer to see firsthand what is occurring. The "show me and let's talk about it" type can acquire the basics that allow them, if interested, to promote the idea among other managers. These managers may ask many questions, and they may turn down a proposal the first time, but with continuous input from the innovator may develop into a staunch supporter. They may also turn down that proposal the second or third time. How many times you go back depends on how passionate you are about pursuing the innovation. Innovators need to understand that upper-level managers decide the future of a potential innovation. They hold the combination to the safe and innovators need to get into that safe. So discover those shortcomings and begin the education process.

Other managers live by paper and paper alone. This is common in major organizations where the final decision makers are divorced from daily operations and depend on others to make recommendations. What's on the paper is what counts. Many managers whose claim to fame is an M.B.A. may be totally numbers oriented. Many corporate controllers may function as judges rather than as participants. Many marketing managers may lose sight of field operations. With the emphasis on quarterly bottom-line performance, decisions that involve risk and uncertainty are often delayed. Many managers are uncomfortable with new technologies, and that includes managers involved in technology and marketing.

What is the scope of the innovation? Introducing a new product with a new technology into an existing market presents many fewer risks than introducing a new product with a new technology into an unfamiliar market. The process becomes more complicated and presents several orders of magnitude in complexity when the new product includes new technologies, new markets, and new distribution systems. Developing a new product distribution system is a costly venture and subject to significant risks and uncertainties. Innovators need to be sensitive to these requirements. The level of risk increases significantly with the addition of every new variable just as it does over the innovation continuum from incremental to break-through.

Innovators need to understand the knowledge level of managers in the approval process. Ideas that reach beyond the approver's comprehension are difficult to sell. They become even more difficult to sell when the typical organizational functions need reorientation and realignment in order to pursue the innovation. Each additional change to current operating methods increases the uncertainties and requires more masterful selling techniques.

Don't Tolerate Mavericks

Mavericks! Who needs them? Every organization needs some. The word *maverick* is not a pejorative word, especially if the modifier *constructive*, as in *constructive maverick*, is added. Any list of mavericks would include the people who made a difference, people who had the vision and the passion to pursue an idea and bring it to fruition, people who questioned the traditional wisdom, people who asked the difficult questions. People often act as obstructionists until success is on the horizon. Think of any major innovator and you quickly recognize the qualities of independent thinking.

Many organizations follow the peace and quiet approach—don't rock the boat. These approaches have led many successful organizations to regret their actions. It takes courage to take a position that is contrary to the majority. The introduction of consensus decision making has in many instances led to a form of communal and incestuous thinking that has isolated individuals who think differently. The mavericks are the individuals who push the envelope, who see the handwriting on the wall, who because of their breadth of interest see beyond the group, and who recognize that change drives the future of the organization—these are the constructive mavericks.

Most innovation comes from constructive mavericks, who are often misunderstood by their immediate supervisors. These people create problems for the supervisor unless the supervisor in some way nourishes the spirit of innovation. It's much easier to go along with the group than to stand up and say that other possible approaches to resolving a problem may provide a greater benefit. These are the constructive mavericks, the ones who do and not the ones who complain. Are they difficult to manage? Yes, but the organization's future depends on them.

It is interesting to speculate why it often takes executives so long to see the light of day that at the same time appears so bright to those in the trenches. But intelligent, proactive, and profit-oriented executives often get caught up with the minutiae and forget to look in the most obvious places—their own organization. Motorola provides an excellent example.[2] Motorola blamed Japan for its problems to the point where it persuaded the United States to impose duties of 106 percent on companies accused of dumping cellular telephones. At an officers' meeting in 1979, a senior sales executive said: "Our quality level really stinks." George Fisher, the CEO, noted that: "We went through a denial process, trying to shout the poor guys down." The issue was rationalized: Motorola's quality was good, so it was good enough. Rationalizing failure to meet expectations occurs daily in many organizations. Motorola decided to do something about it. Motorola instituted the Six Sigma program—3.4 defects per million opportunities. Someone finally had the courage to level with the management team.

Focus Only on the Next Quarter Results

The pros and cons about the emphasis on the next quarter's bottom line can be argued, but employees, suppliers, and all levels of government want to get paid on time. It is also very difficult to recoup what has been lost in one quarter in future quarters. So, the next-quarter mentality is necessary and only becomes an obstacle if management obsesses about it and allows it to rule all other decisions.

Innovation requires long-term thinking, which is why all the participants must understand the implications associated with making a commitment to innovation. Organizations know that their future depends on innovation and that therefore it must be factored into the organization's business model. Innovation can't wait for something unexpected to happen. Focusing solely on short-term results always has its consequences in the future. Innovation cannot live in an environment where next quarter results dominate total thinking. The organization and the innovator both suffer if the money spigot is turned off and on based on Wall Street's projections.

Organizations obviously must be sensitive to Wall Street but need not be dominated by it. Often the problem arises from comments made by the CEO regarding future growth. Hewlett-Packard provides an excellent example. HP was in trouble primarily because Wall Street expected better than single-digit revenue growth and the firm had missed earning projections for several quarters.

In July 1999, a new CEO, Carly Fiorina, arrived with overly ambitious expectations and projected double-digit revenue growth that did not materialize. Why? Over the years the once agile and innovative organization had become overly bureaucratic, was slow to innovate, and faced a product mix that could not justify double-digit growth projections. Perhaps Carly Fiorina through her eagerness to succeed did not realize the magnitude of the problems that would have to be resolved in order to generate that kind of revenue growth. Fiorina's reorganization and restructuring of HP, which were supposed to improve effectiveness and efficiency, mainly created frustration and confusion. Perhaps HP needed a few of those constructive mavericks to tell the CEO about the real problems.

Innovators also need to be sensitive to the approach that management uses to control the progress of any activity. We know that innovation requires a particular kind of environment. If the environment and the infrastructure do not allow for the needs of the innovator, there's only one solution if the innovator really wants to be an innovator: Find an environment that does support innovation. There comes a time when the problems are just too difficult to overcome.

Institutionalize Traditions

Institutionalized traditions and thinking should be reconsidered at intervals to determine their continued benefit. Over the years, national cultures change, and those changes are reflected in how an organization goes about meeting its objectives. The American culture is quite different today than it was in 1950. The question is not whether one culture was better than the other, but to recognize those differences. Organizations now face the existence of new laws governing their operations, political correctness, the two-income family, the decline of the work ethic in spite of all the concerns about stress and overwork, the data overload, demand for more leisure time, and the list goes on.

Much research has been conducted that focused attention on the benefits from institutionalizing traditions, practices, processes, or modes of operation—but this institutionalization can only be effective if viewed in its current business context. What may have been an excellent approach in the past may have outlived its usefulness. What may have been an excellent and powerful tradition in the past may now be creating negative results.

As an example, 3M's policy of allowing their scientists and engineers to take up to 15 percent of their time and work on their pet projects has been praised by many business authors and management scholars. It has paid off very well in the past and brought 3M into the circle of the most innovative organizations. It has been institutionalized. But does this practice need to be modified? Is it providing the same level of benefit as in the past? Yes, many 3M products came about from this policy, but it appears that in recent times it has not yielded any breakthrough innovations. As noted in Chapter 6, Post-it Notes are now over twenty years old.

Over the years many organizations have taken on the responsibility for education and training, health care, day care, and other obligations that in the past were the responsibility of the individual or the family. Did organizations go too far? Consider the emphasis on education and training, such as those institutionalized programs that call for forty hours annually. At one time, personal development was the responsibility of the individual. Organizations began by providing tuition refund programs and other benefits and then basically took on full responsibility. Such institutionalized programs probably need to be reexamined and modified to meet current needs.

Even if innovation has been institutionalized, its continued added value requires periodic reviews, if for no other reason than to determine if the innovation investment is being allocated in such a way as to meet the short- and long-term objectives of the organization. As in the example noted previously, Polaroid was making an investment in the development of instant movies when videocassettes were already available. It is important to invest in the right innovation.

Use Inflexible Hiring Practices

Hire the same kind of people, taught by the same professors from the same schools, focus on the top 10 percent of the class, and you have the beginning of intellectual incest. While there is much talk about diversity, there is practically no emphasis placed on diversity of thought. We want thinkers that we're comfortable with, thinkers that won't upset us too much. We want innovators, but perhaps we don't want them to be too innovative. But innovators are not all cut from the same cloth with the same pair of shears. If nothing else, they have drive and a passion for pursuing an activity far beyond the average person. Organizations need to modify their hiring practices to bring in the innovators. Academic credentials may not be the appropriate criteria. Degrees do not necessarily equate to creativity or innovation. If they did, our academic institutions would churn out more concepts and inventions than industry could cope with. Hiring practices need to focus on the doers regardless of the credentials. Credentials only tell us where people went to school and where they worked, not what people know and what they can do.

At some point, innovation becomes a team effort. Finding the right people in the required disciplines and with a positive attitude and the ability to work together toward a defined objective does not come about by a cursory discussion. The team cannot be just a group of assigned people. The required talent needs to be identified in detail. Saying we need two people from marketing, three from research, five from development, and so on will not build a team. The innovation team needs to be made up of people who have in-depth knowledge and the appropriate levels of expertise and experience.

Make It Hard to Find the Decision Makers

Who are the decision makers? The decision makers will change from the initiation of an idea to the project and launch stages. At the onset of an idea, there may not be a need for a decision maker if the organization provides the freedom to innovate. If the free time is not available, it may be necessary to receive some form of approval. To bring an idea to fruition requires time, use of resources, or perhaps even a small investment. It will certainly require time.

Assuming that an idea is developed into what appears to be a workable concept, higher-level approvals of some type will be necessary. The immediate supervisor will need to become involved because resources will be required. As time progresses, the resource needs will expand exponentially. As an example, other specialists may be required with very specific knowledge. As was noted previously, timing is important and an innovator cannot be a specialist in all the disciplines involved. Those added resources might have to be paid for through some method, be it official or bootlegged. The ability of the immediate supervisor to entice other supervisors to become involved and provide some expertise is important. There are few innovations that can be accomplished through expertise in a single discipline.

But what if the immediate manager has no upper management contacts that can help pave the way? What if upper-level managers don't even know the manager or just what the manager does or has accomplished? The innovator has no alternative but to begin searching for that upper-level advocate. The immediate manager may not be able to spend the time to fight the battles. This manager may also be a single-discipline individual who tolerates the innovator but has little desire to take on new responsibilities.

As an innovator approaches the pre-project stage, knowledge of just who the decision makers are becomes crucial. Will the immediate supervisor lead the way? Yes and no. Yes, if the immediate supervisor is in the loop with upper management and has a track record of successes that inspire confidence. No, if the immediate supervisor is an unknown quantity to upper management. As usual the situation is seldom at the extremes of the continuum. Innovators need to promote themselves and their ideas if they're going to be successful.

Use Corporate Accounting Practices at All Levels

Corporate accounting generally meets the needs of corporate management but does not provide the details needed in operations. It seldom meets the needs of the innovator. In some cases parallel systems may be used. The needs of corporate management are quite different from the needs of research, development, manufacturing, marketing, and project management. The innovator eventually must face up to the numbers that will determine the future directions for the project. At the same time the assigned accountant or controller will play a role in moving the project to the next stages. Resources are limited and only so much can be bootlegged or not accounted for. There are limits and soon some normalization will be required.

In any innovation, thinking time generally can be made available. The problems arise when physical resources are required to demonstrate concepts and perhaps build the necessary prototypes to prove certain principles that are not totally understood. Costs can escalate geometrically. Thinking and modeling and analyzing will only take the innovator to certain limits. Pages of mathematical equations or modeling results will seldom provide justification to management. Management wants to see and feel the idea; they want to get their hands on something. If the management team is technically oriented, it may be easier but they still may not fully comprehend the new technologies and the future potential of a proposed investment. The same applies to management representing marketing and other functions.

Accounting practices can raise havoc with an innovation as it moves to the pre-project and project stages. Accountants quickly find a way to transfer overhead charges to a project that has not yet become viable. All those organizational administrative expenses have just found another home. The innovator now realizes that the project has been assessed some portion of costs associated with the corporate headquarters and perhaps even some for the organization's private fleet of aircraft. This is an easy way to kill an innovation. While accounting's actions may not be intentional, accountants do have a seat at the table of the virtual innovation prevention department.

Keep Decision Processes Secret

There are no standard procedures for making decisions. Decisions take into account many different considerations. Financial projections (return on investment) most likely will take precedence. This may be coupled with the track record of the individual or group requesting the funding. A pet project of someone in upper management may receive more lenient scrutiny and receive approval. Managers recognize that they also may want a project approved in the future and are apt to avoid asking the tough questions. But the actual decision process can include anything from the use of highly mathematical approaches, such as multicriteria decision processes or the analytic hierarchy process, to just a plain gut reaction.

Although some may be critical of the gut reaction approach, it's necessary to understand that someone who has grown up in a business from infancy may have considerably better sources of information than market researchers who do not really understand the industry. Some approach the decision process from a solely quantitative perspective and others may place greater emphasis on the qualitative issues. The fact remains that the innovator needs to know something about management's decision processes and prepare for them. If a manager makes decisions strictly from knowledge and history of the industry, don't bother with elaborate market studies. The opposite is also true.

There is no single decision process that produces better results than others. Excessive rationalism often creates difficulties for the innovator because decision makers focus only on the rational elements—usually the numbers—without looking at the information that justifies those numbers. The history of marketing studies that led firms down the wrong path or took them over the cliff is well known. With the advent of formalized marketing studies by people who know marketing but not the industry or the leaders in the particular industry, many organizations have been focused at the wrong targets. This is not a case against marketing but only to show that marketing studies need to include someone who understands the industry and its history.

Have an Ineffective Bureaucracy

Bureaucracies are probably here to stay, but there's no reason why they have to be ineffective or inefficient. Paychecks must be distributed on time. Employee benefits require timely attention. Other constituencies are entitled to receive quality service. Those administrative duties that people perform that help us do our work need to be performed on time and with little and preferably no interference to our regular duties.

Procrastination and foot-dragging in making decisions or providing information required for continuing an agreed-upon direction not only delay work unnecessarily but also create an environment where it appears that no one cares. Such actions are detrimental to the whole innovation process. Then there are those who are preoccupied with details that cannot be answered in the early stages of an innovation. And too often legal agreements that may be necessary to protect the organization bog down in extraneous details that only delay the decision process.

How many signatures are required for approval of an expenditure of funds, assignment of personnel, or use of experimental or pilot plant facilities? Although the hierarchies of most organizations have been somewhat reduced today, much authorization continues to be rubber-stamped without knowledge of what that signature involves. While the limits of spending authority have been expanded in many organizations, many lower-level managers continue to look to their superiors for approval. This is just another example of uncontrolled bureaucracy.

How many levels must be sold on the idea before work can begin? The scale of the proposed effort probably plays a major role. But at the concept development stage, the immediate supervisor must have the authority to fund the program. Often it's best if the hierarchy doesn't know what's going on. Experience shows that it is easier to kill an idea than try to do an evaluation. Experience also shows that too often the idea becomes a project without adequate consideration of alternatives. Too often good ideas are inadequately framed and thus are bound to fail. Approvals are given but without a clear understanding of the implications of what was approved.

Maintain a Nonsupportive Infrastructure

The impact of infrastructure elements was discussed in Chapter 9. Very simply, without an appropriate supporting infrastructure, innovation cannot take place. It would take someone with extraordinary patience and commitment to pursue innovation in an organization that lacked adequate support. It may also prove to be very disappointing.

There are many threats facing the innovator, and those threats once again depend to some extent on the organization's infrastructure. The infrastructure includes purposes, vision, objectives, strategies, structure, management attributes, attitudes toward managing uncertainties and risks, support for innovation, role of policies and practices, managing essential partnerships, leadership, and communication. Innovation often requires breaking the rules or at least stretching the rules, but the innovator needs to know the limits of the stretch—for example, the limits related to ethical considerations or governmental requirements cannot be stretched. Innovation cannot survive in a status quo organization. Sometimes managers must close their eyes.

Keep Organizational Structures Rigid

Organizational structure can present some roadblocks, but innovators must learn how to bypass them. Anytime an activity tends to impact any organizational entity, roadblocks will be set up to counter the activity. That's the real world. Whenever a proposed action may affect someone's operation, efforts will be made to counteract the action, because you're getting into someone else's sandbox and they don't like it. The response depends on the impact of the proposed action.

That's why innovators need to understand their organizations. They need information, they need expertise, they need resources, and they'll have to get into those other sandboxes. Some may open the door and even participate and get enthused and involved. Others may post a "No Trespassing" sign. The challenge is to find a way to get what's required from those other sandboxes. In the final analysis, rigid structures create problems, but ways must be found to circumvent them—it takes time and patience.

Early stages of innovation usually require unstructured and loosely coupled "adhocracies" made up of people who are supportive and wish to participate, and who can sense the same excitement as the originator. Somehow, these people will find the time to contribute their knowledge and experience to the effort. But the immediate supervision may become uncomfortable with such actions. There's a general feeling, rightly or wrongly, that this new activity is somehow detracting from the routine work that must be completed. Some overly structured supervisors cannot live in such an environment.

Don't Allow Anyone to Break the Rules

Policies and procedures are not only a requirement but also a necessity. But questions arise about the extent and purpose of those policies. Innovators break the rules. They cannot survive without breaking the rules. The question that must be answered is, How far and beyond what point? An extensive and detailed set of policies and procedures can prevent anything from happening, either for good or evil. Unless organizations scrutinize their policies and procedures, there is always the opportunity to add another when some current policy is compromised or some incident occurs. Policies and procedures cannot in any way impede innovation.

One could almost suggest ignoring the policies and procedures and just meeting the business ethical requirements. There may be procedures for filling out forms, but those are insignificant. There may be procedures established for bringing a request to a governing body by a certain date, but that too can be reconciled. Just because it's on the record doesn't mean that it's cast in bronze. There are always exceptions. Policies and procedures will continue to be an obstacle for the innovator. The innovator must find ways to circumvent them, but circumvent them in an ethical manner. It's usually easier to obtain forgiveness than permission. It's a judgment call as to how far the policies and procedures can be circumvented or ignored.

Don't Integrate Organizational Capability

Successful innovation depends on individual competencies being transformed into organizational capabilities. If individual competencies do not add up to integrated organizational capabilities, innovation is dead on arrival. Somehow those individual competencies must provide the critical mass in all the required disciplines. This does not imply that all these competencies must be available internally; they must be available from some source. Most innovation cannot wait for someone to develop competence in an area that's needed. This may be possible on very long-term projects, but in the fast-paced global economy, time is of the essence.

Organizational capability comes from having the right mix of skills and competencies. Assigning a Ph.D. when a technician is needed doesn't work and vice versa. Having sales personnel when marketing people are needed also doesn't work and vice versa. Having manufacturing capability to produce product X but not product Y when Y is what is needed leaves the organization with a serious problem.

Financial capability can also present a roadblock. Innovators must juggle many balls and keep all of them available for a critical evaluation at all times. This is not to suggest that they be preoccupied with any one activity in particular, except with development of the concept. But that concept must be developed within the financial limitations of the organization. If the organization is only capable of funding incremental innovation, it should consider very carefully before funding and taking the risk of a new-to-the-market innovation.

If the organizational purposes, objectives, and strategies are clearly defined, the financial resources should be available. Organizations, in recent years, seldom stray from their core competencies in pursuing new interests. So, innovators need to understand the limitations under which they work. An innovator in a company such as 3M will be quite different from an innovator in an organization such as Intel, General Motors, General Electric, Boeing, Microsoft, or Lockheed.

Refuse to Buy Innovation

The innovator must know how to sell or find someone who can do the selling job. Introducing something new, something that may require changing work habits, or something that may threaten the future of some employees requires the ability to convince, which is salesmanship. Many innovators because of their personal characteristics may not be particularly good at convincing others—they want to sell technology or markets while management wants to hear what the innovation will do to sustain the organization. A very simple question needs to be answered: If the organization invests in this particular program, what are the real benefits? Over my years of 3M experience and years of consulting, I've heard these responses when projects were not approved:

- They didn't know what we were talking about.

- They don't believe in anything innovative.

- It's just too difficult to introduce anything new in this organization.

The problem is that innovators often try to sell something managers do not want to buy, or at least they don't want to buy what was presented. Innovators will have difficulty selling their concepts unless they understand something about the people who make the decisions. What are they looking for? What motivates them? What are their hot buttons? Innovators cannot be demotivated when their ideas seem to be discarded in the wastebasket. They need to go back a second time, maybe a third time, and possibly a fourth time. Every contact with the decision makers is another opportunity to fine-tune the proposal.

Allow Organizational Politics to Drive Decisions

Do internal politics play a role in approving resources for innovation? This depends on how organizational politics are defined. Managers are often accused of forming cliques. They are also accused of allowing social relations to dominate the decision process. The golf course can in fact play a role. But that's life, and not much benefit arises from complaining about it. Managers who espouse to such tactics eventually pay the price. Too much familiarity often extracts its price.

Organizational politics can be either productive or destructive. Innovators need all the help they can possibly receive in order to succeed. Making use of all the possible networks provides an advantage. Many people can contribute both ideas as well as advice. If the sponsor of an innovation has a track record and has influence at the top management levels, obtaining the resources will be much easier. Keep in mind that it's not only the connections but also the track record that matters. Friendship can only go so far when organizational finances are concerned.

Destructive politics, which basically disqualify or disavow a concept, are easily recognizable. Destructive politics generally develop from a previous problematic encounter (a kind of personal vendetta against some previous act), the possible elimination of a pet project, or just a plain power play. Perhaps the most detrimental political ploy involves peers and other colleagues appropriating someone else's ideas or accomplishments. But internal rivalry should not be confused with destructive politics. Some level of rivalry exists in all organizations and basically keeps organizations focused on the market dynamics. From this point of view, rivalry provides the necessary competition to keep all departments pursuing the leading edge in whatever discipline. Yes, functions such as accounting and human resources should be focusing on innovation no differently than research, development, manufacturing, and other product-related functions.

Summary

The obstacles to supporting innovation are not unlike the obstacles that prevent organizations from meeting their other objectives. Each of the actions mentioned either individually or collectively presents roadblocks for the innovator. Many of these will always be present and innovators must find ways of circumventing them. Executives and managers who take action to minimize the impact of these negative factors have the opportunity to build a culture that supports innovation. Managers have a responsibility to manage. If innovation tops the priority list, then they need to act according to the defined purposes, strategies, and objectives of the organization.

Notes

1. Thomas J. Peters and Robert H. Waterman, Jr., *In Search of Excellence* (New York, Harper & Row, 1982), pp. 16–19.

2. C. Morgello, "George Fisher of Motorola: The Quest for Quality," *Institutional Investor*, August 1991, pp. 45–46.

3. Peter Burrows, "HP's Woes Are Deeper Than Downturn," *Business Week*, May 7, 2001, p. 48.

CHAPTER 12

The Innovation Audit

see p. 110 — Measuring Success
p. 73 — Types of innovation.

The innovation audit provides an opportunity for managers to determine whether the organization has the required resources, infrastructure, culture, and processes to seriously consider either focusing on or improving the current state of innovation. Most questions only require a "yes" or "no" response. This is intentional. The most useful approach to conducting this audit, if an organization is serious about embarking on developing a culture that fosters innovation, is to gather a group of ten to twelve managers to discuss each question and then end the discussion with a vote. The sessions will normally take half a day or more, depending on the attendees. The objective is to reach some agreement about the organization's location on the innovation continuum. The audit also allows managers to gain some insight into the organization and how it functions. The audits often show that many managers have developed *denial* as their core competence. It is absolutely necessary that managers challenge each other; otherwise, the audit serves no purpose. The session cannot become personal, and opinions must be based on factual evidence. My experience shows that:

- Managers will claim the organization is very innovative until someone asks that the innovations be identified.

- Many managers have little, if any, idea of what is involved in the innovation process.

- Too few managers think about new-to-the-market or break-through innovation.

- Organizations lack information about their resources, including having insufficient information about the usable competencies of their people.

- Managers lack knowledge about the fundamentals of project management. They know about all the tools but can't do the up-front work effectively.

The objective is not only to perform the audit but also to develop the program to correct the problems and go forward with new opportunities. For this reason, managers need to take time to prepare for the innovation audit. Scheduling a session without some prior study by the participants can lead to voicing of opinions that may not be based on facts. Figure 12-1 illustrates the topics included in the audit. The innovation audit should not be used as a survey. The purpose is not to show raw responses or do statistical studies. The purpose is to discuss each issue to achieve a better understanding, gain some insight into how the organization functions, and develop a realistic program that fulfills the purposes and objectives of the organization.

The Innovation Audit

Organizational Resources
Innovation cannot take place without adequate resources. Chapter 8 covered the issues in depth. The source of those resources can be internal or external. The purpose of this section of the audit is to take a realistic look at the available resources.

1. Does the organization have the proper mix of people to be classified as an innovative organization?

    YES   NO

2. Is the intellectual property of the organization available to all who need it?

    YES   NO

Figure 12-1. Innovation audit questions.

Resources	Power and politics
Infrastructure	Level of bureaucracy
Current environment/culture	Decision making
Growth	Acceptance of change
Leadership	Acceptance of initiative and risk takers
Management involvement	Micromanagement
Managerial creativity	Role of superstars
Managerial literacy	External consultants
Managerial competence	Internal consultants
Support for innovation	Sensitivity to interdependence
Tolerance for failure	Quality of work life
Integration of functions and disciplines	Identifying new opportunities
Scope of activities	Organization drivers

3. Is access to information about business issues available to the innovators?

    YES   NO

4. Does the organization possess the required competencies in technology and marketing?

    YES   NO

5. Does the organization stress the effective and efficient use of time?

    YES   NO

6. Is input from customers sought and analyzed for appropriateness?

    YES   NO

7. Are suppliers audited for competencies and capabilities?

    YES   NO

8. Are pilot production facilities available?

    YES   NO

9. Are the necessary operational facilities (office equipment, etc.) adequate?

    YES   NO

10. Does the organization have sufficient financial reserves to invest in innovative activities?

YES   NO

Organizational Infrastructure

Chapter 9 covered these infrastructure elements in detail. The infrastructure elements include all the nontangible factors that make the difference between success and failure.

11. Are employees knowledgeable about the purposes for which the organization exists?

YES   NO

12. Has the organization developed a statement of just what it wants to be—what some people call *organizational vision?*

YES   NO

13. Does the organization have clearly defined objectives?

YES   NO

14. Are strategies developed to accomplish the objectives?

YES   NO

15. Does the organizational structure fit the needs of the organization?

YES   NO

16. Does the organization operate with a set of realistic guiding principles?

YES   NO

17. Are policies and procedures flexible enough to allow the innovators to function effectively?

YES   NO

18. Does management support innovation by providing the resources?

YES   NO

19. Does management have the breadth of knowledge and expertise to understand the issues related to successful innovation?

    YES   NO

20. Does your management have an attitude that supports innovation?

    YES   NO

21. Has management demonstrated that it can accept uncertainties related to innovation?

    YES   NO

22. Does management at all levels communicate effectively about issues related to innovation?

    YES   NO

23. Although social responsibility probably isn't the major focus of the organization, does the organization maintain a socially responsible posture in the community?

    YES   NO

24. Customer satisfaction is a major organizational issue, especially when innovative products or services are being introduced. Does the organization provide more than adequate customer service?

    YES   NO

25. Vendors or suppliers play a major role in an organization's ability to meet commitments to its customers. Does the organization work closely with its vendors and suppliers?

    YES   NO

Current Culture

The best talent and an abundance of self-motivated employees will not provide innovation unless supported by the culture. Innovation requires both planting the seeds of innovation and providing an environment that allows those seeds to develop. Please consider whether your organization has met the goal of establishing each of the following characteristics of an innovative environment.

26. Allows employees the freedom to act on own initiative
    More than meets   Meets   Partially meets   Does not meet

27. Enforces the discipline of accountability for results
    More than meets   Meets   Partially meets   Does not meet

28. Uses flexibility in enforcement of policies and procedures
    More than meets   Meets   Partially meets   Does not meet

29. Adapts to changing conditions and/or requirements
    More than meets   Meets   Partially meets   Does not meet

30. Has a well-defined set of shared values
    More than meets   Meets   Partially meets   Does not meet

31. Has a set of well-defined beliefs
    More than meets   Meets   Partially meets   Does not meet

32. Has an established set of norms related to acceptable perform-
    ance
    More than meets   Meets   Partially meets   Does not meet

33. Uses organizational pride as a means for motivating
    More than meets   Meets   Partially meets   Does not meet

34. Organizations often develop traditions designated by phrases
    such as hard-nosed, tough-minded, seat-of-the-pants, intellec-
    tual, and other. Circle the appropriate choice or list one that
    more accurately represents your organization.
    Hard-nosed   Tough-minded   Seat-of-the-pants
    Intellectual   Other
    Example(s):

35. Based on the response to question 34, state the extent to which
    the example meets the choice.
    More than meets   Meets   Partially meets   Does not meet

36. Does the organization have a defined set of management tradi-
    tions?
    YES   NO

37. Does the organization have specific rituals?

                                                    YES   NO

38. Does the organization have a particular vocabulary?

                                                    YES   NO

39. Does the organization follow consistent methods in making decisions? For example, are decision process methodologies consistently used?

                                                    YES   NO

40. Are there specific rules of conduct that interfere with innovation?

                                                    YES   NO

41. Does the organization celebrate its past successes to motivate?

                                                    YES   NO

Limitations for Growth

Most organizations survive through some plan for continuous growth. That plan usually involves some level of innovation. How does your organization manage to grow its business?

42. Through new technologies

                                                    YES   NO

43. Through new-to-the-market products

                                                    YES   NO

44. Through breakthrough products

                                                    YES   NO

45. Through new, improved processes

                                                    YES   NO

46. Through incremental innovation for staying ahead of the competition

                                                    YES   NO

47. Through product replacement

                                        YES   NO

48. Through technology acquisition

                                        YES   NO

49. Through technology platforms

                                        YES   NO

50. Other methods. *Please specify.*

Leadership

Leaders push the frontiers, use the available resources effectively and efficiently, and know where they want to go and how to get there. Leadership typically comes from the person who cares sufficiently about something to invest time and energy to explore it, and accepts the risk, including even possible termination, involved in doing that. The leadership role places great demands on the individual and requires a group of followers who in their own way become leaders.

51. Rate your top management leadership on the following scale.
    Proactive   Reactive   Inactive   Complacent   Nonresponsive

52. Does management support taking individual initiative?

                                        YES   NO

53. Does the organization exude a sense of excitement?

                                        YES   NO

54. Are expectations clearly communicated?

                                        YES   NO

55. Does management adopt a defensive posture when problems are encountered?

                                        YES   NO

56. Does integrity begin at the top of the organizational pyramid?

                                        YES   NO

57. Does management stress conformity?

            YES   NO

58. Is more time spent on fighting fires than on the *real work* of the organization?

            YES   NO

59. Does management differentiate between micromanaging and interest in the work being done?

            YES   NO

Management

Management at all levels determines how much innovation will be accepted, nurtured, and eventually funded. Innovation makes certain demands on managers. Please rate your immediate managers on the following management characteristics.

60. Integrity

Excellent   Acceptable   Needs improvement   Not acceptable

61. Courage

Excellent   Acceptable   Needs improvement   Not acceptable

62. Risk-taking

Excellent   Acceptable   Needs improvement   Not acceptable

63. Using information technology

Excellent   Acceptable   Needs improvement   Not acceptable

64. Breadth of business knowledge

Excellent   Acceptable   Needs improvement   Not acceptable

65. Promoting innovation

Excellent   Acceptable   Needs improvement   Not acceptable

66. Establishing organizational objectives

Excellent   Acceptable   Needs improvement   Not acceptable

67. Being good listeners

Excellent   Acceptable   Needs improvement   Not acceptable

68. Making decisions effectively
    Excellent   Acceptable   Needs improvement   Not acceptable

69. Do management's actions support trust and confidence in its
    decisions?
    Always   Usually   Not often   Never

70. How interactive is executive-level management?
    Hands-on   Hands-off

71. How interactive is the organization's management at the de-
    partmental level?
    Hands-on   Hands-off

72. Does management really know what's going on relative to pos-
    sible innovations?

    YES   NO

73. Are decisions made from first-hand knowledge or from reports?
    From firsthand knowledge   From reports

74. Although one does not expect upper levels of management to
    operate as functional specialists, does executive management
    demonstrate creativity in the operation of the organization's
    business?

    YES   NO

75. How has executive management demonstrated its creativity?
    Explain and give examples.

76. How has executive management demonstrated its ability to in-
    novate? *Explain and give examples.*

77. Identify any specific and documented contributions from man-
    agement that led to an innovative product or process. *Explain
    and give examples.*

78. Do you consider your management literate in technological issues?

YES NO

79. Do you consider your management literate in marketing issues?

YES NO

80. Do you consider your management literate in manufacturing issues?

YES NO

81. Do you consider your management literate on product development issues?

YES NO

82. Do you consider your management literate in general management issues?

YES NO

83. How would you rate overall management competence in relation to your organization?

Excellent   Acceptable   Needs improvement   Very limited

Tolerance of Constructive Mavericks

Every organization needs creative mavericks, as long as they're constructive. Think about how your organization deals with them.

84. Does management tolerate the creative and constructive mavericks?

YES NO

85. Does management encourage creative mavericks?

YES NO

86. Does management know how to deal with the creative mavericks?

YES NO

Support for Innovation

Innovation cannot be the driving force of an organization without management's serious attention and support.

87. Does your management adequately support innovation?

YES   NO

88. Is this support demonstrated by providing the resources?

YES   NO

89. Does the infrastructure support innovation?

YES   NO

90. Do you consider your organization innovative?

YES   NO

Give examples to justify your answer.

Tolerance of Failure

Although Tom Peters suggests that organizations should celebrate failure, throwing that party may be difficult. It'll take a creative approach. Learning from failures is absolutely essential. Failure is a necessary part of any achievement and there is no achievement without some failure.

91. Does the organization learn from its failures?

YES   NO

92. Are the reasons for those failures documented and communicated to prevent a possible recurrence?

YES   NO

93. Does management penalize individual failure?

YES   NO

94. Does management penalize group failure?

YES   NO

95. Does management reward exceptional individual performance?

YES   NO

If YES, explain how. If NO, give an example of performance that should have been recognized or rewarded.

96. Does management reward exceptional group performance?

YES   NO

If YES, explain how. If NO, give an example of performance that should have been recognized or rewarded.

97. Does management encourage additional effort when signs of failure become evident?

YES   NO

98. Does management provide additional resources when necessary?

YES   NO

99. Does management disregard failures related to innovation?

YES   NO

100. Does management learn from failures and successes?

YES   NO

Integration of Functions and Disciplines

In the last couple of decades, all functions and disciplines have promoted specialization to the extent that total organizational effectiveness has decreased. Integrating the disciplines and functions requires a new way of thinking. It's not just about teams, it's about looking at a tree but also seeing the forest.

101. Does management focus attention on breadth of knowledge within a discipline?

YES   NO

102. Does management focus attention on understanding within a discipline?

YES   NO

103. Does management focus attention on experience within a discipline?

YES   NO

104. Does management focus attention on those with a proven track record?

YES   NO

105. Which of the following factors take precedence in selecting people for advancement? *Select all that apply.*
Knowledge   Experience   Track record
Leadership   Communication skills

106. Which of the following factors take precedence in selecting people in assembling teams? *Select all that apply.*
Knowledge   Experience   Track record
Leadership   Communication skills

107. Is time available for cross-fertilization between functions?

YES   NO

108. Does management emphasize cross-fertilization among disciplines?

YES   NO

109. Does management promote use of the systems approach in dealing with major projects?

YES   NO

Scope of Activities

The scope of activities that an organization pursues may place severe restrictions on innovation. There are many different technologies and markets to follow. There may also be insufficient resources to meet the needs of some new opportunity in a timely manner.

110. Do the number of projects exceed the available internal human resources?

                                       YES   NO

111. Are external resources available?

                                         YES   NO

112. Does the organization use external resources?

                                         YES   NO

113. Are changes in a project's scope a major issue?

                                         YES   NO

114. Does management schedule work at 110 percent or more of available time?

                                         YES   NO

Power and Politics

Power and politics are inevitable in any organization. But both can be used productively as well as destructively. Politics doesn't have to be a pejorative word.

115. Have there been occasions where the use of power has benefited the organization?

                                         YES   NO

Explain and give examples.

116. Have there been occasions where power has played a destructive role in the organization?

                                         YES   NO

Explain and give examples.

117. Have there been occasions where politics benefited the organization in some way?

                                         YES   NO

Explain and give examples.

Level of Bureaucracy

Bureaucracies are important but must operate effectively and efficiently. Although disparaging remarks are made about bureaucracies, we must keep in mind that they are needed to perform all those activities that we take for granted.

118. Does the organizational bureaucracy generally function effectively?

                                                    YES   NO

119. Does the organizational bureaucracy generally function efficiently?

                                                    YES   NO

120. Does the bureaucracy stifle innovation?

                                                    YES   NO

121. Does the bureaucracy support innovation?

                                                    YES   NO

122. Does the bureaucracy follow the policies and procedures to the letter?

                                                    YES   NO

Rational Decision Making

Decision-making processes and decisions affect opportunities for innovation. Rational decision processes certainly are essential to good management, but not sufficient. Quantifying information can become a costly burden if not used with discretion. Qualitative information cannot be ignored.

123. Does the organization follow any specific method for reaching decisions?

                                                    YES   NO

124. Is decision making based solely on hard quantitative information?

YES   NO

125. Does qualitative information enter into the decision equation?

YES   NO

126. Is there a specific thought process followed by the organization in solving problems?

YES   NO

Explain and give examples.

Acceptance of Change

Since the early 1980s, we've been deluged with all types of advice from the academic community and the industrial gurus about creating change. Some even promote transformational change. Does your organization have a systematic way for introducing changes in the following areas? Explain your answers and justify them.

127. Technology

YES   NO

Explain and give examples.

128. Marketing and related activities

YES   NO

Explain and give examples.

129. Research activities

YES   NO

Explain and give examples.

130. Development activities

YES   NO

Explain and give examples.

131. Manufacturing processes

                                              YES   NO

    Explain and give examples.

132. Product line management

                                              YES   NO

    Explain and give examples.

133. Organizational practices

                                              YES   NO

    Explain and give examples.

134. Policies and procedure

                                              YES   NO

    Explain and give examples.

135. Organizational infrastructure

                                              YES   NO

    Explain and give examples.

136. Developing a culture that fosters innovation

                                              YES   NO

    Explain and give examples.

137. Have changes introduced in the last five years met their goals?

                                              YES   NO

Explain and give examples.

138. Were the changes introduced in the last five years accomplished with a minimum of disruption?

                                                    YES   NO

Explain and give examples.

139. Did the changes introduced in the organization benefit all of the stakeholders?

                                                    YES   NO

Explain and give examples.

140. Does management seriously consider changes before implementation?

                                                    YES   NO

Explain and give examples.

141. Does management involve people from many levels before introducing any significant change?

                                                    YES   NO

Explain and give examples.

142. Do managers make decisions by seeking consensus?

                                                    YES   NO

Explain and give examples.

Innovation Initiative and Risk

There is a linkage between initiative and risk. People who demonstrate individual initiative generally look to the future. They suggest change, and change of just about any type involves risk. Innovation requires individual initiative and risk. If risk is not a factor, then whatever is being planned is most likely not going to yield an innovation. Innovation deals with the unknown.

143. Does the organization promote individual initiative?

                                                      YES   NO

     Explain and give examples.

144. Is there any historical record of how individual initiative has contributed to the well-being of the organization?

                                                      YES   NO

     Explain and give examples.

145. Has the organization risked the introduction of new products, processes, or systems?

                                                      YES   NO

     Explain and give examples.

146. Has the organization introduced something that might be classed as something that built a new business, changed the direction of an industry, or provided some major improvements in organizational effectiveness and efficiency?

                                                      YES   NO

     Explain and give examples.

147. Does the organization have a continuous track record of innovation?

                                                      YES   NO

     Explain and give examples.

Micromanagement

Does your organization need to dot every "i" and cross every "t" before approving any funds that might yield an innovation? The credo that all activities need to be financially justified certainly must be enforced, but with thought and discretion. Organizations also invest in programs because they're the right things to do. We can't put a number on such activities, but we can solicit your responses.

148. Does the organization provide a means for early exploration of ideas or concepts that may eventually prove beneficial?

YES   NO

149. Is there a process that is generally known about within the organization for accessing funds to pursue some exploratory work?

YES   NO

150. Does the approval for minimum amounts of funding for exploring an idea or concept require more than one level of approval?

YES   NO

151. Can such initial and minimal funding be approved within one to two weeks?

YES   NO

152. Does the immediate supervisor of the person seeking the funds have authority to approve some level of funding?

YES   NO

Role of Superstars

Whether we like it or not, there are superstars. These are people who have a track record of accomplishment. These are people who stand out above the crowd in some way that contributes to organizational expectations. These are the people who drive the organization. These are people who can also create problems for managers who live in the comfort zone.

153. Does the organization's culture allow for superstars?

YES   NO

154. Does the organization have any members that have contributed at the superstar level throughout their careers?

YES   NO

155. Have superstars worked well with the rest of the organization?

                                                YES   NO

156. Are superstars rewarded?

                                                YES   NO

157. Does the organization recognize its superstars outside the organization?

                                                YES   NO

158. Are most superstars involved in developing new products?

                                                YES   NO

159. Does the research group provide a climate for superstar level achievement?

                                                YES   NO

Use of Consultants

In responding to the following questions regarding consultants, apply the definition of consultant as a person with a minimum of fifteen years in a particular discipline with a track record of accomplishments. Consultants can be sponsored internally or provided from external sources.

160. Does your organization use external consultants?

                                                YES   NO

161. Is there a record of successful use of external consultants?

                                                YES   NO

162. Have external consultants made a major contribution to the organization in any discipline or function?

                                                YES   NO

163. Has the organization used external consultants for science-related issues?

                                                YES   NO

164. Has the organization used external consultants in engineering?

                                                YES   NO

165. Has the organization used external consultants for research?

    YES   NO

166. Has the organization used external consultants for issues related to marketing and sales?

    YES   NO

167. Has the organization used external consultants for issues related to distribution?

    YES   NO

168. Has the organization used external consultants to develop strategic directions?

    YES   NO

169. Has the organization used external consultants to develop a globally focused organization?

    YES   NO

170. Has the organization used external consultants for education and training?

    YES   NO

171. Has the organization used external consultants for improving the record of innovation?

    YES   NO

172. Does management rationalize the benefit from external consultant services even when the recommendations are not clearly beneficial?

    YES   NO

    Explain and give examples.

173. Does your organization have a group of internal consultants?

    YES   NO

174. Have any metrics been developed to determine the effectiveness of internal consultants?

    YES   NO

175. Have internal consultants made a major contribution to the organization in any discipline or function?

     YES   NO

176. Are the internal consultants generalists or specialists?
     Generalists   Specialists

177. Do internal consultants participate in issues related to science, engineering, or technology?

     YES   NO

178. Do internal consultants participate in issues related to marketing, sales, and distribution?

     YES   NO

179. Do internal consultants participate in developing strategic direction?

     YES   NO

180. Do internal consultants participate in issues related to develop a globally focused organization?

     YES   NO

181. Do internal consultants participate in issues related to developing education and training programs?

     YES   NO

182. Do internal consultants participate in issues related to fostering innovation?

     YES   NO

Sensitivity to Interdependencies

Success no longer depends on the performance by one person. Few business activities can be completed by a person knowledgeable only in some single discipline. Most projects, even some of the simplest, require knowledge from many disciplines. This situation forces organizations to make sure their employees understand the relationships of these interdependencies.

183. Does the organization sponsor any cross-functional or multi-disciplinary educational programs?

                                          YES   NO

184. Does the organization consistently develop operational frameworks for major projects?

                                          YES   NO

185. Are all the players brought into the game at the beginning of major projects?

                                          YES   NO

186. Does the organization use a formal project launch on major projects?

                                          YES   NO

187. In many situations, people in neighboring offices or cubicles are communicating by e-mail instead of face-to-face. Does this occur in your organization to the point where you feel it reduces overall effectiveness?

                                          YES   NO

Quality of Work Life

Much has been written about quality of work life. The work ethic isn't lost but has been diminished in the past two decades. Employee benefit packages have been reconfigured to the advantage of some and detriment of others. The net benefit or loss depends on short- and long-term needs of the individual and what one considers an acceptable benefit package.

188. Does the organization have a metric for individual productivity?

                                          YES   NO

If YES, explain the metric.

189. Does the organization have a metric for measuring group productivity?

                                          YES   NO

If YES, explain the metric.

190. Does the organization teach about the quality of work life issues?

                                        YES   NO

     If YES, describe how this knowledge has affected your lifestyle.

191. Has the organization accepted lower levels of performance to accommodate the quality-of-work-life issues?

                                        YES   NO

     If YES, explain the reason.

192. Have quality-of-work-life programs improved overall productivity?

                                        YES   NO

     If YES, explain how.

Identifying New Opportunities

There is no doubt that problem-solving skills are essential, but they are not sufficient in a dynamic and competitive economy. Most professional schools teach some aspects of problem-solving methodologies. However, problem-finding opportunities are seldom, if ever, addressed. Innovation involves finding those opportunities.

193. Has the organization developed any practices that seek out the problem finders?

                                        YES   NO

194. Is there a process at any management level for screening the output of problem finders?

                                        YES   NO

195. Problem finders are often the constructive mavericks. Does the organization accommodate them?

                                        YES   NO

196. Does the organization provide time for puttering around?

YES   NO

197. Does the organization support the problem finders with re-sources?

YES   NO

Organizational Drivers

Most organizations have what is known as a driving force: the one force that sets the direction and dominates all others. From the following list, select what you consider the single most important driving force of the organization. If the following list does not include your organization's driving force, please indicate one that you feel best describes the organization.

___ Products and services
___ User and market needs
___ Technology
___ Production capacity and capability
___ Sales and marketing methodology
___ Distribution method
___ Natural resources
___ Size/growth/return/profit

13

Making Innovation Happen

Innovation crosscuts all the functions and disciplines within an organization. Making innovation happen begins with adopting a management philosophy that goes beyond considering management as a toolbox of techniques, prescriptive methodologies, and quick fixes. Management is an organizational function and a process, and as such becomes a discipline or perhaps even a technology in and of itself. How that management function operates and how that process is disciplined depends on the context in which it is practiced. There are no prescriptions, but there are some stop, go, and caution signals that provide guidance. The process for making innovation happen is really no different that making anything else happen. The question is: Is innovation on your priority list?

Beginning the Process

As I have stressed throughout this book, innovation can take place from the top down, bottom up, or anyplace in between. So where does the process begin if an organization seeks to become more innovative? The process to make innovation happen will be essentially the same for a large bureaucratic organization, a large non-bureaucratic organization (if there is such an organization), organizations of many different sizes, and a start-up. The implementation will make greater demands on resources as the size and scope of the organization increase. A global organization will obviously have greater difficulty simply because of its size and different cultures. The local organization that operates within a limited geographical area has greater flexibility.

Chapter 1 described innovation as requiring four major inputs: resources, infrastructure, culture, and process, as shown in Figure 13-1. The four inputs individually do not present any new challenges. Innovation presents the additional challenge of integrating these four inputs into a system. The effective use of resources requires a supporting infrastructure, and the integration requires a well-defined process that operates within a supportive culture.

Interest in innovation usually begins when executives review the latest profit and loss statement and conclude that the organization is no longer meeting its financial targets. Somehow the existing products just aren't providing the required revenue and profit. In recent years, many executives have asked what happened to their uninhabited markets. It may take years before managers recognize that their uninhabited markets have become inhabited by competitors. The transition occurs gradually over time and is exacerbated by denial. Quarterly financial targets can be rationalized as blips in the economy. Annual financial targets can then be rationalized because of unfavorable foreign exchange rate fluctuations, competition from global suppliers, lack of raw materials, and any action that justifies the nonperformance. Then annual targets continue to be missed

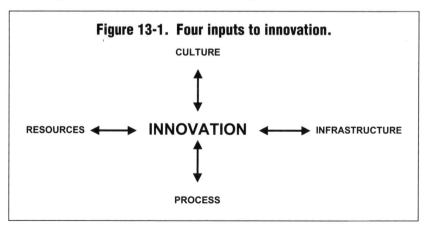

Figure 13-1. Four inputs to innovation.

CULTURE

RESOURCES ◄──► INNOVATION ◄──► INFRASTRUCTURE

PROCESS

until the day of reckoning arrives. It's time to begin the blame game. This is not an uncommon situation, and it occurs at all organizational levels. An argument can be made that not all organizations need to be innovative. This is true, but it is also true that all products have a finite life cycle and all are subjected to the will of the marketplace. Product obsolescence is real—maybe not this year or next, but definitely sometime in the future.

The examples used in previous chapters recognized organizations like Hewlett-Packard, Procter & Gamble, Eli Lilly, and 3M, where innovation became a life force. Innovation originated with the founders as a business philosophy and has been carried forward by generations of managers and professionals. Innovation was not a choice; innovation was an expectation. Innovation was why people joined the companies in the first place, and innovation was the organization. But not all organizations were fortunate to have leaders with such foresight. History tells us that most organizations do not provide a climate that provides the necessary freedom for innovation. So, should the CEO issue a dictum that the organization will become innovative? What would be the impact of such a dictum?

Management dictums have very little impact except under extenuating circumstances. It is possible for a CEO to put together a plan with some forward-thinking managers to move the organization toward becoming more innovative. But if the organization is in a position that it must take such action, it may be difficult to find the cadre of managers and innovators for putting together such a plan. If more forward-looking managers populated the organization, such actions would not be necessary. CEOs cannot expect to bring their top management teams together, hire the latest inspirational guru, go into some breakout sessions, and then put together an innovation plan. Probably no more than 20 percent of the current team would get on this innovation bus.

The best results are most likely gained by finding some group within the organization that has really been pushing to accept the innovation challenge but for many reasons has never received management's support. Now that the CEO has seen the light, innovation may become a possibility. Experience teaches that demonstration of results through sponsorship of innovation may be the best way to bring more people on this innovation bus. It takes a person with particular characteristics to be an innovator, and it takes an extraordinary amount of leadership to sponsor an innovator.

Understanding Organization Limitations

As organizations grow in size, top-level managers receive less and less information from original sources. Some of this comes from a personal choice and some comes from lack of time to meet face-to-face with the people who do the work and make the many decisions that drive the organization's plan. Size prevents the much-wanted personal attention and contact that people expect from their managers. There is only one CEO in an organization. So, CEOs and upper-level managers, to some degree from necessity, must depend on the interpretations of others to learn about what is going on in the organization. They see the organization through someone else's eyes and the picture could be quite different if they viewed it directly. Those interpretations are also subject to biases or partiality that aims to meet other purposes.

Managers need to understand the organization and how it works. They need to know how to traverse those many interfaces, and the larger the organization the greater number of interfaces, each with its own set of peculiarities. If a password is required to cross management jurisdictions, the organization is in serious trouble. Those organization charts don't tell us much about how the organization really works. It's the interaction of the people within those boxes and the interchange between the boxes that determine how the organization functions.

Organizational history reveals what it takes to turn a bureaucratic organization into one that treats innovation as a high priority. Henry Ford said, "History is bunk," but adopting that attitude may require paying a heavy price for ignoring both the positive and negative results from the past. History should provide a table of lessons learned to guide future decisions. The new builds on the past and seldom invalidates it. Fundamentals and basics remain the same.

Over many years, the purposes/mission of an organization become institutionalized, often to its detriment. The original intent served the organization in the past but after many years becomes a barrier to future progress. The usual factors related to competition,

expanding markets, new technologies, changes in customer requirements, and general economic conditions require managers to review
their purposes/mission and the means for fulfilling them. Executives
should ask some serious questions, such as:

- Is the organization's purpose/mission consistent with changing times?

- Does the organization's business scope need to be redefined?

- Are the current organization's drivers valid?

- What are the blind spots of the business?

- Is the organization's management style adequate?

- Does the organization need to differentiate itself in a new way?

- What core competencies are important? What new core competencies are lacking? Is denial a core competence? Is innovation a core competence?

- Are the strategic assets really strategic?

- Has the business model reached a point of diminishing returns?

- Have those mental models of processes or innovations been
  communicated?

Results of the Innovation Audit

One of the most difficult tasks is to get a group of managers to reach
some level of consensus at to where the organization lies on the innovation continuum. The Innovation Audit Questions shown in Figure 13-2 is a tool to help achieve that consensus; see Chapter 12 for
the complete presentation of all the questions that should be considered in such an audit.

The results from a typical audit show a wide disparity of responses among the participants. The replies to many questions will
probably ring the organizational alarm and force questioning the
particular organizational philosophy. Although total agreement will
probably never occur, wide differences indicate that not all managers

---

Figure 13-2. Innovation audit questions.

Resources	Power and politics
Infrastructure	Level of bureaucracy
Current environment/culture	Decision making
Growth	Acceptance of change
Leadership	Acceptance of initiative and risk takers
Management involvement	Micromanagement
Managerial creativity	Role of superstars
Managerial literacy	External consultants
Managerial competence	Internal consultants
Support for innovation	Sensitivity to interdependence
Tolerance for failure	Quality of work life
Integration of functions and disciplines	Identifying new opportunities
Scope of activities	Organization drivers

---

are going down the same road, and these differences need to be resolved. Here is a sample set of responses on selected questions from a typical innovation audit:

1. Are employees knowledgeable about the purposes for which the organization exists?
   YES   6   NO   7

2. Does the organization have clearly defined objectives?
   YES   9   NO   4

3. Are strategies developed to accomplish the objectives?
   YES   7   NO   6

4. Does management communicate effectively about issues related to innovation?
   YES   0   NO   13

5. Although social responsibility probably isn't the major focus of the organization, does the organization maintain a socially responsible posture in the community?
   YES   5   NO   8

6. Are expectations clearly communicated?
   YES   0   NO   13

7. Customer satisfaction is a major organizational issue and even more so when innovative products or services are being

introduced. Does the organization provide more than adequate customer service?
YES   4   NO   9

8. Front-end project work influences level of success. Does the organization consistently develop an operational framework for major projects?
YES   0   NO   13

9. Does the organization have a systematic way of introducing technology changes?
YES   0   NO   13

10. Does management involve people from various levels before introducing change?
YES   7   NO   6

These responses indicate some trouble spots. Those with wide differences create uncertainty among the employees, and those with all negatives indicate areas that need to be addressed for more effective performance. An audit of this type is useless unless new initiatives are introduced to correct the problems. The question of buy-in becomes important, but the buy-in should not be a choice, especially for managers. Malcontents cannot be allowed to obstruct or hinder the need for change. A way must be found to convince them of the benefits of the change or ask them to seek employment elsewhere. Experience has shown that the sooner the opposition is disengaged, the sooner the change process begins. How to disengage the opposition requires leadership.

Feasibility Analysis

The question must be asked: Is it necessary for this company to become an innovator? It's conceivable that a decision could be reached that innovation is a low priority. Do you consider General Electric to be an innovative organization? If you do, identify at least five GE new-to-the-market products. GE has been successful without investing significant amounts in research and development. Most of its successes come from acquisitions and divestitures. If GE is innovative, it is innovative in putting businesses together to optimize the return on investment. Jack Welch, CEO of GE, made a simple statement that defined GE's direction: We will be number one or number two in any industry or we won't be there. If it is important that the organization become an innovator, a feasibility analysis is essential.

A good place to start is with a SWOT analysis that begins with a study of the organization's strengths, weaknesses, opportunities, and threats. A SWOT analysis is only useful if denial is no longer a core competence. Overvaluing strengths and undervaluing the impact of weaknesses destroys the value of going through the process. It's sometimes difficult to identify weaknesses, but they are always present in any organization. They need to be laid out in clear sight of the participants. They cannot be rationalized. Motorola's cell phone experience discussed in Chapter 11 provides a good example. Foreign competitors cannot be blamed for lack of performance. A SWOT analysis requires rigorous discipline and must raise the issues that many would prefer not to raise. The analysis must be a true confession of the pros and cons of everything that is positive and everything that is negative.

The issues related to resources and infrastructure need to be rationalized and integrated. They do not exist as independent operators. Resources without a supportive infrastructure or an infrastructure without adequate resources will not provide the innovators or the culture to support them. Chapters 8 and 9 cover the details related to resources and infrastructure. Figure 13-3 lists the dimensions of the organization's resources and infrastructure.

Consider the relationship between these two interlocking lists. People cannot really do their best if the purposes, objectives, and strategies of the organization or of their suborganizational unit are unknown, disregarded, or not openly practiced. Yet too often the linkage is not clearly communicated. Organizational structure may or may not be a factor in becoming an innovative organization. My experience suggests that with the right people structure does not really pose a problem, but no structure can overcome a lack of talent. Management astuteness and attitude can be contagious. Employees look for these characteristics in their management. If management demonstrates these characteristics, they will probably be emulated. Business by its definition involves dealing with uncertainties and taking risks. How managers respond to dealing with these uncertainties and risks will be emulated. Managers send a strong negative message

Figure 13-3. Organizational resources and infrastructure elements.

Resources	Infrastructure
People	Purposes
Intellectual property	Organizational vision
Access to information	Organizational objectives
Technology	Organizational strategy
Marketing and sales	Organizational structure
Time	Management attributes
Distribution system	Uncertainties and risks
Customers	Support for innovation
Suppliers	Role of policies, procedures, and practices
Production capability	Essential partnerships
Operating facilities	Leadership—systems perspective
Finance	Communication—meaning

to their employees if they cannot deal with uncertainties and risks in a positive manner.

If the infrastructure does not support innovation, it will not happen. But support for innovation goes beyond the manager's ability to approve or reject an investment of resources. Innovation will not occur unless the organization's purpose is defined, the vision is communicated, the objectives are clearly stated, and a strategy has been developed to meet the objectives. Management needs to demonstrate its astuteness in crises with a positive attitude, and deal with the uncertainties and accept the risks.

How managers deal with the essential partnerships like customers, suppliers, regulatory bodies, and community responsibility will be reflected in its employees. If differences of opinion always lead to a confrontation, chances are that internal disagreements will be handled in the same manner.

Leadership and communication crosscut all elements of the infrastructure and the resources. Not much can occur without an astute leadership and system of communication that articulates the wishes of management in an appropriate manner. Communication must meet the needs of the user, not the sender. Jack Welch's comment that GE would be number one or number two in any industry or it wouldn't be there didn't say much to the scientist in one of the

GE laboratories or the sales representative in Duluth, Minnesota. That statement needed to be translated so it had meaning to the individual.

Innovation Actions

Figure 13-4 lists the important actions as an organization considers embarking on the innovation journey. These actions are self-evident but seldom considered in depth. Yes, a critical mass is important, but whether it's available is seldom considered. Yes, we should have a proactive approach, but that's easier said than done. The reasons for not acting are many. An innovative organization needs to consider these actions.

Organize the Critical Mass

The desire of the CEO or any group manager to generate a climate that fosters innovation will only be fulfilled if a critical mass of talent can be brought together and focused on the many issues involved in changing direction. The talent may be available and may be looking for new leadership or a new vision of just what the organization wants to be. *What-the-organization-wants-to-be* must be clearly

Figure 13.4. Innovation actions.

Organize the critical mass
Identify the key players
Support a proactive attitude
Communicate the vision and the plan
Develop support for the vision
Develop a sense of ownership
Understand employee attitudes
Assess performance and affect it
Define the roles
Delineate organizational goals
Educate about the business
Think outside the box
Promote collegiality
Encourage employees to speak out
Make managers role models for change
Delineate potential problems

stated. That statement now provides direction. The talent may already exist and only needs new leadership with a new focus. The Silverlake project at IBM Rochester as discussed in Chapter 6 provides an excellent example of what new leadership can do for an organization. The talent was available at IBM Rochester, but the business direction and the *what-the-organization-wants-to-be* required redefinition.

The process of organizing the critical mass of talent is really the same at the organizational level and suborganizational levels. The only difference is in the magnitude of the task. The people brought into this process must be the change makers. They will come from many organizational functions because creating a change to an innovative culture involves the whole organization. You're looking for people who will adapt, who will help convince colleagues and peers, who will vigorously pursue the change and yet listen to the uncommitted, and who will demonstrate their enthusiasm through their actions. Changing direction in a global organization with thousands of employees will take time and will most likely be accomplished one department at a time. There's nothing in the management toolbox or in that proverbial black box that provides the magic answer. Organizations that begin today will begin improving performance immediately.

A major difficulty that arises in developing the critical mass of talent comes from a lack of usable information on the available talent. What does the organization really know about its players? All those personnel records delineating university degrees awarded, courses completed, discussion of deficiencies, recommended educational programs, and lists of competencies and skills seldom provide the essential information. Credentials have little meaning five years after graduation. Rank has little meaning. The most important piece of information, the track record, is seldom presented. What has the individual accomplished and how? Human resources records usually lack a coherent listing of the contributions during the last five- to ten-year period. Appraisal systems undergo continual changes that in the final analysis, in spite of continual changes from one system to another, provide little value. Appraisal forms have become longer and required more often. All this work exists primarily to fit into a system that has basically transferred merit pay into an automatic progression rate of increase.

Successful examples are the best teachers. Making innovation happen can be initiated more effectively in operational units. Here the manager knows or should know the competencies of the group and not need to obtain information from the human resources department. The manager should know the people and act accordingly. As discussed in Chapter10, innovators require more than technical, marketing, or administrative skills. They need the put-it-all-together competence.

Identify the Key Players

Who are the people who can help bring about the change? Identify them and bring them together to develop the plan and then convince colleagues to adopt it. Making a transition requires support from some people who have a track record and are generally respected by the organization. This team through its actions will determine the level of success. The innovator or innovators, if there are any in the organization, may not be the best people to include in the team. Attempting to bring two innovators to a conclusion may be difficult. The same characteristics that allow them to be the innovators may militate against any effort to reach acceptable conclusions. The ability to communicate is the primary competence of these key players. They bring put-it-all-together competence to the table.

Support a Proactive Attitude

What is the past history regarding support for people with a proactive attitude? If in the past people were in some way humiliated for proposing what needed to be proposed or were ignored, it will be difficult to now convince people that the door is open to new ideas. Every organization is plagued with managers who want peace and quiet as long as certain short-term objectives are met. But innovation requires a proactive approach by many people not directly involved with the innovation. The support people performing administrative services cannot continue to do their work in the same way. They too must recognize their impact on the organization's future and become proactive.

Communicate the Vision and the Plan

The vision—what does this organization want to be and how does it get there—needs to be communicated and indelibly placed in the minds of the group. Managers must decide where the organization is going, how it plans to get there, and recognize that detours are inevitable. Too often this vision lacks adequate communication. Sending out a memo is not communicating the message. Calling a meeting and informing the troops is not communicating the message. Communication involves taking the time to educate the group as to the need for a new vision. It may be as simple as saying that if we don't become more innovative we won't be here tomorrow. Too often the vision is communicated without any passion and without conveying the significance of the decision. In this age of victimization, managers too often fail to apprise their people of the realities. They don't level with their people about the economic and market realities that affect the organization.

Develop Support for the Vision

The purpose of communicating the vision is to develop support for it. Support for any proposal only comes from understanding the implications and the impact of what is being proposed. People must be given an opportunity to raise the issues and even be critical of certain elements of the plan. Often those who raise the difficult question eventually become the best supporters. Support only comes with understanding. People may raise questions about the unresponsiveness of managers in the past when new ideas were proposed. They may ask how come it took so long for managers to recognize the need to become more innovative. Those responsible for communicating the vision need to be prepared to answer such questions. These questions will be asked and they require a response.

Develop a Sense of Ownership

Questions will always be raised and require legitimate responses. *What's in it for me? What do you expect from me? How do I share in the benefits to be derived from this change in direction?* The impossible becomes possible when employees develop a sense of buy-in and ownership. The sense that *there's some action out there and I can have a piece of it* changes the attitude with which people pursue any effort. But the benefits that the individual may or may not derive must be articulated if ownership is essential. Those potential benefits can paint a grandiose picture or they can be as simple as saying you'll continue to receive a paycheck. Hopefully it's not the latter. Expecting people to develop a sense of ownership requires open and aboveboard communication. People must be brought into the action as full partners. As organizations attempt change, whether related to innovation or any other type of change, buy-in and ownership become essential.

Understand Employee Attitudes

Managers bring a particular attitude toward meeting organizational commitments. Leadership and communication are the two principal requirements, but unfortunately not all managers know how to communicate. Each employee exhibits some form of uniqueness that needs to be accommodated at some level. That uniqueness makes the organization function. That uniqueness brings different perspectives. The uniqueness of all the employees combined ultimately defines the culture. So, not everyone can be accommodated in quite the same way. Managers need to know their people—not just by name, but by what makes their clock tick. This is a difficult yet essential task.

People come to the workplace with different attitudes and attitude determines the ability to use competencies effectively. The manager's responsibility involves selecting the individual with the particular attitude that fits the job requirements. Managers who disregard attitudes pay the price. This does not imply that every employee whim must be satisfied. On the contrary, it requires that the manager understand the issues related to the attitude. Let's face it, some people create problems. There comes a time where realistic appraisal of performance cannot be disregarded. It must be resolved.

Assess Performance and Affect It

The best and the brightest were hired, but why did they not fulfill expectations? Bringing the person on the payroll and going through the orientation or indoctrination period does not guarantee performance; managers must manage performance. Management by objectives (MBO), when practiced as it should have been, avoided much of the problem—the manager was part of the objective and in that position played the role of mentor, teacher, and the guarantor that the objective would be accomplished. The manager was in a position to affect performance. It's too late to assess performance at the end of a project, even a small project. Active participation by managers can prevent missing those objectives. Managers who begin the process of innovation need to recognize the significance of their involvement in that process and the need to continually assess individual as well as group performance against the objectives. That assessment includes meeting the manager's personal commitments.

Define the Roles

The roles people can play determine where their talent can be used most effectively both for the person and the organization. Some people are good at detail; others abhor it. Some consider the whole picture; others can only deal only with the parts. Some focus on technology or marketing only; others manage to keep one foot in each camp. Some bring highly specialized competence; others bring breadth of knowledge. These competencies and others can be mutually supportive or mutually destructive. One cannot significantly overshadow the other. Managers need to define roles within the limits of experience and competence of team members and in relation to the project requirements. Putting people into positions for which they have minimum competence, or that go against their desires or exceed their ability to perform effectively, or in which they don't have sufficient project know-how will eventually limit progress. Members of a symphony orchestra have very defined roles. The string section knows its role, the brass section knows its role, the percussion section knows its role, and each member within all the other sections knows their roles. Making innovation happen requires the same kind of discipline; there must be the right mix of people competencies within the organization's contextual limitations.

Delineate Organizational Goals

Delineating organizational goals does not make them a reality. Most organizations can provide lists of goals, many of which have never been achieved. Those action items prepared meeting after meeting somehow don't always make the deadline. They may continue on the list for months without any attention. Part of the difficulty lies in the lack of setting priorities. Then there's the question about setting stretch goals. Research clearly shows that stretch goals provide significant benefits if viewed in a collegial perspective. A manager can set these stretch targets even if they appear to be totally unreasonable.

Consider the case in which an executive asked a production group to reduce their annual costs by 10 percent. The group immediately became frustrated over the seemingly ridiculous request. The group manager responded that the best that could be accomplished was 2 percent. But then the group actually managed to reduce costs by 8 percent without creating any significant problems. The executive hadn't expected that she would get a 10 percent reduction, but the 8 percent that the group achieved was certainly better than the 2 percent that they had projected, and she rewarded the group for their effort. The group had found the resources, exploited the infrastructure, focused on the issues that added value, and developed a plan as to how the goals were to be achieved. Delineating the goals is usually the easiest step. Delineating how those goals are to be achieved is the real work. Was this executive game playing? Possibly. The human species, being what we are, will normally seek a comfort zone. That comfort zone exacts a price at some time in the future.

Educate About the Business

I have always been surprised when I learn how little employees know about their organizations. I have been even more surprised at how little some *managers* know about their organizations. It appears that much of what appears in organizational newsletters and bulletins is seldom read. Yet it is through these publications that management communicates its philosophy, its accomplishments, and its recognition of jobs well done. The question always arises: Do employees really read these publications?

Employees need to be educated about their organization because they convey the spirit of the organization to the outside world. Not all publicity serves a good purpose, but even the bad if presented properly demonstrates the issues faced by an organization. Innovators need to know their top management. Who they are, where did they come from, what is their philosophy, what is their track record, what is their ability to lead, and what are their perspectives beyond the organizational world? Innovators need to know about those attitudes toward excellence, innovation, creativity, customers, suppliers, and the local community and society. Perhaps organizations need to teach about the organization and its fundamental beliefs and its history of how it got to where it is. Too many young people believe those corporate campuses were always there. They need to know what it took to build them.

Think Outside the Box

What does it mean to think outside the box? How do you convince your professionals to transcend traditional boundaries, think strategically, and develop a business perspective? All professionals who live in the domain of research, development, manufacturing, marketing, and the distribution and administrative functions must at times put on the business hat. Innovation by definition involves building a business. It's the opportunity to deliver the full benefit of their professionalism. It's the opportunity to become involved in the whole rather than just the pieces. It's the opportunity to integrate all those independent functions into a cohesive project team that can think about a breakthrough. They have a desire to take the giant step.

Taking the giant step will not be accomplished through traditional methods. Innovators transcend those traditional boundaries, think strategically, and develop a business perspective. To do this, they must get out of the proverbial box. Transcending traditional boundaries requires that professionals in all disciplines develop a level of dissatisfaction and adopt an attitude that there must be a better way and do something about it. Thinking strategically doesn't mean developing a strategic plan. Very simply, understand the significance of the work effort beyond the immediate task at hand. We develop a business perspective by focusing attention on the value added from our work. Ask this simple question: What was the impact of the work effort?

Consider project management as an example. The objectives of the project manager include meeting specification, on time, and within an approved budget. But are these three objectives really sufficient? They say nothing about the business. Can every project that meets these objectives be considered a success? Hardly. Some groups of people may have done an excellent piece of work on something that really never added value to the organization or to those working on the project. From a business perspective, it may even be viewed as a failure except for what may have been learned in the process. Innovation involves the implementation or commercialization of an idea and thus of necessity involves strategy. This implies that on new product innovation the project manager is totally responsible for the business and not just meeting specifications, time, and cost requirements.

Promote Collegiality

For some reason, collegiality, defined as cooperative interaction among colleagues, is seldom mentioned in team-building exercises. Yet, collegiality within any organizational community determines to a large extent the output of that community. The barriers to those functional interfaces must in some manner be minimized, if not completely removed. Every function involved in an innovation project will be required to accommodate related functions. The community needs to resolve any misinterpretations and misconceptions. Does this require compromising principles? It depends.

There are three basic approaches for dealing with conflict: domination, compromise, or reappraisal and redesign. Domination, such as by giving a directive, provides a victory for one side in the conflict and hardly provides support from the defeated. In compromise each side gives up something that ends the conflict but too often compromises the end result. Compromise does work when the involved groups can give and take without compromising the expected result.

Reappraisal and redesign offers a third alternative that too often is disregarded. Going back to the blank sheet of paper can often create something new that fully meets the requirements of all groups. This is a common practice followed by people dealing with technology and science. The reappraise and redesign process is simple: Put all the cards on the table, identify the real issues, and then examine and evaluate them. At times, reconsideration causes certain requirements to vanish. At other times, reconsideration raises new and important issues. The process requires in-depth understanding, commitment, dedication to resolve the conflict, and a good amount of creativity. The process requires collegiality that is built on raising the critical issues, arguing the pros and cons, and reaching a solution that does not compromise the original intent. Above all, collegiality is built on respect for those involved. It's based on resolution of issues and not on personalities.

Encourage Employees to Speak Out

How do managers find out just what their people think about a particular issue? Select a group of people for a discussion and relatively few will volunteer their thoughts. In any group, there are always a few who will be very vocal, but what about the rest who sit and contribute nothing to the discussion? What prevents the others from stating their positions? Are these responses based on the typical distribution curve—10 percent at each end and 80 percent in the middle? Even though managers promote open communication, for some reason most people do not take advantage of the opportunity. There comes a time when some people may have to be forced to voice their opinions. Unfortunately, most of the time opinions from a group are solicited with a phrase such as: What do you guys think? Utter silence prevails until someone finally speaks. Eventually, a few more enter the discussion but the majority sit in silence.

A more appropriate way directs the question to a specific individual. This may be somewhat embarrassing to the individual who seldom contributes an opinion, but it forces the individual to respond. The respondent may need a few moments to organize a response and that time delay should be respected. Often the silent types surprise the group with their thoughts. The person running the session can follow by searching for input directly from others. A manager who attempts to improve the innovation environment cannot afford to disregard the input from the silent majority. The vocal participants are not necessarily the best thinkers. Building the innovative organization will require input from more than just the few.

Managers as Role Models for Change

Should managers innovate? Over the years, much management education and training and primarily the executive M.B.A. programs and related master's programs in manufacturing and technology teach innovation as though it were the responsibility of people other than the manager. Managers don't have to innovate; they only have to make sure they staff the department with innovators. This interpretation demeans the role of the manager into that of an administrator and bureaucrat.

Managers who attempt to develop an environment that fosters innovation will be more successful if they demonstrate in their own way that they too are innovators. This does not suggest competing with the product or process innovators, but innovating within the realm of their functions and responsibilities as managers. The manner in which managers propose a change needs to be innovative. The innovation formula remains the same—idea, concept, invention, and implementation. Introducing a change without thoroughly thinking through the process and the consequences sends the wrong message. Such an approach will not result in an appreciable move toward developing an innovative organization. The manager's role goes beyond merely acquiescing to innovation as a necessary condition for survival. We're talking about building responsive organizations that deliver a continuous flow of new products to the marketplace.

Delineating Potential Problems

What are the key factors that prevent the group from developing an innovative culture? There are no simple answers; the answers must come from an analysis of the organization's competencies in relations to its business purpose. Competencies that no longer provide value are no longer competencies. This exercise is particularly difficult for a group that has a track record of successes. Those successes may have occurred because of a steadily growing economy or because of a lack of competition. The economy may be in a down cycle. Uninhabited markets may have become inhabited by tough competitors. These situations often arise from a lack of strategic thinking and from accepting conventional thinking as wisdom, which can cause executives and managers to lose business perspective. Greater emphasis is placed on management tools with the expectation that the latest one will solve all the problems. Thinking about the issues holistically doesn't even enter into the discussion.

An organization that has managed to reach an acceptable level of success without innovation will have a difficult time listening to those voices of opportunity. The business model may no longer apply but management continues to pursue it. Tweaking the old model because of some type of reverence seldom provides any benefits. A new model must take into account eliminating the roadblocks. The new model requires much more discipline than the old. People really are the greatest asset, and the model only works when the best is extracted from all the participants.

Designing a Transition Model

All of the questions raised will not have immediate answers. If the organization were satisfied with its level of innovation, it would not be designing a transition model. Innovation is not the next quick-fix panacea. Innovation occurs only if you have people who can function as innovators. Likewise, an organization can only develop a successful transition model if it has a cadre of people willing to take on the task. That group requires well-balanced put-it-all-together competence.

Making a transition cannot include tearing the organization apart, integrating people into a new architectural configuration, and at the same time keeping the store open. The organization would be destroyed in the process. At the same time, some definitive actions must be put into place. About two years ago, Hewlett Packard, with $50 billion in sales and eighty thousand people, recognized that its decentralization over the years might have gone too far. Decentralization had provided the growth; decentralization lost its bearings when groups within HP were competing for the same customer. HP found that its legendary engineering competence, its ability to invent and bring new products to market, and its spirit of innovation as structured no longer met the needs of the customer. Decentralization became a liability. As a result, the HP focus changed from products to services and solutions, and from internal people issues to customers and shareholders.

A transition to being identified as innovative does not begin with a major shakeup of the organization. There may be a need to consolidate certain activities for greater effectiveness, but a major attempt to move to an innovative organization by the next morning will prove to be futile. Innovation depends on people, and unless there are some pent-up innovators locked in some closets, nothing will change. Innovation also requires support from the top of the organization. An organization does not become innovative by dictum.

The project management model associated with introducing new products provides a good model for making innovation happen. Engaging in this transition begins with an idea that must then be developed into a workable concept followed by some form of invention and then implementation. The idea is to be qualified as an innovative organization. Making the transition is an innovation in its own right.

One way to approach the process of becoming innovative is to focus on a major project. Focusing on a project changes the approach from a theoretical exercise to one with purposes and objectives. IBM Rochester's AS/400 project, as discussed in Chapter 6, provides an example of how an organization reinvented itself. It took a particular kind of person to focus the group and provide it with new challenges.

A typical new product project involves five major activities:

1. Investigation, analysis, and synthesis

2. Concept development

3. Feasibility—business, markets, technology

4. Development

5. Implementation or commercialization

This simplified model for developing a new product can also be used for successfully introducing innovation.

Investigation, Analysis, and Synthesis. Answer the basic questions: the, why, when, how, and who. Acquire the data, analyze it from the perspective of the organization and the employees, and then synthesize the important information into a crystallized idea just as would be done for a new product.

Concept Development. Take the formalized and tested idea and develop it into a workable concept. Some testing of the concept may be required.

Feasibility—Business, Markets, Technology. Evaluate the impact on current results, which is probably negative. Consider the impact on future business results. Study the impact on employees: They are the market and must be considered. Some actions will work, while others will not. Take into account the timing for introducing the innovation activity.

Development. Develop the plan for launching the project. Set some stretch targets. The plan must somehow bring the majority of people onboard. Although innovation comes from the individual, a team implements it. Identify the problem areas and propose a solution. Specify the expected outcomes. Specifically identify how managers will participate.

Implementation. The work begins on each of the goals that have been established. Implement as any other plan would be implemented. Monitor the progress. Bring people together again and again to keep the action moving.

Like any activity, innovation requires an alignment of:

- Purposes

- Objectives

- Strategies

- Values

- Culture

- Employees

- Systems

- Organizational design

- Human behavior

Measuring Innovation Success

Measuring success in innovation depends on the type of innovation and the organization's approach to measuring success. Since all innovations are different and all organizations have different priorities, the methods will vary. Some will focus totally on the hard quantifiable financial expectations, while others will use a blend of the quantifiable and the qualitative. An investment has been made so some return must be evident. The return could go to the bottom line; it could also go to buy market share. There is no single measure of success for implementing an innovation. However, some criteria need to be established before major investments are approved. Measures of success usually involve a combination from the following list:

- Degree of profitability—plus or minus from some acceptable level

- Payback period

- Return on investment

- Length of time to reach maturity

- Domestic market share

- Foreign market share

- Relative sales for similar products

- Relative profits for similar products

- Sales versus sales projections

- Profits versus profit objectives

- Opportunities for spin-off products

- Opportunities for exploiting new markets

- Opportunities for entering new markets

- Use of existing product platforms

- Basis for future technology advancement

Financial return is the most important indicator of success. That next innovation is desperately waiting for funding, and it won't come from praising the technology or design or the marketing plan. Commercialization success depends on sales and profits. Implementation success depends on savings from the investment of resources.

One More Program

The comments about being overloaded with work are constant. Now, someone wants to introduce a new program into an already overcrowded schedule. Where does the allotted time come from? If the organization's priority list includes innovation, time for it must be allocated, like it is for any other project. The usual response asks for more people. But additional people are really not the answer.

Something probably needs to be eliminated from the daily work schedule of the people already employed in the organization. At first glance nothing can be eliminated. But those low-priority activities that really don't add value should be eliminated. Can they be eliminated? The answer is absolutely yes. The issue involves identifying those nonvalue-adding activities. All types of arguments will be made as to the catastrophes that will occur if certain activities are eliminated. This is where managerial leadership enters the process. Eliminating certain activities after examining and evaluating their impact on the organization's bottom line should be a normal process. Why allocate resources to activities that do not add value?

As an example, education and training now have gained the same respect as apple pie. Yes, they are important, but the important question to ask is what kind of education and training? In my consulting practice, I find a significant investment in education and training with little benefit. In one case, a department head decided to send the whole group (forty people) to a two-day session on PowerPoint. Six months later there was not a single person in the group who could take handwritten copy and transfer it efficiently into a PowerPoint presentation. It may have been more appropriate to send two or three people for PowerPoint training and expect them to develop a high level of proficiency. This point can obviously be argued. But sending forty people used up 640 hours of valuable time. Perhaps most of that 640 hours could have been spent more productively on other training, or another activity altogether.

Making time involves reviewing work habits and processes to eliminate the organizational redundancies and assign people to the real work of the organization. We make time for the things that are important to us. If innovation is important, it will take time to develop a culture that allows it to happen.

What Not to Do

The "what to do" has some corollary actions of "what not to do." Although the "what to do" can spur innovation, the "what not to do" actions often prove detrimental. Some ways for killing innovation are:

- Give short shrift to new ideas
- Reward uniformity in thinking
- Penalize the risk-takers
- Prevent bootlegging of resources
- Manage everything by the numbers
- Practice the "one size fits all" philosophy
- Interpret policies and practices to the letter of the law
- Micromanage
- Discourage departures from accepted norms
- Limit resources
- Eliminate dissonance
- Limit divergent thought
- Disregard the fitness for innovation

How to Work 101

Bring in the clipboard and the stopwatch! Do we introduce Frederick W. Taylor, the reputed father of scientific management, into the organization's professional ranks? Someplace in the last fifty or sixty years, we came to the conclusion that people do not need to be taught how to work. We teach them how to study as they enter college, but we no longer teach people how to work. This phenomenon is especially true of professionals. You've heard the comments, "Tell them what you want done and leave them alone," or similar versions. The only difficulty with that approach is that everyone keeps making the same mistakes over and over. And so we brought on the idea of organizational learning, but organizations aren't learning. Everyone is left on their own.

I'm not suggesting rigid work standards in the professional disciplines but just some rational thought prior to engaging in any activity. There are shortcuts and rules of thumb that can save hours of often very tedious work. Problem resolution requires priorities. The one critical item in an array of problems that might prevent an innovation from being introduced in a timely manner must be solved now. The enclosure for a product isn't really too important at the beginning of a product development program: What goes into that enclosure should take precedence. The design of a stylistic report format isn't really important: it's what's in the body of the report with its recommendations that takes on importance. This is not in any way a statement against creative artwork, but the artwork must fit the content in some way.

Designing a new product is a balancing act, involving decisions about which features will be included and which will be excluded. Excess complexity built into the product only creates problems for the user. Medtronic experienced this situation with its first defibrillator.[1] Medtronic experienced difficulty during the marketing efforts. Usage required a one-hour training program and a half-inch thick manual. A study showed that only doctors and nurses used many of the features. The redesign was reduced to three dial knobs with strong visual graphics. By using a layered menu approach, cardiologists were able to receive more detailed information. Users now had a simple device with limited but essential features that met all of their requirements. This Medtronic example is not atypical of the new-product design process. The first version of any new product is the beginning of a learning experience.

Summary

Making innovation happen requires an astute management and professional staff who possess the competencies for innovation. Both are required. The items outlined in this chapter hold no mysteries. Good management practice focused on doing provides the best approach. Organizations do not need vast training programs to begin the innovation process. Identify an innovation project, assign an experienced and forward-thinking project manager, select the critical mass, provide some guidance, and let them go to work. It may take one, two, three, or more years, depending on the project, but as has been shown in the IBM Rochester case, it can be done.

Note

1. Tom Kelley and Jonathan Littman, *The Art of Innovation* (New York: Doubleday, 2001).

Index